UNLESS VICTORY COMES:

COMBAT WITH A WORLD WAR II MACHINE GUNNER IN PATTON'S THIRD ARMY

UNLESS VICTORY COMES

COMBAT WITH A WORLD WAR II MACHINE GUNNER IN PATTON'S THIRD ARMY

GENE GARRISON

WITH PATRICK GILBERT

NAL
CALIBER

NAL Caliber
Published by New American Library, a division of
Penguin Group (USA) Inc., 375 Hudson Street,
New York, New York 10014, USA
Penguin Group (Canada), 90 Eglinton Avenue East, Suite 700, Toronto,
Ontario M4P 2Y3, Canada (a division of Pearson Penguin Canada Inc.)
Penguin Books Ltd., 80 Strand, London WC2R 0RL, England
Penguin Ireland, 25 St. Stephen's Green, Dublin 2,
Ireland (a division of Penguin Books Ltd.)
Penguin Group (Australia), 250 Camberwell Road, Camberwell, Victoria 3124,
Australia (a division of Pearson Australia Group Pty. Ltd.)
Penguin Books India Pvt. Ltd., 11 Community Centre, Panchsheel Park,
New Delhi - 110 017, India
Penguin Group (NZ), 67 Apollo Drive, Rosedale, North Shore 0632,
New Zealand (a division of Pearson New Zealand Ltd.)
Penguin Books (South Africa) (Pty.) Ltd., 24 Sturdee Avenue,
Rosebank, Johannesburg 2196, South Africa

Penguin Books Ltd., Registered Offices:
80 Strand, London WC2R 0RL, England

Published by NAL Caliber, an imprint of New American Library, a division of Penguin Group (USA) Inc.
This is an authorized reprint of the Casemate hardcover edition. For information, address Casemate Publishers
and Book Distributors, LLC; 1016 Warrior Road, Suite C; Drexel Hill, PA 19026.

First NAL Caliber Printing, November 2007
10 9 8 7 6 5 4 3 2 1

NAL CALIBER and the "C" logo are trademarks of Penguin Group (USA) Inc.

NAL Caliber Trade Paperback ISBN: 978-0-451-22224-4

THE LIBRARY OF CONGRESS HAS CATALOGED THE HARDCOVER EDITION OF THIS TITLE AS FOLLOWS:
Garrison, Gene, 1925–
Until victory comes : combat with a machine gunner in Patton's Third Army / Gene Garrison with Patrick
Gilbert.
p. cm.
ISBN: 1-932033-30-0
1. Garrison, Gene, 1925–.   2. United States. Army. Infantry Division, 87th.   3. United States.
Army—Gunners—Biography.   4. World War, 1939–1945—Campaigns—Western Front.   5. World
War, 1939–1945—Personal narratives, American.   6. Soldiers—United States—Biography.
D769.3 87th .G37 2004

Set in Sabon
Designed by Ginger Legato

Printed in the United States of America

This narrative is dedicated to all the members of the 87th Infantry Division—The Golden Acorns—and especially to those who gave their lives in combat action, and to all the members of C Company.

CONTENTS

FOREWORD

Perhaps Mark Twain said it best when he wrote, "Courage is not the lack of fear. It is acting in spite of it." His observation describes perfectly a combat unit.

The following events are recorded to the best of my recollection. Some names have been changed or purposely deleted. It was not and is not my intent to embarrass or humiliate anyone. Who knows what action or reaction might be taken by anyone in a similar set of circumstances?

Further, it must be remembered that historical data is no more accurate than the information available and the quality of the reports submitted by the company, battalion, and regimental clerks. Also, as memory dims, so does accuracy. In the absence of diaries or journals, which were supposedly "prohibited," chronology, fact, and memory may be in conflict.

It must be understood that I considered all of the noncommissioned officers I served with to be good soldiers, and they performed their duties extremely well. The same can be said about most of the replacement Air Corps NCOs, especially my squad leader, Lyle Jacobs.

ACKNOWLEDGMENTS

The events herein are factual and are related as accurately as possible. Dialogue has been added, but it reflects the situations as they occurred. Most of the events involved the author. Those that did not were either related personally by the participants or were taken from other narratives.

Special acknowledgment is made to Patrick Gilbert, who authored a paper entitled "An Introduction to the Battle of the Bulge," relating the stories of Elmer Zeichner, Tom Katana, and me on New Year's Day 1945. I used his material extensively. Patrick encouraged me, as did many other 87th Division Association members and friends, to have the book published. He volunteered to proofread and edit the manuscript, and make suggestions and revisions as mutually agreed. In the process, he revised paragraphs and chapters for the sake of continuity and transition, and added geographical locations and historical data. Without his many long hours of work and perseverance, this book would have never reached fruition.

I would also like to thank everyone who provided information, be it in the form of conversations or articles, from the following men of C Company: Carl Blanchard, Walter Byrnes, Earl Cate, James Cheatwood, Richard Coble, Pat Collucio, Richard Cunningham, Anthony

D'Arpino, Walter Dippold, Robert Fulton, Bronislaw Jaroz, Robert Jones, Thomas Katana, William Knight, Milton Miller, Norman Panther, William Petrosky, Percy Shue, John Thomas, Armand Verdone, Guy Wick, Charles Yanacheck, and Elmer Zeichner. Earle Hart helped us by providing Signal Corps photos for our use.

We also wish to thank Casemate Publishing and David Farnsworth for their willingness to publish my memoirs, and Theodore P. Savas for his assistance in designing and finalizing this book. Patrick and I would also like to pass along our appreciation to Eric Hammel for his editing assistance.

To my wife, Juanita, who supported my sporadic efforts over the past twenty-odd years, writing while waiting in physicians' offices for my parents to be treated, while on vacations, watching TV, or whenever I could find the necessary time. She volunteered to type my notes into a legible manuscript after having not touched a typewriter for more than twenty years. She even consented to try to use a computer.

To all members of my family who assisted in the compilation of a completed document and especially to my son Geoffrey, who installed the computer, patiently answered my wife's numerous questions, and proofread and assembled the initial documents. To my grandson Brian Short, who has a keen interest in WWII and in my service with the 87th Infantry Division.

To Thomas Fuller, who encouraged me to complete the memoir so he had a more personal narrative to read.

And finally, to Colonel Robert B. Cobb, our battalion commander, whose fearless leadership was our inspiration. The success of the battalion must be attributed to him. His courage was contagious.

PART I

STATESIDE–ENGLAND–FRANCE

CHAPTER 1
Beginning the Journey

It was 0900 hours on a Friday in July 1944. It was hot as usual in the basic training installation at Camp Croft, South Carolina, and rivulets of sweat were on my forehead and temple. I could feel the perspiration on my back under the full field pack.

A dozen young soldiers stood at the edge of the parade ground in front of the neat rows of barracks. We were the next-to-last of the trainees to be shipped out of the latest training class. I had experienced a strange sensation that morning. Although I had made many friends the past three months, I had watched most of them leave over the past two days with a sense of detachment that I had never felt before. I hadn't felt that same indifference when Ed Czarnecki, with whom I had developed a special bond, had left following his father's death. Now I viewed them with no feeling, as if they were strangers. Even John Ehle, who had taken me home to meet his family in Asheville, North Carolina, left with only a brief good-bye and a perfunctory, "Stop and visit if you are ever in Asheville!"

Had I analyzed my feelings, I would have realized that I was building a self-defense mechanism that would be with me throughout my military service—and perhaps forever.

I was shipping out to Fort Jackson, South Carolina, to join the 87th Infantry Division. The men going with me to Jackson whom I knew were Paul Gullet and Warren Little, both from my hometown of Middletown, Ohio; Harold Brewer from Piqua, Ohio; Morris Cole from Seymour, Indiana; and Pat Coluccio of Poughkeepsie, New York. Everyone else was from different training companies.

We stood there, leaning on our barracks bags, waiting patiently for the 6×6 trucks. The only person missing was Brewer. He emerged from the A Company barracks across the compound and walked hurriedly toward the group. "We thought you changed your mind, Brewer," Coluccio kidded.

Brewer ignored him. "What time are we leaving?"

"Ten o'clock. You in a hurry?" Coluccio asked.

"Just thought it was earlier," Brewer answered nervously.

I glanced at him, wondering why he was in such a hurry to leave. Brewer was a likable guy, but the noncoms didn't like him. As my mother would say, "He's just plain devilish!"

A loud screeching sound came from the doorway of the A Company barracks. A fellow by the name of Bonds burst from the building. He was from New Mexico and was the perfect image of a cowboy—tall, lean, a deep tan with crow's-feet at the corners of his mouth, and his eyes frozen into a squint from too much sun. He had been Brewer's best friend over the past few weeks, and had succeeded in keeping Brewer out of trouble most of the time.

Bonds tore out on a dead run across the parade ground, screaming Brewer's name with every step. He was clad only in an olive drab army towel, knotted at his hip, and a pair of combat boots. His elbows and knees jerked up and down; his towel and unbuckled boot tops flapped back and forth. He was Ichabod Crane reincarnated.

Everyone watched in astonishment as Bonds closed the gap between himself and Brewer, who shuffled behind Cole. "I trusted you!" Bonds yelled. "I trusted you! Where's my money?"

"I have it! I was just keeping it for you. I'll get it!" Brewer gasped as Bonds seized him by his field jacket, lifted him, and shook him like a dog shakes a rat.

Brewer tried to reach his combat boot. "It's in my shoe! I was keeping it for you! Put me down! I'll get it for you!"

"In your shoe?" Bonds raged. "You were going to steal it! I trusted you!" He let go of Brewer, who stumbled, caught his balance, and then hopped around on one foot until he had succeeded in removing his boot from the other foot.

"Here! Here!" Brewer yelled as he thrust his hand into his boot and pulled out a folded wad of bills. "I was just holding it for you. Honest!"

"I should have known better than to trust you." Bonds was a little calmer now that he had his money and had switched his concern from Brewer to his towel, which was threatening to come undone.

Brewer sat down to put his boot back on. Bonds turned and stomped back to the barracks. The incident was over as quickly as it had started.

A corporal approached us from the orderly room. "The truck won't be here until 1100," he said. "Take a break. Brewer, the lieutenant wants to see you."

Gullet and I sat down on the barracks steps. "I still think we should have volunteered for paratroop training," Gullet said.

"I told you I'm not going to jump out of airplanes," I reminded him.

"The war might be over before that happens."

"Sure. And what if it isn't?" I responded.

"Uh-oh. Here comes the lieutenant."

"Okay, guys. You two give me your version of what happened," the officer requested. "I've already talked to Bonds and Brewer."

We related what we he had seen to the lieutenant, who looked dejected. "He ever do anything like this before?"

"Not that I know of," I answered. "He's been in some scrapes, but he's never taken anything."

"How about you, Gullet?"

"Same here."

"Damn. I don't want to file charges," the lieutenant said. "It won't do anyone any good. I've talked to him. I'll tell him I'm not pressing charges based on your recommendation, okay?"

"Okay," we responded in unison.

The trucks came a few minutes later and we quickly loaded our gear and ourselves. The trucks moved out through the heat of the South Carolina summer, and basic training came to an end.

The 87th Division had been activated at Camp McCain, Mississippi, on December 15, 1942, the day before my sixteenth birthday. The 87th was a reserve division and had not been in action since World War I. Its shoulder patch was a golden acorn centered on a green background, and thus it was known as the "Golden Acorn" Division.

The trainees from Camp Croft arrived in early July 1944 and essentially completed the personnel quota authorized for the division, which was almost twenty thousand men.

Gullet, Brewer, Coluccio, Little, Cole, and I were assigned to C Company, 1st Battalion, 347th Infantry Regiment. The rest of the contingent from Camp Croft was scattered throughout the division.

Fort Jackson, our destination, was just another Camp Croft—a collection of two-story, white barracks buildings and a canteen where we could buy chocolate milkshakes. The freshly graduated trainees were slightly apprehensive. We weren't on an equal footing with the other soldiers who had been with the division since Camp McCain. We were coming to Jackson as replacements for troops who had been pulled out of the 87th for overseas duty.

Immediately upon reporting to the orderly room we were directed to assemble for interviews for detailed assignments. A sergeant named Van Quekelberghe leaned out of a window with a roster, methodically calling names and assigning everyone to a rifle platoon. Before the sergeant could call my name, Gullet, who was standing behind me, spoke up: "Sarge, could Garrison and I be assigned to a machine-gun squad?"

Van Quekelberghe looked surprised, but he quickly said, "Yes, you can. I was going to ask for volunteers. Report to a Sergeant DeVine—first building on the right."

"Damn it, Paul, I should have left you in Camp Croft," I uttered.

"Easy. Think of all that machine-gun firepower."

"Sure, and think of all the incoming enemy firepower falling on us. This is almost as bad as you wanting us to volunteer for the para-troops."

"Stop and think," Gullet said. "In Basic, they told us that there were always two men assigned to a machine gun. One of us will be on guard and the other one can sleep!"

"Oh? I bet some sergeant will screw that up."

Van Quekelberghe continued to make his assignments. Brewer, Cole, Collucio, and Little were all assigned to rifle platoons.

Staff Sergeant Henry DeVine, the machine-gun section leader, was wait-ing for us. He had two squads under his command. "You guys will be in the 1st Squad. This is Sergeant Kelly, your squad leader. He'll show you around. Need anything, ask him."

Robert Kelly greeted us and introduced us to Bill Carollo and Jack Crooks. "Bill's first gunner, and Jack is second. You two are ammo bear-ers. Chow is in about twenty minutes. Stow your gear and wash up."

It didn't take long to get acquainted with the rest of the 4th Platoon members. There was another machine-gun squad and three mortar squads. Most of the men in the weapons platoon had not been assigned to the division for long, except for the noncoms, who were members of the original cadre and had been with the 87th since Camp McCain. The other troops were mainly former ASTP (Army Specialized Train-ing Program) members who had been attending college until the Army cancelled the program in April. At least they had gotten some college. I had passed the ASTP test and was scheduled to go to college after completing basic training, but the program was terminated before I finished.

The 4th Platoon members seemed to be very compatible, perhaps because the average age was nineteen, and a few had been in ASTP and had college backgrounds.

The 1st Machine-Gun Squad leader, Sergeant Kelly, was a twenty-year-old from Detroit. He came from an Irish background. He was red-faced and thinly built but durable. He was outgoing, and the men liked him because he was easily approachable. They found that none of their problems were too small for him to discuss.

Private First Class Bill Carollo, the first gunner, was from Diamondville, Wyoming. He was a well-built, nineteen-year-old six-footer. He was constantly brushing his brown hair away from his eyes and took delight in making sarcastic comments about the Regular Army cadre.

The second gunner, nineteen-year-old Private First Class Jack Crooks, was from Bethlehem, Pennsylvania. He resembled Carollo in build but had a shock of blond hair. His glasses never stayed in place and he fought a constant battle to keep them on his nose. He could match Carollo in sarcastic wit, but he was usually more reserved.

Private Paul Gullet and I, the ammunition carriers, were eighteen. Gullet was dark blond with a complexion that always seemed tan. At five foot ten, he was a good athlete, and had endured the training exercises better than most. Generally quiet, Gullet nevertheless could instigate lively arguments about sports.

A couple of days after the Camp Croft contingent settled in, a group of replacements arrived from Camp Roberts, California, and the last member joined the machine-gun squad. Private Tony D'Arpino was another eighteen-year-old who was instantly likable and fit right into the squad. He came from the small town of Voorheesville, near Albany, New York. D'Arpino had several brothers, which might have accounted for his gregarious personality. He had a dark complexion and a ready smile.

D'Arpino, who also was assigned to be an ammo carrier, had a comment or an answer for everything. He called Carollo, the recruit from Wyoming, Cowboy.

Carollo retorted, "Just because a person is from Wyoming doesn't mean he's a cowboy."

To which D'Arpino responded, "True, but look at those bowed legs!"

I was about the same size, five foot eight, as D'Arpino, but more low-key and with light blond hair. I was athletic and had played intramural basketball with Gullet in high school.

There wasn't much difference between the regimen at Fort Jackson and the one at Camp Croft. We arose at 0530 hours, showered and shaved, dressed, made up the bunks, had breakfast, cleaned the barracks, fell out for roll call, exercised, and hiked with full packs—*always* full packs.

A major requirement for members of the weapons platoon was to qualify in our own specialty, either the 60mm mortar or the air-cooled .30-caliber light machine gun. But with rumors flying around that the division would ship out shortly, the 4th Platoon sergeant, James Pearson, passed the word to DeVine, who, in turn, chewed out Kelly about his squad not being fully qualified.

The next morning, immediately after breakfast, the 1st Squad (minus Carollo, who had previously qualified) headed to the firing range. Four targets were distributed at various distances for each squad member. Kelly hovered like a mother hen, adjusting targets and selecting gun positions. Crooks, the second gunner, fired at his group of targets. Small clouds of dust puffed up beyond the targets. It was impossible to determine the accuracy of his shooting except for one target, which fluttered away in the wind.

I fired next. I pressed the stock of the .30 caliber firmly to my shoulder and thought of hunting on the farm with my dad and uncles. Hold the gun tight, aim slightly low to the left, and squeeze the shots off. The targets jerked with the impact of the bullets.

Gullet and D'Arpino took their turns, Gullet with his serious look and D'Arpino laughing after each short burst of gunfire.

The firing session ended and Kelly scrambled to collect the targets. A passing score was 110. Kelly clucked as he examined the sheets. "Well, I'll be damned. Crooks, 100. Gullet, 85. D'Arpino, 75. Garrison, you are the only one to qualify. You had 125. Good shooting."

Crooks complained, "You didn't count the target that blew away. I only need ten points, and you know I shoot better at the longer distances."

"I know, but we can all use the practice, and I would rather be out here than picking up cigarette butts," Kelly said.

Everyone laughed as we headed back to camp.

The company supply sergeant was Samuel Breen. He could be very overbearing, especially to the replacements. He owned a monkey and kept it in the supply room, which the monkey thought was his exclusive domain. Breen, most of the time, kept him on a chain. That monkey chased more than one person from the supply room. His sharp-tooth grin and bright beady eyes were very convincing.

The monkey also liked to drink whiskey, but only with one person at a time. Once the monkey found a bottle someone had stashed under the barracks building where the 2d and 4th platoons were billeted. That time, he drank alone and became "drunk as a skunk." No one claimed ownership of the whiskey.

On another occasion, Corporal Norman Panther, one of the jeep drivers, was in the supply room and completely forgot about the monkey, who was sitting quietly at the end of the counter. Panther picked up his supplies and turned his back to leave. The monkey leaped, landed on his back, and sank his little dagger teeth into Norm's shoulder. Startled, Norm lunged forward and the monkey, still on his chain, was yanked off his shoulder.

Panther used some uncomplimentary language and started for the monkey, who disappeared behind the counter. Breen and Corporal Frank Watson, the company armorer, charged through the door to the monkey's rescue. Panther left, rubbing his shoulder and muttering threats to the monkey.

I had played enough penny-ante poker and blackjack the last couple of years to consider myself a decent player. One evening, a couple of 2d Platoon noncoms invited me to play a game of blackjack. I stayed even for a while, and then the stakes went from a quarter to a dollar. That might not seem like much, but I already was down ten dollars and had only twenty to last me the rest of the month. I decided to drop out. As I started to leave, Lloyd Sylva, the platoon sergeant for the 2d Platoon, who had walked into the game a few minutes earlier, stopped me. "Don't quit now. Wait until your deal."

Sylva, who was much older than me, bunked on the floor below me, and we had become friends. He stood behind me and monitored my play. By the end of my deal, I was only down two dollars. "Now is the time to quit," Sylva snapped. "Don't play with these guys again. As for you three," the sergeant snarled to the noncoms, "you know better. Do it again and I'll have your ass."

I scooped up my money and headed for the safer confines of my platoon. I didn't blame the noncoms; I blamed myself for not leaving when the stakes were raised.

Later that night, I decided to stay in the barracks to read a mystery novel. I waited until everyone had left for town, the theater, or the post exchange to take my shower. I collected my clean clothes and stuffed my billfold in the bag with my toilet articles. I hung my clothes on the hook next to the shower door and placed the bag on the windowsill.

No one was around except one of the Regular Army cooks, whom I knew only as Pop. I showered quickly, dressed, and reached for the toiletry bag. My billfold was gone! I felt crushed. First, the card game, and now this.

Upon leaving the shower room I met Sylva as he entered the rear door. "You look down. You play some more cards?"

I told him what had happened.

"You're having a bad day, aren't you?"

We moved away from the shower room, and I stood with my back to the door. We talked for a while and Sylva said, "Maybe you had better check for your billfold again and then go to bed before something else happens." He turned and went to his bunk. I went back to the shower room, moved a scrub brush from the windowsill, and there lay the billfold with all my money. As I started up the steps, I held up the billfold so Sylva could see it. Pop was lying on his bunk, apparently paying no attention.

As I climbed the stairs, I realized that Sylva had taught me two lessons that day.

The days passed rapidly, each filled with calisthenics, marches, field-stripping weapons, and general bitching. Field exercises were common, and the jeep drivers, Panther and Corporal Carl Blanchard, requested me as the third man on their jeep. Their primary job was to transport supplies.

On one field exercise, the jeep was carrying food and hot coffee to the company command post. Panther—an expert at hitting every pot-hole and bump in the road—drove while Blanchard and I desperately attempted to hold the trays of hot food and scalding coffee in the jeep. Panther steered the jeep over a large bump. The lid on the coffee canister I was holding flew off, sending coffee splashing on my hands and legs, inflicting severe pain, especially on my legs. I never let them know how badly it hurt, because I was afraid that I would be removed from the temporary duty on the jeep. The job did have its advantages, such as missing drill and forced marches. Luckily the burns were not severe.

Amid rumors that the division had received its overseas orders, personnel changes continued. Additional men, mostly from the defunct ASTP program, were assigned to the company. The Red Cross notified a sergeant from Indiana that his hardship discharge to work his parents' farm had been approved.

In mid-September, I received an order to report to the Red Cross office, where, to my astonishment, I was told that my request for hardship discharge had been disapproved.

"What request? I never requested anything," I told a Red Cross worker.

"Well, the request was actually initiated by a Herbert Schafer from

Woodington, Ohio, to have you released to help him on his farm," the worker explained. "The request says that he is your uncle."

"Oh. I didn't know anything about this, but it seems a good idea. You sure it's been disapproved?"

"Yes, sorry."

I'm glad my uncle had never told me. Had I known, I would have been disappointed. I grappled with mixed emotions as I slowly made my way back to the company. My uncle was only fifteen years my senior, and I had been his constant shadow back on the family farm. I would very much have liked to go back to that farm.

One recently arrived replacement was given a Section 8 discharge as a homosexual. Bill Carollo said that the soldier was "crazy like a fox." They never caught him doing anything; he just knew what to say and what to do to deceive the Army.

D'Arpino, because of his typing expertise (which meant he could use more than one finger), was occasionally asked to lend a hand as an extra clerk. As D'Arpino reported for work at company headquarters, the recruit angling for the Section 8 bolted through the door, waving a handful of papers. D'Arpino stepped aside, but the recruit stopped and tapped D'Arpino's chest. "You think I'm crazy, but this fall I'm going to be watching the Chicago Cubs play in the World Series. You bastards are going overseas and have your asses shot off."

He was still laughing as he entered his barracks to pack for his trip home.

The next day, rain poured down as it can only in South Carolina. The division marked time by packing equipment until we received departure orders. The day was supposed to be spent on more weapons orientation. Kelly was summoned to meet with DeVine and Pearson. He quickly returned and called out names: "Crooks, Gullet, D'Arpino. Get on your rain gear. Bring the gun. You guys have to qualify, and today is it. We ship out tomorrow. Carollo, you and Garrison make yourselves scarce. We'll be back whenever these guys qualify."

Carollo never cracked a smile. "It'll take them two hours, and that includes driving time," he said. He missed his prediction by an hour, because they stopped at the PX on the way back. They returned, drenched but qualified. Crooks scored 130, Gullet 126, and D'Arpino 124. They later confessed that they could barely see the targets. They each fired one burst and Kelly exclaimed, "Good shooting. Let's get out of the rain."

In the Army, a requirement is a requirement.

The rain had stopped and the company was granted a blanket pass for the rest of the day. Surprisingly, very few men left camp, just the married men and the hard-core drinkers.

I decided to attend the movie at the base theater, but as I left the mess hall, Lieutenant Roland Baxter, the 4th Platoon leader, stopped me. "Garrison, I need some help at the BOQ [bachelor officers' quarters]. You have any plans?"

"Just the movie, sir."

The lieutenant smiled. "Good. Come with me."

I spent the next two hours carrying Baxter's and some other officers' belongings to a truck for transportation to the rail terminal. Finally, Baxter released me from duty. "You have ten minutes to make the movie, Garrison. You'd better leave."

"You're all heart, Lieutenant," I said. "You owe me."

Baxter laughed. "Get out of here before I find something else for you to do."

I made the movie just as the lights dimmed.

When I returned to the barracks, I discovered that I had been assigned to guard duty along with one of the riflemen. Our four-hour assignment was to guard a tent in which all of the company's weaponry was boxed and stored to await transport.

A couple of hours into the post, I realized the rifleman was missing. The huge storage tent was square, and we patrolled on opposite sides. I found him asleep on a storage box. I left him alone for a while, and then nudged him. "It's your turn. Get." It took some more nudging to get him moving.

I sat down and thought I would rest a couple of minutes and go back out to join the rifleman. I awakened with a stiff neck and, for several seconds, didn't know where I was. I heard someone snoring. The rifleman was sound asleep. I saw a shadow through the tent and realized it might be the sergeant of the guard. I whacked the rifleman in the ribs, stepped outside, and shouted, "Halt, who goes there?"

It was perfect timing mixed with luck. The relief guards had arrived and our infraction of sleeping on guard duty was not discovered.

The countryside slipped past the train windows, displaying its fall colors. Although the mid-October scenery was nice, the train was stuffy and the ride was uncomfortable. Some of the troops read, others bantered back and forth, especially those from the New York and New Jersey area. They were close to home. Would they get leave? How easy would it be to "go over the hill"? Many men merely stared out the windows, lost in their individual thoughts as the brilliant reds, yellows, and oranges of autumn flashed by.

The train was blacked out at night, and the men settled into their bunks. Foul, stale air filled the car. I struggled with a window and managed to open it a small crack. The odor of coal soot permeated the air, but at least the area around my bed was cool. I awoke in the morning to find my face blackened with soot: the grit was in my eyes, nose, and mouth. I longed for home and my own bed. Fear of the unknown clutched at my stomach and crept throughout my body.

That afternoon the troops disembarked from the train and loaded onto 6 × 6 trucks for the short trip to Camp Kilmer, New Jersey. We were assigned to transient quarters and quickly given "make-work" tasks. Rumors immediately circulated that those troops who lived close by would be given overnight passes. It never happened.

Two days later, 6 × 6 trucks arrived to take us to the dock area. There we boarded a ferry that took us to the *Queen Elizabeth,* which had been converted into a troop ship. We thought the *Queen Elizabeth* was the largest ship in the world until British sailors later told us that the *Queen Mary* was three feet longer.

On the ferry, one of the mortarmen became very excited. He had grown up in the Hell's Kitchen area of the lower west side of Manhattan.

As a kid, he had ridden the same ferry for a nickel. He recognized the New York City skyline and started counting off the streets. "Forty-second, Forty-third, Forty-fourth. I live on Forty-fourth between Eight and Ninth avenues," he yelled. "I can almost see my house."

Onboard the *Queen Elizabeth,* Company C was deposited in the bowels of the ship, right above the engine room. Early the next morning the ship moved smoothly out to sea. The thumping of the engines awakened me. It was October 7, 1944.

The thumping became monotonous, so most of the troops stayed topside as much as possible. But two men from the mortar squads were so seasick that they never left their cots for the duration of the voyage. D'Arpino wisely volunteered for KP [Kitchen Police] in the officers' mess. He ate better than his comrades. Everyone else ducked details by roaming the decks. They soon discovered that certain areas were off-limits, such as a section for nurses and the officers' quarters.

I discovered an outside passageway that led to the aft section of the ship, where the officers had established a trap-shooting range. I spent as many hours as possible watching their attempts to shoot the white clay birds from the sky. Despite the size of the *Queen Elizabeth,* the rolling action of the waves was more than a match for the shooters. A hit was rare.

The *Queen Elizabeth* used speed as its best defense against German U-boats, so we traveled unescorted. The fourth night out, a jerking motion almost threw me from my metal cot. Then the throbbing engines accelerated, but soon the thumping noise became more rhythmic. The sudden maneuver had awakened everyone in the compartment, but not a word was said. The unconfirmed report the next morning was that the crew had detected a U-boat and had made a sudden course change to outdistance the danger.

On October 22, five days after leaving New York, the *Queen Elizabeth* passed the northern coast of Ireland and entered the Firth of Clyde, docking at Greenock, Scotland, the port city for Glasgow. Disembarkation started that evening, as soon as it was dark.

"Wonder why we waited so long," Gullet said as they started down the gangplank.

"I've been thinking about that," Kelly responded. "I imagine it makes it more difficult for any 'fifth column' to count the troops. They might know that there are troops, but they might not know what kind of troops or how many."

"That's probably the smartest thing you ever said, Kelly," Carollo commented.

We laughed at Carollo's jibe as we filed into the relatively dark streets of Greenock before heading to the nearby rail station. Across the street, a wooden sign that bore the name of a local pub hung from a wrought-iron frame. Brewer and another rifleman quietly left the column and disappeared into the shadows. "What the hell do they think they're doing?" Kelly muttered.

"Getting a beer," D'Arpino replied with a laugh.

No one else, apparently, noticed their departure. Kelly growled, "Let's go. It's none of our business. They have their own sergeants. We'll see if they made it when we get off the train."

We marched to the station, boarded a blacked-out train, stored our barracks bags, and found seats. Soon we were all asleep. The train departed into the dark Scottish countryside on its way south to England.

On the Eve of Combat

Numerous small towns and villages near Manchester, England, served as billets for the 87th Division. C Company was located in a village named Hale, while other 1st Battalion units were stationed in the nearby town of Altringham. The 4th Platoon occupied a large, three-story, private home that had been stripped of its furniture and refurnished with military-issue bunks and miscellaneous chests and chairs. A large fireplace dominated each room, and the ceilings easily reached twelve feet high. Each floor had one bathroom.

Surprisingly, a liberal leave policy was adopted. The more adventurous immediately obtained passes and ventured into Manchester. The U.S.O. Club sponsored dances every evening, and the working-class city supported numerous pubs.

Letters home now were subjected to the tight censorship of a war theater of operations. Military censors cut out even the vaguest references to troop location, strength, designation, and movement. A bigger problem in maintaining military secrecy concerned conversations among men in pubs and at dances, especially those whose tongues were loosened by alcohol. There were so many men that it was impossible to prevent information leaks.

Letters from the 4th Platoon looked especially shredded after 1st Lieutenant Jack DiNola, the company executive officer, finished censoring them. My first censored letter home prompted my mother to ask in her return letter what I could possibly have written to have so many words cut out. She commented in a later correspondence that Lieutenant DiNola must be a nice person since he had added a comment to my letter that, "Gene was feeling much better after a touch of the flu."

A couple of days after arriving in England, I joined several members of the 4th Platoon on a visit to the U.S.O. Club in Manchester. Fog settled among the trees as we left the house. By the time we had walked halfway to the Hale station stop, it was impossible to see more than a few feet. D'Arpino, Gullet, Abraham "Red" Blum, one of the rifle platoon members, and I clustered together as we walked across a small bridge. Suddenly, I felt myself being jerked back from the curb. A large, dark touring car loomed out of the darkness and brushed against my leg. It disappeared into the fog as rapidly as it had appeared. Blum had just happened to look over his shoulder in time to see the car. Luckily, he had instinctively saved me from injury.

The U.S.O. dance was crowded; it seemed that the ratio of GIs to English girls was one hundred to one. The four of us decided to go to an English pub. As we entered from the darkened street, the glare of the pub's lights blinded us.

"My God, the entire army must be in here," Blum blurted out.

Military personnel—English, Canadian, and American—packed the pub. The male-to-female ratio was still one hundred to one. Despite the crowded conditions, it only took minutes to be served a beer. D'Arpino and I sipped the warm, bitter liquid and simultaneously made faces to indicate our displeasure. One English beer was more than enough for the evening.

We heard a commotion in the pub and stood up. Blum was performing a Russian kick dance. He was an instant hit. Although others in the pub who had too much to drink tried to copy him, none measured up.

Despite the "bad beer," I learned to sing the English pub song of "Roll Me over in the Clover," and it turned into my most pleasurable evening since being in the service.

On a second visit to Manchester, Blum, Gullet, and I were drinking at another pub when Blum decided to go table-hopping. He soon reappeared with a peroxide blonde. "We have to help this girl," he announced. "Her boyfriend is home on leave from the British marines and he thinks she has been going out on him."

Gullet and I glanced at the girl and exchanged looks. A British marine, along with some civilian friends, was sitting next to the door. "How are we expected to help her?" Gullet asked.

"We'll walk out and she'll follow us in a couple of minutes. Her bus should be leaving in a few minutes, and she can get away from him," Blum explained. "Her father's a bobby."

"Oh, good," I said sarcastically. "How do you keep getting involved in this type of thing? We don't even know her. You brought her to our table and her boyfriend is going to think we're involved."

"Come on, Gene. Let's get out of here," Gullet whispered.

The marine was watching us intently. To leave the pub, we would need to pass his table. Gullet and I rose and quickly passed the marine, followed closely by Blum.

"Let's get to the U.S.O.," I said as soon as we were out the door.

"Too late," Gullet growled.

I turned just as Blum and the girl passed us, running for the double-decker bus. The marine, meanwhile, had reached the hallway. Gullet and I sprinted for the bus and boarded it as it pulled away from the curb. The marine and his friends were left standing at midstreet, shouting obscenities.

The bus was a limited express, and about an hour passed before it circled back past the U.S.O. Club. The girl rejected all of Blum's offers to escort her and got off without him at the last stop on the line.

On another trip to town, I became separated from my friends. I stopped at the U.S.O. but quickly grew tired of the place after eating some doughnuts. I didn't like frequenting a pub alone, so I decided to return to Hale. The fog was exceptionally thick that evening as I alighted from the train. I realized that I had never walked alone from the station to the platoon billet. After a few blocks, it was obvious that I was completely turned around.

I paused at a street corner under a muted streetlamp. I figured a total blackout was unnecessary because the fog was so thick.

"Good evening." A shadow appeared out of the fog. "A bit thick this evening, isn't it?"

"Yes, it is," I replied. "Makes it a little difficult to find your way around."

"Yes. Could I be of assistance?"

The stranger from the fog was about six feet tall, with dark hair graying at the temples. He wore a tweed suit buttoned to keep out the damp chill. He spoke with a middle-class English accent.

"Well, seems like I can't find Bandy Lane."

"Come, I'll direct you there. It's only three streets away." Within minutes we were standing in front of the billet.

"I appreciate your kindness," I said.

"You are more than welcome," the stranger said. "If I might impose, I have a son in the RAF somewhere in the Pacific theater. My wife passed away last year. Perhaps this weekend we could share a cup of tea and a game of dominoes."

I stumbled a bit and then responded, "I would be glad to. This Saturday?"

"Seven o'clock. Here is my name and address. If the soup is this bad, I'll meet you here. It's quite easy if you know the landmarks."

I glanced at the card. The name on it read "Thomas Burnett."

"Good, my name is Garrison. I'll see you Saturday at seven o'clock. Thank you again."

"My pleasure. Good evening," the Englishman said as he disappeared into the fog.

On Saturday night I found my way to his neatly kept flat. Burnett said he was employed as a civil servant but added no other details about his job. I didn't press. I enjoyed the tea and learned to drink it with milk. I ate crumpets, discovering they were similar to muffins and quite good. The game of dominoes was interesting but took some practice.

I visited Burnett on three occasions, and we discussed many things, but never anything pertaining to the war. We were scheduled for another dominoes game, but the division shipped out, and I never had a chance to thank Burnett for his hospitality. In our brief time together, he had become my temporary father figure.

Romances between some of the men and English girls flourished. At least one member of the company married an English girl. It was rumored that he also switched his ten-thousand-dollar GI insurance policy from his mother to his new wife.

I had my own encounter. At one of the U.S.O. dances, I noticed an English girl standing at the edge of the dance floor. She was small— about as big as a minute. I also noticed that she glanced at me from time to time, so I worked up my nerve and asked for a dance, which she accepted. Her name was Dorothea, and she lived in the country. I never saw her anyplace except at the U.S.O. We prearranged our evenings so we could attend the dances. I saw her three or four times. It was a safe relationship for both of us.

As Thanksgiving approached, troops of the 87th prepared to celebrate their last holiday before combat. On Thanksgiving eve, I was walking guard duty. A guard—no one knew why—was always posted to walk the block behind the mess hall. My sentry duty proceeded routinely until my toe came in contact with a loose cobblestone. I tried breaking the fall with my carbine, but I landed flat on my stomach and skinned my knuckles. Later, I half-seriously asked for the company's first Purple Heart, but I was told that I wasn't in combat—at least with the enemy.

The company entered the mess tent on Thanksgiving and found that Forsythe, the assistant cook, had cut out life-size paper turkeys, colored them, and hung them in the mess hall. None of us knew Forsythe's first name; everyone just called him Forsythe.

Carollo sat down with his plate of turkey in front of him. "You know, this is just like being home in Wyoming; turkey, my family, and there's even a big, fat mountain at the head of the serving line."

We laughed as we looked first at Carollo and then at Leland Fry, our rather large mess sergeant. We quickly fell silent and attacked the plates of turkey.

The next morning we packed our gear and boarded the 6 × 6 trucks. The move was carefully planned so there was no chance for any good-byes to newfound friends. I never saw or heard from Burnett again, but I did correspond for a while with Dorothea.

The trip from Hale, made in blackout conditions, proved uneventful. The troops of C Company knew we were headed for France and that we would depart from Southampton. The trucks traveled slowly over the uneven streets as they approached the dock area. They came to a full stop for several minutes. Then they moved forward, turned a corner, and stopped again. We were weary from the long ride and were glad to un-load. Our full packs were cumbersome and slowed our movement. Within minutes Lieutenant DiNola issued instructions on boarding the transport ship, which was visible only by its silhouette.

C Company lined up by twos, or as Kelly was yelling to us, "Queue it up! Queue it up!" We "queued it up," climbed the gangplank, and spread out on the deck, each of us seeking a comfortable spot. Some soldiers jostled for rail positions, but it was all friendly.

Kelly's squad gathered as far from the rail as possible. Being from the heartland, we had no great love for the ocean. I settled in and dozed. When I awakened, the ship was getting under way. I was appre-hensive about crossing the English Channel. We all had heard many stories about German U-boats.

A hatch opened, sending a shaft of light skyward. A British sailor shouted, "Here, mates, have some hot bread." He quickly passed out several dozen long loaves of freshly baked bread. "Good luck, mates." He grasped the hatch, pulled it shut, and disappeared belowdecks.

The rest of the voyage passed quietly until it was time to disembark. As we berthed at Le Havre, we were told there would be no gangplank walk onto the soil of France.

"C Company, get to the rail," First Sergeant John Trojnar ordered. "Get ready to go over the side."

I hoped that our obstacle-course training was going to pay off. We had to go over the side using rope netting. A misstep would mean a hard fall in the landing craft below, or worse, in the icy English Channel. The water was deep enough that a man's pack would quickly pull him under.

The other men seemed indifferent; it was just another task someone had decided we should accomplish. The soldiers moved forward.

"Over you go!" Trojnar shouted. "Stay in place. Don't hurry, but keep moving! Hold on to those ropes!" He continued giving words of both encouragement and admonishment. As the boats filled, they pushed away from the ship and headed shoreward.

The 4th Platoon approached the rail. When my turn came, I bellied over the rail and squeezed the ropes with all my might. I sought footholds in the swinging rope netting. My only thought was to get down safely and not embarrass Sergeant Kelly, the squad, or myself. Hands grabbed my legs and guided me into the landing craft. I, in turn, helped the man behind me. The boat was loaded and drifted away into the darkness.

Minutes later, the landing craft scraped to a stop on the beach. The bow ramp flopped down and we disembarked. We were on land again. Company C quickly assembled and marched toward the bivouac area.

The 1st Battalion camped in an orchard beneath two-man pup tents stretched irregularly through the trees. The topsoil was frozen, but it softened with daylight and turned to mud under our GI boots.

Various members of the 4th Platoon huddled around a small fire of K-ration boxes. The wax-covered cardboard burned furiously, taking some of the morning chill from our stiffened joints.

Crooks, Carollo, and Private First Class Harold Barr, an ammo bearer in the mortar section, were engaged in their usual banter when a single rifle shot echoed through the orchard. "Ten-to-one someone killed either Fry or Breen," Barr quipped.

"My money's on Fry," Carollo returned.

We placed facetious bets on the victim, but kept an eye out for any unusual activity that might provide a clue about what happened. We noticed several men milling around a tent a few rows away. A call went out for a medic. The banter was silenced. It was impossible to see what was happening. Platoon Sergeant James Pearson left the warmth of the fire and went to the company command post. Pearson was from Florida and talked with a Southern drawl. He was older than the other members of the platoon, and one of the few who was married.

Almost an hour later, Pearson returned to clarify the various rumors circulating about the shot.

"All right everybody, listen up," Pearson said, although he already had everyone's attention. "We've been trying to drill this stuff into your heads for months. Bill Herman just paid with his life for someone else's dumb-assed mistake. Some guy in A Company a couple of tent rows over decided to clean his rifle and didn't clear the round from the chamber. The rifle went off and hit Herman in the head in his own tent, while he was reading a letter from home. Totally unnecessary. And Stork, who was lying on his blanket next to Herman, is a basket case. You guys use your heads. We don't need this kind of stupid crap. You all understand?"

There was a murmur of acknowledgment as we quickly returned to our assigned tasks or went back to our pup tents. Stay out of sight and avoid any fallout. Stork was evacuated that afternoon, but he returned to the company a few days later.

Our five-day stay in the tents was wet, cold, and muddy. During this time, I realized that Captain Ruffin, the C Company commander at Fort Jackson, was no longer with us. The only officers I remembered seeing in England were DiNola and Baxter.

Private First Class Richard Cunningham, the company runner, had been Ruffin's jeep driver back in the States. The two never got along. Ruffin constantly criticized Cunningham's driving, accusing him more than once of intentionally hitting every pothole in the road. Dick finally went to 1st Sergeant Trojner and requested to be reassigned before he did something that might get him charged with insubordination. From that time until the division landed in France, Cunningham was the company bugler.

The morning of December 6 found us on the "40 or 8" boxcars (40 men or 8 horses), headed toward the front lines. The train rumbled along most of the day, crossing the French countryside of fencerows and dairy cows.

That afternoon the train stopped and everyone jumped off to relieve themselves. Lieutenant DiNola was called to meet with the new company commander, Captain John Wilkins. Pearson immediately issued instructions that everyone must stay in the vicinity of his assigned boxcar.

DiNola returned at dusk and informed us that we were headed for Metz. That information didn't mean much to us, so Private First Class Elmer Zeichner, of Baltimore, Maryland, a member of the mortar section, pulled out a pocket atlas. We found Metz on the map, but it still didn't mean anything to us.

"Garrison, have you brushed your teeth yet?"

I turned and saw DiNola squeezing toothpaste on a toothbrush.

"Well?" DiNola insisted.

"Right away, sir," I responded.

"That goes for everyone," DiNola loudly added. "Just because it's inconvenient doesn't mean you shouldn't do it."

"Who are those people camped in that clearing?" D'Arpino asked.

"Gypsies," DiNola answered. "See their dress? Red, black, and white. Bandanas around their heads. Wagons look like circus wagons, don't they? See those horses? Big, aren't they?"

"Those are Belgian draft horses," Cole spoke up. "We have four of them on our farm. Probably have tractors before I get back. Dad was talking about one before I left."

The men crowded by the open door and watched the gypsies prepare a meal over their red-and-orange fire. The gypsy men grouped by the wagons to talk occasionally glanced at the troop train. The women did the work, moving about quickly in their bright clothing. Soon they were eating.

The train jerked to a start and the troops settled to the floor of the boxcar and slept.

DiNola informed the platoon that Metz was part of the Maginot Line and that several forts in and around the city were still under German control. The lieutenant named several of the forts—Driand, De Plaffeville, St. Quentin, and Jeanne D'Arc.

The 87th, ordered to relieve the 5th Infantry Division, which had captured some of the forts, was supposed to finish the job. Metz was in that part of France that over the course of history was sometimes under French control and sometimes German. The dominant language was German, and the men were told they could expect some Nazi sympathizers.

We boarded trucks at the rail station in Metz. The convoy made its way through the jumbled streets of the city, crossing a canal two or three times. We stopped by a large stone building. As we unloaded, Sergeant Pearson announced: "Welcome to the Third Army and General George Patton. Be alert, someone said he's in Metz now."

"Wonder if he needs an aide?" D'Arpino quipped.

C Company was assigned the third floor. The center of the building was open, and I thought it must have been used in some training capacity. We were told later that the building formerly had been part of a German officer candidate school. An outside walkway was protected by a parapet surrounding it at the third-floor level. We could hear artillery fire in the distance. Noncoms established two-hour guard-duty assignments and the troops settled in to await further instructions.

A member of the mortar squad had a crystal radio and he managed to pick up a BBC broadcast. To everyone's surprise, President Roosevelt was speaking. During the course of the speech, he said that eighteen-year-old soldiers were not being sent overseas. There was an immediate uproar from the eighteen-year-olds—D'Arpino, Stec, Coluccio, Verdone, me, and others. Because of a static interruption, we didn't hear the President end his statement with the words "as replacements." In fact, eighteen-year-olds could be shipped overseas as a part of a unit, such as the 87th Division.

The sarcasm-laden discussion ended almost as quickly as it began. We soon drifted back to our card games, paperback novels, and casual conversations.

That evening, Gullet and I walked around the parapet while on guard duty. The sky was exceptionally bright, filled with stars.

Gullet broke the silence. "What's that red streak?"

Plainly visible in the northern sky was a bright streak of red moving west over the Allied lines. The walkway began to fill with soldiers, who also watched and wondered. Lieutenant DiNola soon appeared with the answer. "You can be glad you aren't in London tonight. Those are V-2 rockets."

Most of the troops watched in silence as several rockets crossed the sky. When they were gone, only the stars remained overhead. We could hear the booming explosions from heavy artillery. Soon, Gullet and I were alone again, pacing the walkway and peering into the dark street below.

The next day, Captain Wilkins called the company together to introduce himself. Part of his talk concerned what the enlisted men should call the officers. They had been warned that if the Germans heard an officer called by rank, they would become primary targets. Wilkins decided that he should be called "Skipper," and that we were not to salute any officer. What to call the platoon leaders, he said, would be left up to each lieutenant.

Two days later, the troops boarded the 6×6 trucks and proceeded north toward the German lines. During the journey, the convoys were split into two columns to travel on parallel country roads. The rough road bounced members of the 4th Platoon up and down in our truck. Three small deer leaped from cover and sprinted for safety, moving parallel to the convoys. At first, they were treated with indifference, and then someone, probably a cook, opened fire with a carbine. Soon, the valley was filled with gunfire as soldiers from both columns fired at the fleeing deer. A few members of the weapons platoon joined in, more to relieve tension than to hit the deer. Everyone watched in amazement as the deer disappeared safely into a wooded area. We laughed and joked about the deer and felt relieved that they had escaped. DiNola interrupted with a caustic comment: "I hope to hell your shooting improves when it counts."

At a road sign reading ACHEN, 8 KM, the trucks pulled off the road and the troops were instructed to take cover. The weapons platoon scattered along the crest of a hill overlooking a broad valley. Gunfire sounded in the distance. To our surprise, we could see several aircraft at the eastern end of the valley as they spiraled and rolled about in the sky. We were witnessing an aerial battle, or dogfight, between two cigar-shaped American P-47 Thunderbolt fighters and a German Messerschmitt. The aerial combatants twisted and turned and tried to gain advantage on one another. It was a great show as the Messerschmitt held its own.

Another American plane, a twin-fuselage P-38, joined the fight. The Messerschmitt pilot decided it was time to leave and sped toward German lines with the P-38 in tow. The two P-47s disappeared to the south. The P-38 soon gave up the chase and followed them.

We all chatted excitedly about the planes, forgetting for the moment that we now were a part of the war. We reboarded the trucks and continued to our next bivouac area.

PART II
THE SAAR

CHAPTER 3

Turning Nineteen in Battle

On December 12, 1944, the 87th Infantry Division relieved the 26th Infantry Division in the Saar Basin, close to the Franco-German border southeast of Saarbrücken, Germany. We were to be part of the Third Army's drive to breach the Siegfried Line and thrust toward the Rhine River. The division represented the right wing of the U.S. XII Corps, which occupied the dividing line between the Third and Sixth U.S. armies. Opposite the inexperienced 87th were elements of the veteran German 17th SS Panzergrenadier Division and the 25th Panzergrenadier Division.

The 347th Infantry took up positions east of the Blies River around Weisviller, France, an area of gently rolling farmland topped by forested hills. The 1st Battalion's objective was to secure the area around the border village of Obergailbach, then advance across the frontier to take the high ground overlooking Gersheim and Walsheim, Germany, along a rail line that led into the heart of the Saar industrial region.

The 1st Battalion disembarked from trucks and deployed in the vicinity of a small town called Woelfing, a few miles southwest of the German border, and immediately established guard posts. As C Company slogged toward its assigned positions, the brisk air blew flurries of snow across the plowed fields and pastureland, leaving a fine white dusting on the furrows of black soil. The ground appeared frozen, but with every footstep our GI boots sank to our ankles. Our machine-gun squad, ordered to set up a position on the company's flank to protect against a surprise attack, moved cautiously along a fencerow. We weren't expecting anything from the Krauts.

As Carollo walked along quietly, he refrained from making his usual wisecracks. I could tell from his silence that he was badly shaken by the wounding of his friend, Sergeant Robin Nichols, only the night before. Nichols was an aspiring pianist. Carollo had heard him play Stateside, and admired his musical ability. Nichols had been detailed to guard the battalion CP. No danger; all he had to do was stay awake for four hours. A stray German artillery shell had landed short of the CP. No one else was hurt, and even Nick's wound wouldn't be considered serious unless you played piano or did anything else that required the use of both hands. One piece of shrapnel had mangled the bones in his left hand. In that one brief second, his entire lifetime of plans and hope disappeared.

"Well," Carollo muttered to no one in particular, "he's out of here. He's going home alive. That's better than what might happen to the rest of us."

This comment was punctuated by the whine of an incoming shell.

"*Hit it,*" Kelly bellowed. His words were unnecessary, inasmuch as everyone had already dived for cover along the fencerow.

It was the first shot fired at us.

We hugged the ground for every bit of protection. The shell passed over our heads and plowed a furrow in the grass.

My heart pounded as if I had just finished the hundred-yard dash. My stomach twisted in fear, the kind I had felt in the sixth grade when the class bully pounded my head into the gutter. I had cried then. I hoped I would react better now. I cautiously raised my head and peered through the fencerow. The field, which led to a wooded area about two hundred yards away, was clear. There was no sign of movement. There had to be a German gun emplacement, a tank, or *something* out there. I saw nothing. Maybe it was just a chance shell, like the one that had been Nichols' misfortune.

Kelly shouted: "Garrison, get down."

Minutes passed. D'Arpino, in his usual jesting manner, murmured, "Wonder if we can still make it to the U.S.O. dance in Manchester?"

"How about it, Kelly? We can do it on a three-day pass," I added.

Kelly ignored us. He watched for a few more minutes. "Gullet," he barked, "move up to that big corner post. Stay low and let me know if you can see anything."

Gullet held his carbine at the ready in his right hand and half crawled, half ran for the scant cover of the large post. He stood slowly and watched the woods intently. Still nothing. Gullet finally turned. "Can't see a thing."

"Okay, let's move up," Kelly said.

"You sure, Sarge?" Crooks cut in.

Again Kelly ignored the question, and everyone moved slowly to join Gullet.

"Must have been a stray," Kelly said as the squad gathered around the fence post. "Let's set up the machine gun on that little knoll. Looks like a good field of fire."

Carollo busied himself placing the gun. Crooks slid in to the left of the gun and made sure the ammo box was lined up so the belt would feed properly. Both Carollo and Crooks wore glasses. Carollo was good with the air-cooled .30-caliber light machine gun. He was especially good at long distances. D'Arpino's favorite comment to keep Carollo's ego in check was "How can you hit something that's so far away and not the side of a barn?"

"Dig in," Kelly ordered as he pointed out positions for foxholes. We broke out our combination GI shovels and picks. With slow deliberation, we began digging shallow excavations just long enough to sleep in. We piled excavated dirt in front of holes for extra protection.

The holes were only inches deep when the next shell exploded. No one heard the 88mm shell come in. The trajectory of an 88 is flat, similar to small-arms fire, and because it's a high-velocity weapon, the shell travels faster than sound. The noise of its explosion is heard before the high-pitched roar of its approach. When the shell exploded, D'Arpino was kneeling in his foxhole. The impact of shrapnel hitting the freshly piled earth in front of D'Arpino splattered dirt in his face. Shrapnel splintered my shovel handle in two.

"Spread out," Kelly yelled. "Get behind the fencerow!" A second shell whined overhead. "They're zeroing in on us. Move!"

I half climbed, half leaped over the fence. Carollo and Crooks had already taken cover behind the heavy foliage that grew along the fencerow. D'Arpino and Gullet sprinted several yards along the fence. When they reached a spot where the wire was broken, they dived through to the other side. Kelly, who had gone the other way, crouched behind a tree trunk.

Minutes passed. As before, there was no movement in the woods or the surrounding area. "You know, I bet they have a forward artillery spotter in that woods," Crooks said.

"Probably right," Kelly answered. "You wouldn't think the Krauts would waste shells on four or five people like us. Stay down and keep out of sight. Let's see what happens."

The squad maintained its position for about fifteen minutes; then Kelly decided it was time to move. Using arm signals, he regrouped the squad on the back side of a small hill, out of sight of the German artillery spotter and safe from the direct fire of the 88mm gun. Kelly posted D'Arpino and me on guard duty at the fencerow with special instructions to listen for tanks. If the panzers were on the move, our position might not be secure. He didn't need to add that if there were tanks, we had more than a position to worry about.

Kelly and Gullet started their hole west of where Carollo and Crooks were digging in the machine gun. Their shovels tore large bites out of the damp clay with each stroke. While Crooks added a little more depth to their foxhole, Carollo carefully scanned the surrounding terrain. He didn't like the idea of a German spotter in the woods, although he knew they were screened from direct observation by the fencerow. The squad had an escape route if the Germans did attack; a small gully behind us led to another fencerow, and then on to another wooded area.

Kelly and Gullet completed their foxhole. "Hey, Bill," Kelly said to

Carollo, "Gullet and I are going to relieve D'Arpino and Garrison on outpost, so they can dig in. Best you and Jack eat and get some sleep. You will be on in two hours after us. No fires. It's too dark."

Kelly and Gullet loomed out of the gathering dusk to relieve us. D'Arpino and I hurried back to the squad. "Hey, buddy," D'Arpino called out, "where's our foxhole?"

"What foxhole?" answered Carollo, who was still awake and sitting on the edge of his hole.

"The one you and Jack were supposed to dig for us."

"Up yours," came the reply.

"Some buddies you are."

The banter continued unabated until D'Arpino and I finished our work and started to eat our K rations. Exhaustion hit us even before we collapsed into our shallow foxhole. The night dragged on with an agonizing slowness that becomes all too common in combat. Every two hours, men groggy from sleep stumbled out of their foxholes to relieve men numb from cold and struggling to stay awake on guard duty. Everyone was concerned about German night patrols, but the night remained quiet.

I opened my eyes to the pale light of morning. D'Arpino was gone from the foxhole. I could hear voices telling me it was safe to come out, inviting me to share the warmth of a fire. I tried to rise, but I couldn't move. The shelter half over the bottom of the hole was submerged in freezing cold water, which covered my entire right side. I had no feeling in my right arm, and none in my right leg. I felt numb all over. I struggled frantically to get up. Only my left arm responded.

"Tony. Paul. Help me. I'm paralyzed. I can't move." Responding to my desperate cries, the entire squad rushed to my foxhole.

"Come on, buddy, you don't get a Purple Heart for freezing your rear end. Get your butt out of there," D'Arpino laughed. Hands grabbed my heavy overcoat and hauled me to a standing position. I promptly fell down. They picked me up again and took turns walking me back and forth.

Gullet and D'Arpino walked me to the fire that had been built up with K-ration boxes and twigs. D'Arpino shaved some chocolate D bar into a hot cup of water and handed it to me. Gradually, the feeling seeped back into my body, but I was still unable to walk without help.

"This is sure a hell of a way to start my birthday," I grumbled.

"Hey, that's right!" Gullet said. "Nineteen."

"That's everyone but me," D'Arpino noted. "Hope I make it to my nineteenth." His melancholy comment brought glances from the rest of us.

There was a momentary silence, interrupted by Kelly. "That's in January, isn't it?"

"Yeah, the nineteenth," D'Arpino responded.

"There's someone in the field," Carollo blurted out. "There! Next to the fence!" He had already repositioned the .30-caliber. "These damn bipods. You have to stand up to move the gun," he growled.

He was right. The short-legged bipod mounted on the end of the barrel prevented rotation. The gun had to be picked up and moved. But it was quicker to set up by merely flipping down the mount, and therefore it could be operated by only a two-man crew—a gunner and ammo carrier. The tripod-mounted weapons had a much wider radius of movement, but it definitely took a three-man team to operate: the gunner, the ammo carrier, and a man to carry the tripod.

Kelly said: "It's Stec. Hold your fire." Steve Stec was the 4th Platoon's runner.

"Hey, you guys, Sergeant Pearson wants you back with the platoon right now!"

"Pack it up. Let's go!" Kelly ordered. "Somebody help Garrison."

Stec left immediately, followed by Carollo and Crooks. Kelly checked the abandoned position to make sure nothing was left behind. Gullet and D'Arpino took turns helping me. We cautiously made our way along the fencerows. By the time we joined the platoon, I was walking without help.

We found C Company spread out on a densely wooded hill. No specific orders had been issued, but the rumor was that the company was to attack and occupy the small village of Obergailbach, in the valley on the other side of the hill.

"Over here, Kelly," Pearson called. "Kelly, we're moving out in about fifteen minutes," Pearson said. "Sergeant DeVine will brief you."

"Okay," Kelly responded, then turned to the squad. "You guys have about ten minutes to get done whatever you have to do."

All five members of the squad plopped to the ground and shoved steel helmets under our heads for pillows.

Before Kelly ever got to DeVine, he noticed that the rifle platoons were assembling, and he saw Captain Wilkins and the other officers moving through the trees toward a narrow ravine before they disappeared from sight. Squads of riflemen followed.

"Hey, Henry, get your men," Pearson called to DeVine. "You're supposed to bring up the rear with the mortar squads."

"What the hell," DeVine growled. "We aren't supposed to leave for another ten minutes. Kelly, let's go!"

We filed along the ravine. There wasn't a clear path, so the men were soon scattered at different intervals among the tall pine trees. As I threaded my way through the trees, I felt a stinging sensation in my right leg and realized that my leg had stiffened. I knew I had to stretch the muscles and walk it off.

I had to readjust the grip of my right hand on the ammo box. The pace quickened and the weapons platoon had to trot in an effort to maintain pace with the riflemen. Intermittent rifle fire could be heard ahead. It was hard to judge, but I thought that we had gone about a half mile before we emerged from the forest into an open field.

The field sloped downhill about two hundred yards to a road that bisected the valley. A small plateau stretched to our immediate left for about twenty yards, obstructing the view of most of the opposite hillside and forest. To the right was the remnant of a fencerow overgrown by bushes and small trees. C Company was scattered from the edge of the forest to the road in the valley.

The earth was cold and saturated with water. By the time the 4th Platoon reached open ground, the rifle platoons ahead of us had turned it into a quagmire. Our boots were almost sucked off our feet with each step. We were falling farther behind the riflemen. The mortar men stripped their packs, keeping only a shelter half or blanket. Soon, our path was littered with packs, shovels, 60mm mortars and shells—anything to lighten the load.

The gunfire grew heavier. I realized that the rest of the machine-gun section was rapidly leaving me behind. "Gene. Stop and rest," D'Arpino yelled. "Paul and I have enough ammo. Bring yours when you can."

I just stood there, unable to pull my right foot from the sticky mud. I slammed both boxes of machine-gun ammo into the mud and slipped my pack from my shoulders. I folded my blanket over my ammo belt, fitted the blanket in the small of my back, and then rebuckled the belt.

A sense of helplessness swept over and engulfed me. I felt ashamed. My squad was going into battle without me. I couldn't keep up. That couldn't be. I was never last. I was never left behind. I was always in the lead. I picked up my ammo boxes and jerked my right foot from the mud. My foot came halfway out of my boot. I jammed my foot back into my boot, grasped the back of the leather-backed legging and jerked the boot from the mud. As I did so, I noticed a bag of mortar shells lying in the mud with a mortar tube carefully placed on top of the bag to keep it out of the muck. I placed one of my ammo boxes on top of my shelter half. I laboriously made my way toward the small plateau on which numerous C Company men were gathering.

Just ahead, I could see Kelly, Carollo, Crooks, and Gullet approaching the road. D'Arpino was about twenty yards behind them and struggling to catch up. Several riflemen were taking cover by a culvert in the side ditch. The mortarmen and I hurried to catch up.

I heard Carollo shout out: "Kelly, there's a German machine gun down there! It's pointing along the road!"

Before he had finished his sentence, bullets ricocheted off the road and plowed into the mud close to Kelly's feet. Carollo threw his machine gun in front of him as he hit the ground and fired several bursts toward houses located about three hundred yards down the road. He didn't see any Germans, so he sprayed bullets at the windows. There was no answering fire.

The rifle platoons were scattered all over the hillside. Many men had been hit. Some lay motionless in the mud, either dead or afraid of being shot again if they moved. The walking wounded scurried to find any position that offered shelter.

Kelly watched two officers approach, each helping the other through the half-frozen mud. He recognized Lieutenants Morrill and Lester, two rifle platoon leaders. Both men had shrapnel wounds and were having difficulty walking.

"You need some help?" Kelly called.

"Thanks, Sergeant. We'll make it," Morrill replied. "You men stay down, and remember to zigzag. Don't let them get a bead on you."

As they passed, I noticed Morrill's ashen face and thought he might be more seriously injured than he thought.

D'Arpino, who had fallen behind the rest of the squad while trying to avoid the worst of the mud, finally caught up to the firefight. He ran into Carollo, who was firing the .30-caliber light machine gun along the narrow road. He could hear small-arms fire coming from the woods, but he couldn't see any enemy troops.

When Kelly signaled to continue the advance, D'Arpino rose and approached the road. Suddenly, his right leg was knocked from under his body, and he landed hard on his back. Surprisingly, he didn't feel any pain. He lay motionless for several seconds, not sure whether he could move or whether his leg was still there.

"D'Arpino, you okay?" Red Blum came to a sliding stop next to D'Arpino. "You hit anywhere else besides your leg?"

"Is it still attached?" D'Arpino asked as he cautiously rose on one elbow.

"Yeah, let me put a tourniquet on it," Blum said. "Looks like the bullet went on through. Give me your handkerchief."

D'Arpino fished a handkerchief from his pocket. Blum quickly tied it to his own and placed them above the wound. He pulled the makeshift tourniquet until it was snug around the leg and tied the ends. "Loosen that every ten minutes or so."

"Why?" D'Arpino asked.

"The medics said so. You have any water?"

"None left."

"Here, have mine. I made chocolate this morning. Gotta go."

"Thanks, buddy."

"Anytime." Blum rose and continued up the hill.

D'Arpino watched Blum leave as he sprinkled sulfa powder on his leg. By now, some GIs had entered the woods at the top of the hill. But several never made it. He could see them scattered over the hillside. Other wounded soldiers who could walk made their way back along the route of attack, heading for the aid station. Using his carbine as a crutch, D'Arpino pushed himself erect and followed, his head down. He gazed at his muddy boots as he limped along.

In the confusion of the brief firefight, I had lost sight of D'Arpino. As I neared the road, I spotted him gamely trying to keep up with the other wounded.

"Tony!"

D'Arpino looked up at me and the mortarmen.

"Hey, Gene, how's your leg?"

"Better than yours," I answered, gesturing toward D'Arpino's blood-stained pants. "You need any help going back?"

"Sure, come on." We both laughed.

"Cole got hit," D'Arpino said after an awkward moment of silence.

"Bad?"

"Yeah. He wasn't moving. I better go. I don't want to be in those woods after dark."

D'Arpino and I looked at each other.

"Take care," D'Arpino said.

"You, too, Tony. With your luck, they will probably send you back to England."

D'Arpino laughed and continued on his way. I watched him go, wondering if I'd be lucky enough to get a wound just bad enough to warrant a month or two in clean sheets, hot food, and some pretty nurses to tease.

"Kill the bastard!" The startling words interrupted my thoughts.

A rifleman with a shoulder wound was taking a German prisoner to the rear. One of the mortarmen was venting his frustration on the prisoner, who was also wounded and looked extremely pale.

The rifleman stopped. "The bastard was dug in at the corner of the woods," he blurted. "He kept shooting at us until we were right on him, and then he stuck up his hands. Pearson wouldn't let us kill him. Said to take him back; he might have some information. He shot Garrett and Smith and Cole."

"You better let him rest, too," I said, pointing to the prisoner.

"Let the bastard stand," the mortarman snarled.

"A dead prisoner can't give much information," Zeichner interjected.

I motioned for the German to sit down. "Sitzen!"

More American wounded passed on their way to the rear. The rifleman nudged the German with his M1. The two of them slowly rose and joined Garrett, who was bleeding profusely from a head wound. The group trudged off toward the rear.

Artillery shells, fired from behind our lines, whistled over our heads as they headed for somewhere beyond the wooded hill on the opposite side of the valley. A lieutenant rushed up to us. He was dressed in a relatively clean uniform with sharp creases in his trousers. "What outfit is this?" he demanded to know. His trenchcoat was neatly buttoned and extended below his knees. I noticed that his new, rubberized winter boots were muddy.

"Part of C Company, sir," a mortar sergeant answered.

"Where is the rest of the company?"

"In the woods, sir."

"Why aren't you with them?" the lieutenant snapped.

"We couldn't keep up," the sergeant responded, dropping the "sir."

"I bet," the officer barked.

The sergeant stood up, his eyes alight with anger. Before the sergeant could spit out a response, the lieutenant quickly said, "You men stay here and move up with A Company. We will move out as soon as it is dark." He turned to walk away through the muck, followed by his runner.

"Goddamned ninety-day wonder," the sergeant spat. "What does he know? He wasn't here. They load us up with full packs, mortars, ammo, and everything else they can think of. And that goddamned Wilkins takes off on the run to meet a time schedule, leaving us strung out behind him. I'll bet he wasn't first going into that woods. Why didn't they set up the mortars and machine guns to give supporting fire?"

The lieutenant, who hadn't gone far, couldn't help but hear the sergeant's tirade, but he seemed intent on pulling his new boots from the sucking mud.

I had never cared much for the mortar sergeant, but the man's sudden outburst reflected my thoughts. At that point, I gained a lot of respect for him.

During the pause in the attack, we tried to rest, but the excitement of the day and the expectation of moving forward again kept most of us alert and in a ready position.

I noticed Rich Fleming, a mortar ammo carrier, crouched as if to run. "What are you doing?" I asked.

"I belong over there," Fleming replied.

"We all do," Zeichner chimed in. "We'll be leaving soon."

Fleming seemed to relax, but suddenly he sprang forward and ran toward the opposite woods. The ground, refrozen by the evening drop in temperature, allowed Fleming to move quickly, and he disappeared into the woods.

Dusk came quickly in the gloom of early winter. The day had gone rapidly. The mortar sergeant stood in the gathering darkness and looked back at our line of departure.

Although there were other sergeants among the group, this sergeant had taken charge. "A Company is coming," he said. "Let's move out."

No one questioned the order. No one wanted anything to do with A Company and the snotty lieutenant with his cleanly pressed uniform. We moved slowly and cautiously across the road. The footing was good. The only sound was our own breathing. It was completely dark in the shadow of the woods.

The sergeant raised his arm and the thirty-odd soldiers melted into the darkness. In a loud whisper he gave instructions to spread out in a line parallel to and about a hundred feet from the edge of the woods. "Dig in, two men to a hole. Best we not try to enter the woods. Our own guys might shoot us."

I paired with a mortar ammo bearer named John Cormack. He was an older man, around twenty-five. The noise of the pick shovels digging into the frozen ground seemed to reverberate in the darkness. I was sure we would draw fire—if not from the Germans, from our own troops. Nothing happened. Our foxholes finished, we settled in to wait for morning. This time, the foxholes were deeper. The silence was absolute. We knew their troops were in the woods along the top of the hill, and we couldn't help thinking that the Germans would come charging at us out of those same woods at any second.

My nineteenth birthday had been a long day. I pulled my canteen from its canvas holder. Empty. I couldn't even remember taking a drink. I didn't want to ask Cormack for a drink; it wasn't his problem. If any member of my squad had been present, I would not have hesitated. No reflection on Cormack, but he just wasn't a close buddy. I remembered stumbling in a wheel rut filled with water as I moved across a field toward the woods.

"I'm going to get some water," I whispered.

"Water," Cormack said. "Where?"

"I stepped in a puddle not far from here."

"Puddle of what?"

"Don't know and don't care. I'm thirsty. I'll put a couple of halazone tablets in it."

"I'd give you a drink, but I don't have anything, either."

"Thanks. You want me to fill yours?"

"No, thanks. I saw hoofprints out there."

I chuckled and slithered into the darkness. I thought I knew where the closest foxholes were and about where I had stepped into the water. Cormack was probably right about the source of the water, but my throat was so dry that I could barely swallow. As I crawled through the dark night, I could hear my heart pounding heavily against my chest.

I removed my glove to run my hand over the muddy ground in search of the rut. I didn't want to wear a wet glove in the freezing night. I felt a wagon wheel rut and followed it until there was ice, and then water. It was deep enough that I could insert my canteen. The water made a gurgling sound as it filled the canteen. I dropped in two halazone tablets and vigorously shook the canteen. I lay quietly for two or three minutes. I was supposed to wait two hours for the tablets to dissolve and purify the water, but thirst made me impatient. Wait two hours! The hell with that. I tilted the canteen and drank. It was water.

Several minutes later, I was back in the foxhole. Cormack refused my offer of a drink.

"I'm not sleepy," Cormack whispered. "If you can sleep, go ahead. I'll wake you if anything happens."

I wrapped myself in a blanket and fell asleep almost at once.

CHAPTER 4

Bloody Woods

The **C Company attack** had lacked organization; each man had to fend for himself. When the lead platoons had entered the woods, the resistance had been light. The Germans had inflicted enough damage during the initial attack, and then retreated. What was left of C Company was scattered along the other side of the wooded hill.

On the near side of the woods, Cormack reacted to the sudden eruption of firing and shook me from my deep sleep. We grabbed our weapons and prepared for an attack. The screams from the woods made me cringe. I found myself praying: *Please don't let it be Gullet or Kelly or Crooks or Carollo.* The names and faces of my friends flashed in my mind. I watched as the tracers darted from the depths of the woods.

The gunfire suddenly increased in intensity and the tracers coming from the German weapons stopped. B and C companies were counterattacking. For several minutes, the gunfire was heavy, then it dwindled to occasional bursts. The Germans had retreated again. There would be no more sleep that night for the men of the 1st Battalion.

* * *

Dawn slowly parted the dark sky, and with daylight came artillery shells that hit the treetops and sent their deadly shower of sharpnel down to the ground. The initial barrage lasted only a few minutes, then tapered off to sporadic, widely spread bursts.

The 4th Platoon mortar sergeant left his foxhole and carefully approached the shadowy woods. Minutes later, I could hear him talking, and then Red Blum walked out of the woods. "Garrison. I thought you were hit. Someone said you had a head wound. Damn, you're all right." He hugged me.

Blum guided me into the woods to the machine-gun section foxholes. Gullet saw me before any of the other squad members. "About time you got here. You have anything to eat?" Gullet asked in a nonchalant tone, as if I had never left. "Carollo and Crooks ate everything in sight."

Kelly looked haggard from a night without sleep and the tension of combat. He stepped toward me and asked, "How's your leg?"

"Better," I told him.

"Let's get back to food," Carollo growled.

"Right," Crooks said.

"Sorry," I said, for not bringing more food.

"Figures," Carollo muttered as he gnawed on a chocolate D bar.

I glanced around the immediate area, mentally checking off members of the 4th Platoon. "Where's Bialk?"

Kelly lowered his eyes and studied a rip in his overcoat. "He got it this morning with a tree burst, hunting for firewood. He didn't even hit the ground. Thought the burst was too far off. Got him in the chest."

"Crap." I wondered who would write the letter to Bialk's parents in Wisconsin. "That only leaves Sullivan in the Second Squad. I noticed that he's dug in with Gullet. Where's their machine gun? I haven't seen it."

"It was captured last night," Kelly replied. "We also don't have any mortars. They were either discarded during the attack or lost to the Germans during the night."

"I don't see Fleming," I said. "Didn't he join you just as it got dark last night?"

"Yeah, but he's missing," Kelly said softly. "They captured a bunch of guys last night. Wick, Verdone, Trojnar, Goodfriend, some riflemen, and some guys from B Company. It was a real mess."

Kelly paused to get his frustration under control, then continued his story. When the order had come down to dig in, everyone scooped out foxholes on the spot. No sentries were posted, no patrols were ordered. The only men who were alert and on guard were those like Kelly, who couldn't sleep. He had braced his back against the shallow wall of the foxhole and waited.

Several hours passed. Kelly had begun to relax when he heard someone moving in the darkness. It was Armand Verdone, the C Company runner.

"Anything going on, Kelly?" Verdone asked.

"No. Hope nothing does."

"I'm going to check up ahead," Verdone said. He slipped into the darkness. Kelly waited, alert and nervous. Suddenly, flashlight beams sliced the darkness.

Kelly heard Verdone scream, "Counterattack! Counterattack," as he crashed through the undergrowth toward the company command post. Kelly raised his carbine and fired at the beams of light, which seemed to be everywhere. Carollo's machine gun joined the din with short bursts. GIs vacated their foxholes and stumbled through the darkness. "Bill! Cease fire," Kelly yelled at Carollo. "Fall back. We're shooting into our own troops. Fall back!"

The Germans had pierced the defense perimeter, causing confusion and panic.

"The Krauts caught some people in their foxholes and bayoneted them," Kelly continued. "You know Crawford? He and Sawyer were in the same hole on the perimeter. Didn't have time to bail out and decided to play dead. A Kraut bayoneted Sawyer. He missed Crawford on the second try and hit Sawyer again. Then the Kraut sat down on the edge of the foxhole, put his boots on Crawford's rear, and went through his pockets until he found some cigarettes. When B and C companies counterattacked, the Kraut left them. He thought they were both dead. Sawyer bled to death before morning. Right before he died he asked Crawford to write to his wife and tell her that he loved her. Crawford was a basket case. They walked him out at daylight."

There was complete silence after Kelly finished his story. Reference to a loved one seemed inappropriate in this forest of shadows. They were from another place, another time.

Kelly went on: "Pearson told me that John Thomas [one of the rifle platoon sergeants] was captured and then escaped. Just stepped behind a tree and the Germans never missed him."

Again there was silence. Cormack finally asked, "Did Byrnes get it?"

"Yeah, so did Hengeveld and Panebianco," Kelly replied. "Did you see D'Arpino?"

"He got hit in the leg, but he was walking pretty good and talking about his two-million-dollar wound," I said.

"Two million?" Crooks asked.

"You know Tony," I said with a grin. Everyone laughed. "Tony said Cole was hit pretty bad."

Gullet looked up from cleaning his carbine. "Cole's unconscious. I just came back from seeing him. There are eight or nine wounded at the edge of the woods. The medics haven't been able to get them out."

"Paul, what about Coluccio, Brewer, and Little?" I asked.

"They're all okay," Gullet said. "But Fulton and Jaroz got hit."

Pearson, newly promoted to first sergeant to replace Trojnar, suddenly interrupted the casualty report. "You troops better spread out. We've lost enough men already." The men drifted to their positions.

"Kelly, I'm going to see Cole," I said.

"You stay with me when you come back."

I carefully made my way through the woods toward the spot at which the wounded had been collected. I spied the group of wounded soldiers lying in a shallow depression at the very corner of the woods. Only one man appeared to be alert. He rose on one elbow as I approached and pulled a blanket over the man next to him, who turned out to be Cole.

"How is he?" I asked the wounded GI as I pointed to Cole.

"Not good. He's been delirious all night. They should have taken him on the last ambulance, but there just wasn't enough room."

I looked at the other wounded. They were all asleep, and I didn't recognize anyone. "Looks like B Company took a hit, also."

"Yeah. Some of the fellows were captured last night, too."

I sat there for some time, watching Cole moan and thrash his arms. "I had better go," I said, my voice cracking.

"I'll take care of him the best I can," the wounded B Company soldier promised.

"Thanks." I rose to go. Tears trickled down my cheeks as I made my way back to the squad.

I later ran into an ambulance driver who told me that Cole was safely evacuated to a field hospital and, at first, was progressing well from his wounds. After the 87th Division withdrew, the Germans counterattacked and the field hospital was forced to relocate. The rigor of the relocation was too strenuous for Cole, who died before reaching another hospital.

When I returned, Private First Class Bill Petrosky, a platoon runner, was relating an incident that had happened that morning. Petrosky's platoon leader had been caught in his foxhole when the Germans counterattacked and bypassed his position without discovering him. The lieutenant decided that the most damage he could do at that point was to throw grenades at the Germans. He took a grenade in each hand and pulled the pins with his teeth. Just as he was about to toss the grenades, C and B companies counterattacked, and suddenly there were GIs all around him, so he couldn't throw them.

By this time, the pins were somewhere in the bottom of his foxhole. With a grenade in each hand, the lieutenant couldn't search for the pins, and with all the confusion he didn't want to try to attract someone's attention. He placed the hand-clasped grenades in his overcoat pockets to keep his hands warm and waited for morning. The first person he saw was Petrosky, who had been looking for him. The officer explained the situation, and the runner finally found the pins and reinserted them into the grenades. Petrosky said he would have found the pins sooner, but he was laughing too hard.

By the time Petrosky finished his story, everyone else was laughing. They would never again view the lieutenant the same way.

The Germans had been firing tree bursts into the woods atop the hill for at least two hours. The shelling caused more of a morale problem than it did casualties. Nerves were wearing thin. Shrapnel from the tree bursts scattered over a wide area. Archie Gilbert, one of the company medics, was the only known casualty. He was a small, wiry, cocky twenty-four-year-old from Parkersburg, West Virginia. Doc Grieco dressed his wound, and while he waited to be evacuated, Gilbert told us an incredible story.

During yesterday's disorganized attack to take the high ground around Obergailbach, Gilbert had become separated from C Company after he took wounded soldiers to the rear. As Gilbert made his way back to the front lines, Robert Taylor, a kid from his hometown who also was a medic attached to C Company, joined him. As they passed through B Company, they were stopped by an officer and asked to bring in a wounded forward artillery observer. The officer explained that B Company has lost all its medics. A sergeant told Gilbert and Taylor that the wounded soldier was over the next hill near a tree about twenty yards off a road. The whole area, the noncom warned them, was under German observation.

Gilbert and Taylor climbed over a fence, crossed nearly fifty yards of furrowed ground, and started up the knoll. As they neared the crest, the medics crouched low and scurried for cover behind some bushes. They peered through the bare foliage and saw a wide, shallow valley ringed by hills, the highest of which lay to the north, behind the German lines. About a hundred yards from the bottom of the knoll was a shell-shattered tree. Beneath it they could see a brown figure that appeared to be sitting up against the tree's trunk.

The medics broke from the cover of the bushes, ran down the knoll, and reached an unpaved road that twisted its way through the valley. Moving in rushes, they reached the wounded GI.

The soldier, his eyes half open, pointed to his leg. Quickly checking him over, the medics found that a piece of shrapnel had dug a six-inch gash in the man's thigh, nearly to the bone. The wounded man had sprinkled sulfa powder in the wound and stuffed it with bandages in a crude attempt to stem the bleeding. Gilbert put a tourniquet above the wound, removed the blood-soaked bandages, and wrapped clean ones around the gash. Taylor stuck a syrette of morphine into the man's leg.

"Can you walk?" Gilbert asked him.

"I'll try," the wounded GI replied.

Gilbert and Taylor got on either side of the man and grabbed him underneath his arms and gently lifted him to his feet. He moaned and cursed. The medics supported his weight and started down the side of the road as the wounded man, whose strength was quickly ebbing, tried to keep pace on one leg. The whistle of an approaching artillery shell sent them to the ground. The shell exploded across the road from them. They lay for a few minutes, then got up. The medics placed their hands under the wounded man's buttocks and lifted his body to carry him down the road. Another shell, closer this time, exploded behind them.

"We gotta get off this road," Gilbert said, breathing hard from his exertion. "They got it zeroed in." Taylor said nothing.

They lifted the wounded man again in the chair-carry, and cut across a fallow field as another shell hit directly on the road. The field rolled gently down to a cart trail used by local farmers to move their farm equipment. When they reached the other side of the field, the medics sat their casualty down and collapsed in exhaustion. After catching his breath, Gilbert rose and looked around.

"Jesus!" His exclamation caused Taylor to sit up and look in the same direction. About two feet away was a sign in German script. It read, ACHTUNG! MINEN! The blood drained out of Taylor's face. Walking abreast, the medics had carried the wounded man across a German minefield. After looking at each other wordlessly for a time, the medics slowly rose, hoisted their human cargo over their arms, and struggled down the cart trail in the dwindling light toward the battalion aid station.

After the German barrage lifted, Kelly went to talk to DeVine and Pearson. I sat next to a large pine tree and watched Gullet and Sullivan try to dig through tree roots to enlarge their foxhole. The noise of their shovels hitting the half-frozen ground echoed through the woods. The distinct crack of an M1 rifle brought an immediate stop to the digging. The machine-gun squad jumped into our holes with weapons ready, peering in the direction of the German lines, expecting the worst.

Kelly returned in a few minutes. "Relax. DeVine was cleaning his rifle and shot himself in the hand."

"DeVine?" Sullivan said in disbelief.

"Yeah, DeVine. He said he had forgotten to eject the bullet from the chamber."

Sullivan resumed digging, making Gullet dodge dirt that flew in his direction.

We heard the whine of the incoming shell and knew it was going to be close. It burst in the top of the tree next to Kelly and me. A sharp pain in my right thigh caused me to lunge forward. I was afraid to look. "Kelly, you alright?"

"Yes, are you?"

"Hit in the leg."

"Medic!" Kelly screamed. "Let me look at it."

Kelly scrambled over to me and looked at my leg. "There's nothing but a little hole. Drop your pants."

I obediently lowered my trousers and long underwear. "Your leg's just cut a little, but it's worth a Purple Heart," he added.

"It felt like it was more than a little cut," I muttered.

"You just want to go back to England," Kelly laughed.

"Try Ohio," I shot back.

"Go see a medic," Kelly said.

Gullet moved quickly toward my gun position. "How bad is it?" he asked. He noticed the bloody spot on my leg and realized that the wound was not serious. "You better pull up your pants or you'll freeze your rear," he laughed.

Another shell whined over us and exploded. Shrapnel rattled through the trees. Someone let out a scream that was instantly muffled.

Kelly checked the squad for casualties. Finding none, he looked at me. "Find out what happened and who got hit when you see the medic."

"Okay," I called back. I was already walking toward the company CP.

More artillery bursts came in, but they were scattered and did no damage. It was obvious the Germans didn't know how the company was deployed and were trying to strike all parts of the woods. I passed DeVine. He sat on the side of his foxhole with an almost apologetic smile, his hand covered by a bloody bandage. Neither of us spoke at first. Then DeVine asked: "You get hit?"

"Yes," I replied. "A small piece of shrapnel in my leg."

"A medic is over there, taking care of Musselman and Fitzgerald."

"Thanks. You take care."

I saw Blum and Doc Taylor at a nearby foxhole and made my way toward them. The damage inflicted by the last tree burst was obvious. Musselman and Fitzgerald had been crouching in their foxhole. Shrapnel had torn into their backs, leaving gaping wounds. Both men were conscious and joking with Taylor and Blum. Musselman suddenly began shaking and his face became almost white. Blum placed his gloved hand in Musselman's mouth and said, "Bite."

Taylor worked rapidly. The shrapnel had ripped through Musselman's overcoat and underclothing, exposing torn flesh and muscles. I noticed Taylor begin to shake almost in unison with Musselman. The strain of the previous night and the pressure of tending critically wounded men while under fire were taking their toll. Gilbert's evacuation earlier that day had left Taylor as the only medic in the company.

Two riflemen appeared and prepared a litter with their rifles and blanket. Musselman had stopped shaking and seemed to be stabilized. Taylor turned his attention to Fitzgerald, whose wounds were as bad as Musselman's.

I had never fastened my trousers. I was transfixed by the scene in front of me. There was nothing I could do to help. No one even noticed me. I stepped backward, feeling embarrassed that my wound was so insignificant. I adjusted my clothing, buckled my belt, and made my way back to my foxhole. I passed DeVine again. The sergeant hadn't changed his position or expression.

With the exception of Blum, I never saw any of them again. Taylor suffered a gunshot wound to the foot later that day. He, Musselman, Fitzgerald, and DeVine were evacuated that evening.

Shortly after dusk, Kelly received word that a hot meal was being served. The men of the 4th Platoon were last to eat, leaving their foxholes two at a time. Kelly and I were together, using the trunk of a huge pine tree as shelter from possible shelling. Mess Sergeant Fry, the head cook, was his usual blustering self. His assistant, Forsythe, trembled so badly that he missed the mess kits as he tried to serve a version of GI hash.

Kelly tried to reassure Forsythe that he was safe. "The Krauts haven't shelled us for a couple of hours. Besides, they know your cooking will do more damage to us than their shelling."

I chuckled. Forsythe forced a smile but didn't seem to relax much.

"You're always wising off, Kelly. If you don't like it, eat K rations," Fry snapped.

"Up yours, Fry," Kelly snarled.

"Keep it down, Kelly," Pearson drawled. "We don't need any more incoming shells."

Kelly and I both laughed, and in a few minutes we made our way back to our positions.

The next day was relatively quiet. A few shells came in, but there was only one casualty—shrapnel wounded John Thomas. The Germans couldn't keep him captive, but they did get him off the line.

Kelly returned from the CP with news that C Company was being relieved. The excitement in his voice revealed that he had had enough of exploding shells and shrapnel. We all felt the same. After the first two days of combat, we were surprised by the way we had remained so calm and controlled during the shelling. Now it was time to get out before the odds tipped against us.

"Listen up," Kelly called. "We're pulling out. We're moving into a little town down the road. Everyone but the machine-gun section goes."

"Hey, why not us, Kelly?" Carollo asked.

"We have the honor of defending this lousy place until morning. No one wants it, anyway," Kelly said.

Sergeant George Burden, one of the mortar squad leaders, smiled. It was the first time he had felt like smiling for several days. He rose and motioned toward the CP. "Let's go guys. Hey, Kelly, don't do anything dumb."

"No problem. I did that when I got into the infantry," Kelly retorted.

We watched in silence as the rest of the platoon departed. They were gone in seconds. The stillness after their departure was oppressive. The woods stayed quiet through the night.

Kelly and I took the last guard shift before dawn. It seemed reasonable that if there was to be an attack, it would be at first light. The early morning shadows could be deceptive, but there was no movement and no sound. It was as if both sides, tired of the carnage and sapped of energy, had no fight left. As I stared across the valley, the darkened hills grew lighter with dawn. The wind created sounds as deceptive as the morning's shadows.

"Let's get out of here." Kelly shook the other squad members awake and issued quiet instructions. It seemed imperative that we leave as quietly as possible. Kelly surveyed the area, making sure that nothing was left behind. This wooded hillside had taken a tremendous toll from C Company.

The bulk of the troops moved into a small town north of the bloody wooded hillside. A broken sign hanging from a single hook on a pole identified the place as Walsheim. Another sign pointing back along the road read Obergailbach. It was the same road we had crossed in our initial attack on December 16, and the same town from which enemy machine-gun fire had helped whittle down the company.

Daylight also brought intermittent shelling. The Germans seemed reluctant to shell the town itself, but explosions in the adjacent fields and the roads leading in and out of Walsheim were enough to keep us on edge.

Our platoon occupied a railway terminal building, which housed various pieces of railroad equipment. The building sat on the banks of the Blies River, which ran along the edge of town. One set of tracks ran to the north and disappeared into the wooded countryside.

Because of the shelling, troops dashed to a hot breakfast by ones and twos. Gullet and I were prepared to leave the terminal building when Kelly burst through the door. His eyes were full of anger. "Sullivan's dead!" he shouted. "A goddamned 88 got him. One lousy piece of shrapnel hit him in the back of the head. The shell landed so far away that he didn't even get down. He thought he was out of range. Goddamned bastards."

Kelly stood there shaking with anger. The rest of the men took the news in stunned silence. Sullivan was well liked. Carollo inspected his combat boots, adjusting them carefully. Crooks and Gullet stared into space. I adjusted the carbine on my shoulder, wondering how many more times there would be such periods of grief. I thought, When the last man is gone, will there be anyone to miss him?

"Here, Gene, this is yours." Kelly handed me a .45-caliber pistol, a holster, and ammunition. "It was Sully's. Some goddamned lieutenant from A Company was taking it. I told him to back off, and damn if he didn't. I said this was a C Company man, and the weapon was going to stay with C Company." Kelly's words still rang with emotion. "Give your carbine to Watson when you go to eat."

I buckled the .45 around my waist. I was sure Sully wouldn't mind. Gullet and I left immediately for breakfast. We ran along the tracks, using empty railway cars as cover until we reached the middle of the town. We both listened intently for the whine of any incoming artillery.

The company mess hall was set up in a commandeered house. We ate hurriedly and silently. Sullivan's death was on our minds. He was the last C Company casualty in our brief campaign in the Saar. The 1st Battalion moved out that evening, loaded onto trucks, and disappeared into the darkness.

The 347th Infantry Regiment had been pulled off the line and the 87th Division went into U.S. Army reserve, replacing the 82nd and 101st Airborne divisions. The unexpected German attack into the Ardennes on December 16 had forced General Eisenhower to commit these divisions to help stem the enemy offensive.

Losses sustained by the regiment had been heavy. Company C casualties in dead, wounded, and missing amounted to the equivalent of nearly two platoons. The 4th Platoon had lost all three of its mortars and one machine gun. Kelly's squad was still intact, except for D'Arpino.

The troop trucks rumbled slowly along the twisting road. Each turn of the wheels sent a separate wave of pain through my body. I pulled my blanket more closely across my face as a gust of wind tried to tear it from my grasp. In that brief second I caught a glimpse of a lonely star in the blackened night. I wondered vaguely what the fool thing was doing out on such a cold evening.

The convoy crossed the German border back into France and stopped in a small village with cobblestone streets choked with other military vehicles. The balconies on the two-story houses loomed over the convoy.

We crawled stiffly over the sides of the truck. I pressed both hands over my stomach. I wasn't sure whether I should pray or just swear. I pulled myself up with great effort and wretched violently into the snowy mattress below. A hand grasped my arm and I dimly realized that I was entering a building. Someone threw blankets in a corner and I sank down against the wall, murmuring my thanks. My mind was numb; I wasn't aware of the activity going on in the room. A sudden knot in my stomach brought me to a sitting position, and I growled my anguish. The fellow next to me was snoring loudly, but besides that there wasn't a sound.

I began thinking about Cole and how he had always snored. I covered my eyes with a hand and attempted to shut out the vision of Cole's face. It didn't do any good. I rolled over on my side and a tear trickled down my cheek. After a while my mind stopped working and I slept.

Upon awakening in an upstairs bedroom, I pulled myself to a solitary window facing the town square. I could see a Red Cross truck parked less than a hundred feet away, next to the small fountain. Two Red Cross volunteers were distributing doughnuts on Christmas Eve. Despite their rather bulky clothing they were easily recognizable as American women, and, as usual, officers escorted them.

Every time I moved, my stomach sent sharp reminders of my last hot meal. I lay back down. Gullet brought me my allotment of two doughnuts, but, seeing my condition, he also ate them. I drifted off to sleep again.

A mess tin clanging against the wall brought me back to reality. Fragments of conversation floated up the stairway. One thing puzzled me: Why should they be talking about turkey? A smile broke my lips, and I started for the mess line. This was Christmas Day; we could have all the food we wanted. There was nothing to do all day but eat. I grabbed a slice of white meat and took one bite. A small revolution hit my stomach, and I remembered the nausea of yesterday. I walked toward the door, hurriedly gnawing at the slice of delicious turkey, but I knew it wouldn't stay down very long. Minutes later I returned with a satisfied but sickly look on my face. Satisfied because I knew that I wasn't the only one in the outfit who couldn't eat that day.

Gullet finished my meal and Kelly was sympathetic, but Carollo and Crooks groused that Gullet had two meals. I crawled back under my blanket. As the aroma of roasting turkey came up the steps, I held my nose and went to sleep.

PART III

BATTLE OF THE BULGE

CHAPTER 5

In the Cold Shadows of Night

The day after Christmas, the 4th Platoon was squeezed into yet another 6×6 truck, which rumbled along in the lengthy line of vehicles. The closeness provided some warmth against the extreme cold, which was magnified by the movement of the trucks into the brisk wind. Canvas tops did not cover the trucks, so we had only the cab as a shield from the biting wind and swirls of wet snow.

Each truck had a .50-caliber machine gun mounted at the back of the cab. Every member of the machine-gun section who had survived the first combat in the Saar—Kelly, Carollo, Crooks, Gullet, and I— took turn's manning the gun on the truck.

The convoy had departed the rest area at daybreak and had made only quick rest stops. The hot meals had given almost everyone the GIs. At each stop, there was a mad scramble of men over the tailgate and a rush for whatever cover they could find. Apparently, the convoy leader must have been afflicted with the same malady, for the stops were frequent.

Eventually, the vehicles pulled to the side of the winding road and came to a stop. This time, there was no cover, so those with the more serious cases of the GIs barely cleared the side ditch before relieving themselves. Soon, soldiers covered the entire hillside.

Crooks, Carollo, and Gullet were the only people in the platoon who had cast-iron stomachs. They didn't pass up the opportunity to chide the less fortunate, and their laughter could be heard clearly amid the cries of intestinal agony. "Use your shovels! Cover that stuff up!"

The trucks were reloaded and our convoy pushed toward its destination, which was unknown to us.

The winter night descended quickly, and soon the convoy was enveloped in pitch darkness. I was posted on the .50-caliber. I wondered how the trucks could stay on the road in the inky blackness. At least the driver had the protection of a windshield and could keep his eyes open. The snow and wind, much heavier and gustier than before, slashed my face, making it impossible to keep my eyes open. I wrapped my scarf about my face for protection, leaving only my eyes visible. The icy wind froze my eyebrows and sent searing pain into my sinus cavities.

Visibility was nil. I rested my head on my forearm. The cold so numbed my senses that I didn't know whether my eyes were watering from the wind or if I was crying. My thoughts again returned to Cole. I knew that he had been evacuated. I had last seen him delirious with pain, lying on the ground among the other wounded in the corner of the woods near Obergailbach. I replayed Kelly's description of how Cole was wounded. Out of ammo and caught in the open, Cole kept charging up that damned hill with nothing left to protect himself. He was only about twenty feet from the edge of the woods when he went down. I could picture Cole running toward the woods. He was strong as an ox. He could make it. He had to.

Suddenly, I was alert. Something was wrong. What? Where? A noise, a whining motor. "Airplane!" I screamed. The shadow of a plane loomed in front of the truck and was gone in an instant. The plane's engine roared above us. I swung the .50-caliber around on its mount, but all was blackness. Behind us, there was a burst of gunfire, and then another. Then quiet.

Lieutenant DiNola abruptly appeared, placing his arm across the breech of the gun. "Don't fire. Don't fire."

"I can't see anything, anyway," I replied.

"How the hell can they see to fly?" DiNola's question was rhetorical; it went unanswered.

"Was that Bed Check Charlie?" someone asked from the truck.

"That's what they call them," DiNola responded. "They go out at dusk and create as much havoc as possible. This guy is a little late to-night. He may not have seen us because of the darkness and snow flurries. These pilots fly pretty routine patterns and try to pick targets wherever they can. Whoever fired at him back there sure let him know something was down here."

"Gullet, it's your turn on the gun," Kelly called out from the back of the truck.

I looked down at Kelly. All of a sudden, I didn't feel cold anymore. My heart was still beating rapidly from the unexpected intrusion of Bed Check Charlie.

Gullet rose from the darkness of the truck bed and moved toward the gun. Just then, the roar of the aircraft engine mixed with the dull, thudding chatter of the plane's guns filled the night sky. Bed Check Charlie hadn't gone home to bed. The plane was gone so quickly no one had time to return fire. He had missed his target. The German pilot finally had spotted the convoy, but he probably couldn't see the road well enough to make an accurate strafing run. DiNola learned later that the convoy had suffered some casualties, but no deaths, from Bed Check Charlie.

We settled back against the hard seats, each wrapped in his own private thoughts. The trucks continued their journey into the night.

The next morning was dreary but it didn't seem as cold, and the snow had stopped. We woke up griping and hungry, indicating our stomachs had returned to normal. Breakfast consisted of standard K rations, but eaten cold. Semifrozen scrambled eggs from a can in a wax box were better than no food at all.

Midafternoon brought the convoy to the French city of Reims. The streets were filled with clean-shaven American troops wearing clean uniforms and highly polished boots.

"Suppose those are our replacements?" Carollo cracked, using his best dry humor.

"I doubt it," Barr replied. "They wouldn't have time to fight and keep their shoes polished."

Carollo laughed sarcastically. "This is another morale booster, even better than the Red Cross doughnuts."

"What doughnuts?" I quickly asked. My question sparked laughter from the other men, especially from Gullet.

The buildings in Reims seemed huge compared with those in the village in which we had spent Christmas. The narrow streets were filled with numerous small shops and cafes. I noticed few civilians as the trucks passed slowly through the narrow streets. They were older men with caps pulled over their ears and their hands stuffed into their pockets.

The convoy reached the town square, where a large semi-truck was parked next to the fountain. A long line of GIs stood at one end of the truck. Every few minutes, one or two GIs exited the other end of the vehicle.

When our trucks stopped, DiNola slipped over the tailgate and disappeared toward the front of the convoy.

More men joined the line entering the trailer. The men coming out the other end seemed almost jovial.

Barr watched intently. "Those guys are laughing. I thought for sure there were doctors in there giving more shots."

"I know!" Carollo shouted. "They have girls in there. Look at that guy's face. Doesn't he look satisfied?"

Everyone roared. "How would you know, Cowboy?" Gullet asked.

"Bill should be a scout," Kelly said. "At least he's always looking for the right thing."

DiNola's head appeared over the tailgate. "Everybody out. That trailer over there is a portable shower. We get clean."

"With all those women?" Barr queried.

"What women?" DiNola asked.

"That's all right, sir. You wouldn't understand; you're an officer," Carollo answered.

"What does being an officer have to do with understanding women?" DiNola questioned.

"Remember, Lieutenant, you were the one who told us we had to clean our teeth and take a bath in our helmet every day," Carollo said.

"Take a bath from a helmet full of water, not in the helmet," DiNola corrected, amid laughter.

"Bill, I told you, you didn't have to get in that helmet," Barr said.

"Let's get back to the women," DiNola interrupted. "Where are they?"

"In the trailer," Barr reminded him.

"Oh?" DiNola answered. "Let's go see."

The men laughed as they jumped from the truck and headed for the trailer, where they pushed and jostled for a position in line. The tension was gone. For the moment, the pain and memories of the past days were buried. The simple pleasure of thinking about a shower had worked wonders. I was as eager as any of them. It had been more than one month since I had bathed—except out of a helmet—the last night before leaving Hale. It seemed as if years had gone by.

I glanced back along the line of irregularly spaced soldiers. Maybe they were going to shower, but I noted that every last man had a weapon. Crooks was even carrying the machine gun.

The line moved slowly. Finally, I tromped up the wooden steps into the warm trailer. There were no women. I stripped and entered the shower.

Warm water flowed down from overhead taps and washed away the grime and smells of the past month. The minutes now passed all too quickly. I wanted to pretend I didn't hear the order "Next man." On the other side of the shower, I was issued clean underwear and socks. They even had a selection of sizes. New trousers and boots were available for those who needed them, but the choice of sizes was more limited. The young soldiers exited the trailer with big smiles and a greatly improved disposition.

* * *

Soon, we loaded aboard the trucks again and the convoy was under way. DiNola informed us that we were headed for Belgium. Were we still going to be in Patton's Third Army, or were we headed to Hodges' First Army? No one seemed to know and no one really cared. We would still fight, no matter which field army we were in.

The convoy rolled on into the lengthening shadows. My turn came to man the machine gun. "It's *always* my turn," I grumbled as I climbed over seated bodies stiff from the cold. No one paid any attention. I hated to give up the little warmth the bodies packed against me provided. At least the wind had subsided.

The next hour proved uneventful. When my stint on the machine gun was over, I climbed back over the same bodies to my seat, bringing a few complaints from those I jostled awake or on whose feet I accidentally stepped. I was wedged between Gullet and Kelly, listening to their tales of female conquest. Some stories were so strange that they might have been true. The stories gradually seemed to drift into the distance as I rested my chin on my arms folded across my chest.

It was New Year's Eve, and it seemed as if C Company had been on the truck for days. The 87th Division had been rushed more than one hundred miles from Reims, France, to Libramont, Belgium, to join the VIII Corps in the fighting around Bastogne. The monotony of our ride was interrupted by artillery fire some distance in front of us. The horizon erupted in a continuous flash of light and explosions. What we didn't know was that General Patton had ordered every artillery piece along the Third Army front to fire a prolonged New Year's greeting to the Germans.

The effect the artillery barrage had on the Germans was unknown, but it struck a certain amount of fear in the young 87th troops. Experience had taught us that an outgoing barrage could result in an enemy response. The convoy finally stopped by the side of a narrow, rural road. It was a few minutes after midnight, January 1, 1945. The cold shadows of isolated buildings stood out in sharp contrast to the snow-covered ground. The road was lined with tall pine trees, their branches weighted with snow.

The men from C Company slowly crawled over the tailgates of the trucks. Stiff muscles reacted slowly in the cold night air. A church spire was visible against the skyline to the rear of the convoy, indicating we were near a small village. Quiet orders were issued, and we moved up the road for several hundred yards in single file. The bitter cold easily penetrated our two pairs of OD (olive drab) pants, OD shirt, two pairs of long underwear, sweater, and overcoat.

The pine trees gradually thinned and ended by the remains of a two-story hay barn on the outskirts of a Belgian village called Remagne. Along the edge of the road, Staff Sergeant Thomas Katana, a squad leader in the 1st Platoon, stretched his aching muscles and wisecracked with his friend, Sergeant Arnold Van Quekelberghe. Captain Wilkins, the company CO, appeared from out of the darkness.

"Katana, take some men and sweep this village. Make sure it's secure," Wilkins ordered.

The order seemed strange to those of us who heard it. The 345th Infantry Regiment, which we were relieving, had kicked the Germans out of the town a day earlier. Katana shrugged, grabbed Van Quekelberghe and several riflemen, and they headed down the street.

A long mound of dirt led from the edge of the road to the barn. Helmeted soldiers were crouched behind the dirt. Lieutenant DiNola waved the 4th Platoon off the road and toward the barn. The 2d and 3d platoons, and the rest of the 1st, disappeared to the left of the road. Administrative, supply, and kitchen personnel already had settled somewhere else in the village. They always seemed to find a building in which to sleep.

Sergeant Eugene Black, a squad leader, led the mortar squads into the barn. They nestled into the hayloft, letting everyone who would listen know that they had soft mattresses to sleep on.

Kelly directed our squad to take positions behind a two-foot-high dirt mound. As we moved forward, shadowy figures rose from the darkness and filed toward the road. "What outfit are you guys?" I asked.

"A Company, 345th," someone replied. "I'm sure glad you're relieving us."

"Why? You going somewhere?"

"Yeah, anywhere away from those damned woods over there. There are at least two or three Tiger tanks in there."

"How do you know?" Gullet asked.

"You could hear them earlier," the A Company soldier said. "They make an eerie noise. We think maybe one of them left. Everything has been real quiet for the last couple of hours. Probably getting some sleep before you guys go in tomorrow. I'm sure glad it's going to be you instead of us. Good luck."

"Thanks," I responded. "That's the most information I've had since I've been in the army." The thought of Tiger tanks made me shiver.

To the vast majority of GIs in the Ardennes, every tank they saw and heard was a Tiger. The legend of these tanks, with their high-velocity 88mm cannon and thick armor protection, created a myth far exceeding reality. Out of the more than eighteen hundred tanks deployed by the Germans during the Bulge, only about 250 were Tigers. The Panzer Lehr Division, which opposed the 87th in this sector west of Bastogne, had only a complement of Panzer IVs with 75mm cannon, and Panther Vs with 75mm long-barrel, high-velocity guns.

Kelly, Crooks, and Carollo crowded toward me and Gullet.

"What was he telling you?" Kelly asked.

"Tanks in the woods," Gullet responded.

"Hell," Carollo muttered.

Crooks looked at the woods but kept his thoughts to himself. A half smile tugged at the left side of his mouth.

Kelly asked, "How many?"

"Two or three. Said they could hear them moving," I answered.

"Nothing like the sound of a tank," Kelly said with mock delight. He nodded his head toward the mound of dirt. "What's in there?" he asked.

Carollo handed him a dirt-covered turnip. "Try one. They're pretty good." Kelly held the vegetable up for closer inspection, then tossed it into the darkness. Carollo laughed.

Back from having "secured" the village, Katana and Van Quekelberghe looked for some shelter from the cold. They walked into a house on the outskirts of Remagne, but it was full. Outside, they spotted a barn attached to another house. Katana nudged Van Quekelberghe, and they walked over and went inside. The two company medics, Frank Grieco and Archie Gilbert, were bunching hay in a loft. Katana and Van Quekelberghe climbed into the loft and claimed a corner for themselves.

Gilbert looked out a crack in the loft wall and noticed a jeep on the street below. "Rations," he cried, and darted from the loft. Outside, Gilbert surveyed the back of the jeep and found it was loaded with C rations. Front-line infantrymen rarely saw these individual cans of mainly hash, beans, and spaghetti. They were more appetizing than the small cans of eggs and Spam found in K rations, which came in a waxed box about seven inches long. The breakfast K ration contained the eggs, a packet of powdered coffee, a cracker, cigarettes, and toilet tissue. The dinner K ration included the Spam, coffee, powdered lemonade, and a bitter-tasting chocolate D bar.

Gilbert rummaged through the contents until he came up with two cans of spaghetti, a meal highly prized over the other fare offered as C rations. He stuck the two cans in his pocket, scooped as many cans as he could cradle in his arms, and quickly returned to the barn. With great difficulty, Gilbert climbed the rickety ladder to the loft. The sound of cans dropping on the floor startled Katana. Turning, he saw Gilbert standing there, grinning, with a pile of C rations around his feet.

"We're going to eat good on New Year's Eve," the medic announced. He pulled a small Bunsen burner from a bag that had once held his gas mask. Gilbert heated cans for the men in the loft. He savored the can of spaghetti, eating it with deliberate slowness.

After dinner, the riflemen cleaned their weapons and talked. The conversation centered mostly on the cold. No one wanted to talk about what might happen after dawn. The medics checked the articles in their first-aid bags. It made the riflemen uneasy.

As the night was about to give way to dawn, everything was quiet except for the occasional far-distant rattle of gunfire. I stared intently at the distant woods. I had slept fitfully and only for a few hours. I looked at the squad dug in behind the dirt mound and wondered how any of them could sleep. Kelly, Carollo, and Crooks hadn't stirred. Gullet had been awake more than asleep.

I turned my attention back to the dark woods and listened for any telltale sounds that might indicate the presence of tanks. There was only silence. Maybe, I thought, the armor had pulled out earlier. Or maybe the departing soldiers had been wrong about hearing tanks. Why would the Germans want to protect these woods? On the other hand, why would we want to take them?

Movement on the road interrupted my thoughts. DiNola and Pearson appeared out of the gloom.

"Kelly, you awake?" Pearson called quietly.

Kelly stirred at the sound of his name.

"Here, Sarge."

"Wake 'em up and tell 'em to eat," Pearson instructed. "We may have to move out soon."

"Back on the trucks?" Kelly laughed nervously.

"I doubt it," DiNola answered. "We may just check out that woods."

"Can't we just go around it?" Kelly pleaded. "There's supposed to be tanks in there."

"Maybe they left during the night," Pearson suggested.

"Nothing left last night," I said.

DiNola and Pearson disappeared in the cold shadows. Bodies began stirring, and Sergeant Black's voice could be heard exhorting his sleeping comrades. "Get some chow, but no fires," he called out. "And try to keep it down, will you? Those Krauts aren't deaf."

The men pulled K rations out of their pockets and gas mask bags. Cold cans of scrambled eggs were better than raw turnips for breakfast. I gnawed on a D bar for dessert, while Gullet and Crooks huddled under a blanket to smoke. A cold, raw wind kicked up. Was it an ominous signal of the day to come?

CHAPTER 6

The Farmhouse

The first streaks of dawn crept over the horizon, but the woods in front of C Company appeared even darker, framed as they were by the snow in front and the faint daylight on the sides.

Lieutenant DiNola, the company exec, approached from the direction of the village. "Fourth Platoon, front and center. The First and Fourth platoons have been volunteered for a combat patrol."

"Patrol!" Kelly snorted. "We aren't riflemen. Why us?"

"We're expendable, that's why," DiNola retorted. "We don't have any mortars, only one machine gun, and no rifles. That's why we're going. Hell, I don't know. The captain said us, so it's us."

The objective was to reconnoiter the patch of woods between two roads that led north from Remagne—the same woods from which the infantrymen from the 345th had heard the sound of tanks. The two roads connected beyond the woods with a major highway that ran from southwest of Bastogne to the town of St. Hubert, about twenty kilometers to the west. The highway marked the main line of German resistance.

The men gathered around DiNola. "We're splitting up into two groups. Kelly's men will approach the woods on the left. Stay off the road. Swing out through the field and then in. I'll take the mortar squads and Katana's squad to the right corner and then into the woods. If you run into anything, get out fast. Any questions?" There were none.

The two columns quietly, almost reluctantly, began to form. I saw Doc Gilbert join DiNola's group, his medical bag secured over his shoulder.

"Let's move out," Kelly ordered. He slowly started north on the road out of Remagne and, after a few yards, veered left into what appeared to be a pasture. Carollo, Crooks, Gullet, Stec, and I spread out behind him. The woods ahead no longer looked like one large dark shadow. Individual trees now stood out in the gathering light. There still was no sound or movement. For all the infantrymen knew, the woods were clear of Germans.

DiNola and the rest of the platoon moved to the right and started on a diagonal line toward the woods. Zeichner, who was walking a few paces away from me, was looking at footprints in the snow that led to the woods. A few minutes before moving out, we had talked about encountering antipersonnel mines. I saw Zeichner deliberately step into each footprint. I wondered if I should do the same.

Ever since awakening, I had felt very tense. I remembered my birthday, the attack on the woods in the Saar, the mortars, the .30-caliber machine gun that had been lost in the assault and never replaced, and how much better I'd feel if we had those weapons for support. My stomach tightened as I watched the woods and the individual pine trees, with their swooping branches covered with snow. It was impossible to see beyond the first row of dense trees. Was someone watching us?

Kelly called, "Bill, do you have the wire cutters?"

"Sure," Carollo answered. "Why?"

"There's a fence up here. Cut through it. I don't want to be caught on top of a fence if someone starts to shoot at us."

Carollo laughed and trotted forward, muttering, "This is the most useful thing I've done since I've been in the Army." He produced the heavy-duty cutters and clipped through the wire.

My tension disappeared. I felt almost relaxed as everyone laughed at Carollo's exuberance.

The squad crossed through the cut strands of wire. Carollo followed the fence to the road and disappeared into the woods beyond. The remainder of the squad began to move at a faster pace, angling toward the woods.

Suddenly, a laughing Carollo emerged from the trees, holding his carbine to the back of a German soldier. "This guy was sound asleep. What should I do with him?"

"Take him back to the CP," Kelly replied. "Did you see anything else?"

"No more Germans, but DiNola's group is about even with us."

"Well, get that guy back as fast as you can. Maybe he'll tell where those tanks are."

Carollo prodded the German in the back and headed down along the road toward Remagne.

"Let's join DiNola's group," Kelly said. We moved quickly into the woods. I felt relieved that we were out of the open field. I felt a sense of protection among the trees. The pine branches touched the ground and there were patches of dense undergrowth. Visibility was poor, but I thought it worked both ways. The enemy couldn't see me any better than I could see them.

"Garrison. Gullet. Take positions here," Kelly ordered. He pointed to a pine tree about twenty feet farther into the woods. "Be sure no one comes down that road. Stec, over here. Crooks, you come with me. Bring the machine gun with you." The two of them disappeared among the trees.

Gullet slumped against the trunk of the huge pine to watch the road. I moved to the side of the same tree trunk so I could see Stec, who crouched low behind a snow-covered pine branch. I peered at the opening through which Kelly and Crooks had disappeared. I could hear voices, and recognized Sergeant Barr as he greeted Kelly.

Lieutenant DiNola's men had filtered through the dense woods until the trees abruptly thinned to a clearing. Ahead, they saw the back of a two-story stone farmhouse. The snow around the house had been churned up by tank treads.

Zeichner spotted part of a tank protruding from the back of the farmhouse. DiNola also saw the tank and motioned the bazooka teams 'forward. One team set up and inserted a round into the tube. The assistant bazooka man slapped the gunner on the shoulder. He fired. The *whoosh* from the discharge broke the silence. The projectile missed the tank and exploded against the corner of the house.

The Germans, inexplicably caught unaware by our patrol, quickly reacted. Tank engines coughed to life, the sound splitting the cold air. One tank wheeled into the side yard. A second tank, its track throwing snow as it pivoted, came around from the front of the farmhouse.

Both tanks fired, their thunderous cannon blasts accompanied by the heavy staccato of machine guns, which was immediately followed by small-arms fire.

Stec plunged under the pine branches. Gullet and I dove behind the tree trunk as shrapnel cut through the trees. We could hear the electrifying clanking noise of the tanks' metal tracks and the screams of the wounded.

The tanks fired again in a slightly different direction as they swept the woods. Someone was shouting. The screams abruptly stopped. The small-arms fire from the Germans died away and a lone machine gun fired only sporadic bursts. The sound of shrapnel still tinkled down through the ice-laden branches, like glass chimes ringing in the wind.

The second bazooka team readied its weapon, but it wouldn't fire. The extreme cold had weakened the batteries. Kelly fed ammo to the .30-caliber as Crooks fired at the German panzer grenadiers. A bullet smashed into Crooks' metal helmet just as another tree burst exploded in front of them, wiping out one of the bazooka teams.

Shrapnel from the same shell hit Kelly in the face, blinding him. He leaped up, shouting, "I can't see! I can't see!" and stumbled forward toward the farmhouse. Gilbert ran after him through the slippery snow, stumbling in the dense underbrush, screaming for Kelly to get down. A burst of machine-gun fire from one of the tanks killed Kelly instantly and barely missed Gilbert, who dove for cover.

Katana helped Crooks to his feet and picked up the .30-caliber machine gun, ripping what was left of the ammunition belt from the ammo box. He heard DiNola calling for everyone to fall back. Another cannon blast and more shrapnel rattled through the trees. Men leaped from their vulnerable positions and helped the wounded as everyone stampeded through the dense woods.

Whether or not the men misinterpreted DiNola's order to fall back as one to retreat, it was too late to countermand it. The troops were leaving the woods.

Stec appeared, dodging among the trees and heading toward Gullet and me. His face was ashen, his expression frozen in disbelief. "Lieutenant DiNola said to get the hell out of here," Stec yelled. "Kelly's dead! Crooks is hit! They're all dead or wounded. Damned Tiger tanks! They didn't have a chance!"

The three of us bolted from the forest's edge and ran along the road toward the safety of Remagne. The suddenness of the savage attack had completely unnerved us. While on the road, we were plainly visible from the woods and well within rifle range if the Germans moved forward. But fear had replaced caution.

I frequently glanced backward, but I saw no one exit the woods after us. I felt numb as I went over in my mind the names and faces of the men who had entered the woods, and those who must still be there.

Stec, Gullet, and I arrived at our jumping-off point on the edge of the village, when we ran into First Sergeant Pearson. We excitedly described the terror we had encountered in the woods. "Calm down," Pearson ordered. "We need to know what happened. They just brought out a group of wounded. I understand Kelly got it?"

"Yeah," Stec answered. "He got hit by shrapnel and when he jumped up he got hit by machine-gun fire. I saw Crooks get hit, too. A bullet hit him in the head. Turned his helmet around."

"Crooks isn't hurt badly," Pearson said. "His helmet deflected the bullet. His bells are ringin', though. How many tanks did you see?"

"Two Tigers, I think," replied Stec. "The trees pretty much blocked our view, but we could hear them well enough." Gullet and I nodded in agreement.

"There was one tank behind a two-story stone house and another one across the clearing," Stec added.

The whine of an artillery shell sent everyone scattering to the ground. The shell exploded without causing damage.

"Spread out!" Pearson yelled. I threw myself behind a small shed located several yards to the left of the road. Another GI lay next to the shed. A second artillery round exploded, splattering the old shed with steel splinters. I cringed, but I didn't feel the sharp bite of shrapnel. The soldier next to me gasped. His body began to jerk with spasms. A cone-shaped wound was visible on the nape of his neck.

"Medic!" I cried. Grieco and Gilbert were close by, but as they rose to answer the cries, another shell landed, and then another.

I felt helpless. I knew the man was dying, but there was nothing I could do. I didn't even know him. "Medic!" I repeated.

"We're here! We're here!" Grieco yelled as he and Gilbert suddenly arrived and examined the stricken soldier. "We have to get him to the aid station now," Grieco said.

"Who is he?" Gilbert asked.

"Don't know," I replied. "Never saw him before. Maybe he got out of that jeep over there."

"The only jeep here is Major Chapman's," Gilbert said. Chapman, the battalion CO, had come up to the edge of the village to visit with Captain Wilkins and observe the combat patrol. Wilkins had his CP in a shelled-out house about a hundred feet behind the shed where I had taken cover.

"That's who this guy is," Grieco said. "Chapman's jeep driver. Get a couple of rifles. We'll make a blanket stretcher." They rolled a blanket under the wounded soldier and wrapped the edges of the blanket around the rifles to make a stretcher.

The shelling stopped as quickly as it had started. I watched silently as Gilbert and Grieco carried the wounded soldier to the jeep for the ride back to the aid station.

Zeichner was digging his foxhole about twenty yards away from me when the first shell came in. While he frantically dug, he glanced toward the soldier closest to him. He had found a foxhole deep enough to stand in, dug the day before by someone from the 345th. A shell exploded nearby. The soldier in the ready-made foxhole didn't duck quickly enough and caught a piece of shrapnel in the chest.

Zeichner yelled for a medic and the ever-present Grieco appeared. He borrowed Zeichner's trench knife to cut away the wounded man's clothing, then tossed it back. The knife was covered with blood. Zeichner cleaned it in the snow before putting it back in its scabbard.

When the GI gasped, Zeichner heard air escape from the holes in his chest. Grieco looked at Zeichner and shook his head. In a few minutes the wounded man stopped breathing. Grieco hurried on to treat another casualty.

"Gene," Gullet called. "Over here. Katana is taking a patrol back to the woods to check on Kelly and see who else is still there. Wilkins wants us to go since we know where he is."

"That figures," I said. "Is Stec going?"

"Yeah," Gullet replied.

"When do we go?" I asked.

"Right now," Katana answered as he and Stec approached. "Lieutenant DiNola said you guys volunteered to do this."

"Sure we did. Didn't you?" Gullet asked in a mocking tone.

"Let's go," Katana barked. "No playing around. We go straight up the road as fast as we can go. We'll stop at the edge of the woods and decide how to go in."

The four of us started off at a trot, but we were soon at a dead run.

We spread out so a machine-gun burst wouldn't wipe us out. I thought I heard someone behind me and looked over my shoulder. Gilbert was following us. We reached the woods, ducked into the underbrush and stopped beneath a large pine branch to catch our breath.

Katana signaled for quiet. The only sound was our heavy breathing. Katana motioned us forward. Silently, we parted the branches and proceeded in crouched dashes. We were almost to the spot at which we had been surprised in the morning.

The sound of German voices carried very clearly in the cold air. The patrol froze. "Our orders are to determine casualties and get out. I'm going on ahead," Katana whispered.

"I'll go. I know exactly where Kelly is," Stec cut in, and before Katana could answer, he moved ahead.

Katana motioned for everyone to stay in place and followed Stec. Gilbert went with him. Gullet and I also moved closer to the clearing, our .45s drawn to provide fire support if needed. Katana swore under his breath. This patrol was a stupid idea. If only we had a machine gun.

We found Kelly lying on his back in the same position in which he had been left. The color had drained from his face; he was a pasty gray. We could see the evenly spaced line of bullet holes that the German machine gun had stitched across his body.

Four other bodies were visible. The crumpled forms left little doubt that they were dead, but Gilbert checked each body anyway. Katana removed their dog tags, keeping one and placing the second in their mouths so they could be identified. He glanced at the names on each tag: Kelly, Baertlein, Byrnes, Dobson, Zudneck.

"If we had some firepower, we could stay here," Katana muttered as he stared menacingly at the farmhouse barely visible through the trees.

We filtered back through the snow-laden branches and crouched low as we hurried down the road. When we arrived back at the edge of the village, Katana reported the information about the dead to Wilkins and DiNola, who in turn relayed it to Major Chapman at the battalion CP. A short time later, two medics from the battalion aid station, in a jeep plainly marked with a Red Cross insignia, drove through C Company's line. They advanced cautiously along the road to the edge of the woods, looking for bodies.

Several Germans rushed from the trees with weapons at ready. The driver slid to a stop. The Germans motioned them to get out of the jeep. Hands raised, the two medics were herded back into the trees. A German soldier hopped into the jeep, drove along the road, and disappeared behind the woods. That brought a surrealistic end to a very chaotic morning.

CHAPTER 7

A Priest Is Giving Me Last Rites

After the disastrous combat patrol and the intense shelling that marked the morning of January 1, the soldiers of C Company secluded ourselves in the small houses and outbuildings of Remagne, tending to our weapons, writing letters, sleeping, or staring vacantly across the snow-covered fields. No movement was discernible in the woods that just a few hours earlier had been the scene of so much sudden violence and death. The landscape appeared very peaceful, a beautiful scene waiting to be placed on canvas.

I noticed that the officers and what was left of the senior noncoms had disappeared. That usually meant that something was up, probably another attack on the woods. My conclusion was confirmed a few minutes later when a screeching, metallic noise announced the approach of several tanks. This time they were American. Four Shermans from the 761st Tank Battalion rumbled through the village and stopped at the shed in which the mortar squad had spent the previous night.

In a matter of minutes, Lieutenant DiNola called the company together. Only 48 out of the original 187 men who had left Fort Jackson answered the call. I noted that DiNola seemed to be the only officer around. Lieutenant Baxter had been hit that morning, and we hadn't seen Wilkins or Chapman since Katana's patrol had returned.

"Platoon sergeants! Squad leaders! Over here," DiNola shouted. "On the double!"

The remaining noncoms gathered around DiNola. "The whole company is going into the woods again, but this time we have a little help. The Second and Third platoons, go through the field to the left. The First and Fourth platoons, go to the right. We'll have a pincer movement in the woods. Two tanks will support each group. Stay behind the tanks as much as possible. When you get on the far corners, enter the woods. We will be in contact by radio and will coordinate the attack. Any questions?"

"What about riding the tanks?" someone asked.

"Put one man on the .50-caliber, and one rifleman," DiNola responded. "No more questions? Get ready to move out."

The noncoms returned to their platoons and the tanks maneuvered into position. "Let's get two men on each of these tanks," DiNola ordered.

Sergeant Burden clambered up the side of a tank, followed by Carollo, who was almost immediately encouraged to come back down by Sergeant Barr. I replaced Carollo on the tank. As I began to check the .50-caliber machine gun, the turret hatch opened and the helmeted head of the tank commander appeared. "That gun is in good working order."

I glanced at the tanker and nodded.

To my surprise, the tanker was black, the first black soldier I had encountered in the service. The tank moved slightly. The tanker muttered to himself as much as to me, "I don't know why they can't wait until our gas supply catches up. We can't go very far." He pulled his head into the tank and slammed the turret hatch shut.

Pat Coluccio was checking his Browning Automatic Rifle (BAR) when a sergeant instructed him to mount the tank. Another voice barked out an order: "Keep that BAR on the ground!" A rifleman named Laird scrambled aboard the tank in Coluccio's place.

I heard DiNola's shout to move out. The tank lurched forward, almost dislodging both Burden and me. I grabbed the twin handles of the .50-caliber to retain my balance. The barrel tipped up, caught either a telephone or an electric wire and snapped it like a broken violin string.

The left flank, with two Shermans, moved out first to form our side of the pincer movement. DiNola's men followed the two tanks to the right flank. My tank took the lead. I settled behind the .50-caliber, wondering if the Germans were still in the woods. Where were the Tiger tanks? I knew that to put the Shermans out of commission, the Tigers must come around the woods. They couldn't come through the woods or fire through the trees. From everything I had heard, if Tiger tanks made an appearance, the Shermans were mismatched.

The Sherman's gun roared. Since I had one foot braced against the turret, the recoil knocked me off balance. I fired my first burst and realized I was at least ten feet too high. I lowered my sight and fired burst after burst at ground level.

Burden, who knelt on one side of the tank, fired his M1. I heard him shout, "Stay down! Stay down!" I looked back at the second Sherman, which had stopped. There was no one on the tank. Bodies lay scattered along the attack route. Only then did I realize that the Germans were firing back.

I could see Katana and Carollo a few yards away, firing at the woods. German machine-gun fire ripped the snow around their feet. I heard Katana yell at Van Quekelberghe, who walked erect in front of him and to his right, to get down. The words no sooner left his mouth than Van Quekelberghe stumbled backward as a machine-gun burst hit him across the stomach and knocked him back on his buttocks. Van Quekelberghe slumped over on his side. He bled to death in minutes.

Katana moved to his right to put the tank I was riding on between him and the fire coming from the woods. As he took a step toward the tank, I saw him suddenly hit the ground hard. Shell fire, probably from the German tanks in the woods, burst around the Sherman. I ducked as shrapnel buzzed around me. The Sherman veered slightly as if to get out of the line of fire, and I lost sight of Katana.

After the war, Katana finished the story. Machine-gun slugs had torn into his upper arm and chest. He lay on the ground with blood trickling from his mouth. He struggled to his knees. That was as far as he could get. Katana leaned on his M1 for support. German mortar shells began landing among the advancing infantrymen. Lieutenant Lidster, the 1st Platoon leader, came stumbling by on his way to the rear. "Lieutenant, Lieutenant, help me, will ya," Katana called.

Pointing to his shoulder, Lidster yelled, "I'm hit pretty bad. Can't help you." He kept going, spurred on by the shelling.

Katana watched the lieutenant run across the field. Bullets continued to whiz all around him. The Sherman nearest him had stopped. He rose unsteadily to his feet, using his rifle as a crutch. He stood for a minute, trying to gain strength to move on. The sound of an explosion rang somewhere in the back of his mind, like the noise from a faraway dream. Katana had the sensation of his body floating lazily through the air. He felt detached. He was no longer a part of the madness around him. There was just darkness.

Still standing on the deck of the Sherman, I continued to fire short bursts with the .50-caliber into the woods. The tank's cannon fired continuously. I had no idea how long the battle had been going on. Time seemed to move in slow motion. The barrel of the .50-caliber was hot; I could feel the heat through my two pair of gloves. I fired another burst, and the weapon jammed. I twisted the barrel to try to clear the jam. At that moment, the tank came to a stop, but it still fired its cannon.

I heard Burden, who had been crouching alongside the tank's turret, firing his carbine, scream. I saw his body twist around from the impact of a slug. Burden's overcoat was ripped open at the left shoulder. He looked at me, his eyes asking for help, as he pitched over the side of the tank. I thought it odd that I had never before noticed how blue Burden's eyes were.

Other men were being knocked off the Shermans. Now I knew why Carollo had gotten off the tank. I knew I had to get off. I felt a sharp pain in my left hand as I pushed off the Sherman's turret. At that instant, the Sherman fired. The combination of my push and the gun's recoil sent me hurtling through the air. My helmet flipped from my head and followed my falling body. I stretched my arms above and caught the helmet as I hit the ground, back first.

Stunned by the hard landing, I lay in the snow for several seconds, allowing the cobwebs to clear. The tank turret opened and the tank commander's head and shoulders emerged. "What's wrong with the .50-caliber?"

"It jammed," I yelled over the noise. "You better get down; they're trying to shoot everyone off the tanks."

The tanker started to adjust the calibration on the barrel of the .50-caliber, but a bullet ricocheted off the open turret door and he quickly dropped back into the tank, slamming the hatch shut over his head.

I twisted my head to one side and saw Carollo crouched in a firing position about ten feet away. After Carollo emptied the clip in his M1, he pivoted and took a half step toward our tank. As he moved, the force of a bullet arched him backward and slammed him to the ground. He lay crumpled in the snow within a few feet of Burden's motionless body.

I heard someone shout, "They got Garrison, too!" I rolled to my right to stay behind the stationary tank and shield myself from the intense fire coming from the woods. Then I jumped to my feet and saw Lieutenant DiNola huddled behind the tank, using the portable field phone. His radioman, Ferguson, and a rifleman flanked him. They seemed astonished to see me standing. Gullet, who was positioning the .30-caliber at the front of the tank, looked over his shoulder at me. "If you aren't dead, get over here and feed this ammunition," he shouted. I picked up the ammo belt as Gullet started to fire into the trees.

DiNola screamed into the phone, "We need support! When is B Company attacking? What do you mean Chapman doesn't want to commit them yet? If we don't get help soon, there won't be anyone left!" He slammed the phone back into its cradle.

Zeichner and Bill Petrosky walked next to the other Sherman. The gunfire accelerated. Men in front and beside it fell. One of the men on the tank tumbled off. Petrosky later told me that Zeichner asked him if they should get behind the tank. Before Petrosky could reply, a bullet made the decision for Zeichner.

The bullet passed through Zeichner's left side and out his back. The impact spun him counterclockwise through the air. He started to yell for the medics even before he hit the ground. Painfully, he moved his legs around so that his body wasn't fully exposed to the incoming fire from the woods. Zeichner pulled his helmet tightly over his head and buried his chin in the snow.

Coluccio walked slowly next to the Sherman, firing his BAR in short, rapid bursts at ground level where the snow-covered field disappeared into the pine forest. Amid the crescendo of battle, he kept hearing a pinging noise nearby. It took him a few minutes to realize it came from bullets ricocheting off the tank.

One of the men riding the Sherman pitched backward and landed on the ground a few feet in front of him. As Coluccio stepped over the man, he looked down and saw that it was Laird, from the 3d Platoon, who had replaced him on the tank. He had been killed instantly. Blood poured from a wound in his throat.

As the German fire increased in intensity, Coluccio ducked and scrambled for safety behind the tank, which had temporarily halted. A bullet slammed into his back at his left shoulder and drove him to the ground. The initial shock of the wound left Coluccio incapable of moving.

Coluccio lay motionless as he waited for the medics to find him. The numbness in Coluccio's shoulder slowly wore off, replaced by almost unbearable pain. He decided his best chance was to make it back to an aid station on his own. Coluccio rose, stepped over the body of a dead comrade, and stumbled toward the village.

DiNola picked up the phone and Ferguson cranked until the CP answered. "What with?" DiNola said. "All five of us!" He slammed down the phone.

"They're committing B Company now," he said to the men around him. "They want us to press the attack. Let's go!"

None of the men around DiNola said a word. Gullet picked up the machine gun, and he and I started at a run toward the woods. "Paul," I yelled, "remember basic training? Zig!" We took two steps to the right. "Zag!" We took two steps to the left and hit the ground while Gullet fired into the trees. We leaped up and repeated our zigzag movements at a dead run.

How close would we get before the Germans opened fire again? It took forever to reach the protective branches of the huge pines.

Several minutes passed. We couldn't tell whether anyone from the other platoons had penetrated the woods. DiNola waved us forward and disappeared among the trees. Ferguson and the rifleman followed him. Several rifle shots echoed from deeper in the woods.

A lone figure appeared from among the trees. He was one of the platoon sergeants, and he was furious. "The bastards are in the treetops," he roared. "I killed one of them. He almost got me. Look." He held his helmet in front of him and pointed to a fresh gouge in the metal. "Where are the rest of your men?"

"This is it," Gullet answered. "DiNola and Ferguson are over to our left somewhere. Didn't you see them?"

The sergeant stomped away and disappeared behind a tree. Seconds later, two shots rang out and he reappeared.

"What happened?" I asked as Gullet brought the machine gun to the ready.

"Don't go back there," he snapped. "Two less Germans." He wheeled in the direction DiNola had taken, stopped, and turned. "Don't ever say a word about this. You understand?" He glared at us. "Understand?" he repeated.

We nodded our assent as the irate sergeant disappeared among the trees. We exchanged looks and proceeded deeper into the woods. As soon as the sergeant was safely out of sight, we returned to where we had heard the shots.

We discovered two blond German soldiers in a two-man foxhole, sitting upright, side by side, with their heads tilted backward. Both were dead. Their rifles rested on the sides of the foxhole. Had the sergeant killed them, or had he fired into their dead bodies in sheer frustration?

We never mentioned the incident. We never saw the sergeant again.

Sergeant Katana regained consciousness in the cold snow. He raised his head slightly and saw his left leg lying at a crazy angle across his lap. His eyes were only a few inches from his boot top. He yelled for a medic. No one came. With his left hand, Katana grabbed his left leg and put it back down beside his body. He fumbled with the buttons of his overcoat, reached inside, and pulled out his little first-aid kit. He was trying to get it open when Gilbert ran up next to him.

"You got the million-dollar wound," the medic said to Katana. "You're going home."

"But am I losing my leg?" Katana cried.

"Don't know," Gilbert answered. He tore open an envelope and sprinkled sulfa powder on the wounds in Katana's arm and chest. He jabbed a syrette of morphine into Katana's other arm.

Gilbert pulled Katana's belt off and tied it tightly around his chest. He worked quickly. He found a thick stick and made a tourniquet on Katana's thigh near his crotch. The femur near the hip had been shattered by the blast and was sticking out through the skin. Gilbert gently pushed it back in and bound the leg.

As the medic worked on him, Katana noticed men moving through the field. It was B Company, moving around the woods to protect C Company's right flank. One of the soldiers changed direction and jogged over to Katana. It was Clair Beeghly, a friend from his hometown, Latrobe, Pennsylvania.

"Tom, what happened?" Beeghly asked as he knelt down beside his wounded friend. Beeghly touched Katana's hand. "Can I do anything for ya? Need anything to eat?" Beeghly pulled out a couple boxes of K rations and laid them on Katana's stomach. "How about a drink of water? Want some water?" Beeghly asked, loosening his canteen.

"Don't give him water," Gilbert ordered. "He's got a chest wound."

Beeghly looked helplessly at his friend, then slowly stood up. "I'll be back. I will," Beeghly said. "I'll see ya." Katana nodded through his pain. Beeghly turned and trotted across the field. Katana felt a lot better.

Gilbert picked up Katana's helmet and placed it over the sergeant's face. He grabbed the collar of Katana's overcoat and pulled him across the frozen snow. An occasional bullet whined through the air. After several dozen yards they arrived at a shallow ditch. The medic made Katana as comfortable as possible at the bottom of the ditch, and disappeared. A few minutes later he returned.

"I'm going to leave you here," Gilbert said. "The litter jeeps will be up the road in a few minutes. Good luck." Then he hurried back across the field to help Grieco with the other dark mounds that littered the snow. The medics would earn their meager pay this day.

B Company, along with A Company, bypassed the woodlot and gained a road junction, the battalion's objective, a quarter mile beyond. Moving past the T intersection, the two companies entered the thick, foreboding Hais de Tillet Woods. The forest guarded the vital hilltop village of Tillet, which commanded the area. It was from these woods that German tanks and self-propelled assault guns of the Panzer Lehr Division's 902d Panzer Regiment laid down accurate fire on the advancing 87th Infantry Division. No sooner had A and B companies entered the woods than the Germans counterattacked with tanks and infantry and drove them back to the treeline bordering the highway. The two companies dug in there for the night.

Gullet and I stopped to rest in the thick forest cover near several dead Germans, one of whom hung from the top of a pine tree. It was impossible to determine whether some Germans had retreated or whether they had fought to the last man.

DiNola returned and said orders were to stay put. "Don't go any farther into the woods. Dig in for the night and wait until daylight."

Gullet and I realized only then that in the darkness of the thick woods, dusk had come, and what little light remained was reflecting off the snow.

We dug in under a large pine tree, next to its massive trunk. Our field of fire included the clearing next to the stone farmhouse.

"What happened to your hand?" Gullet asked.

"Got hit just as I jumped off the tank," I said.

"Jumped? You weren't too graceful," Gullet laughed. "Besides, I pulled you off that tank. Does your hand hurt?"

"Yeah, it's beginning to throb. So you pulled me. I wondered why I came down so hard. Thanks."

"Why don't you find a medic?"

"With my luck, I'll find more Germans." I rose to leave. "I'll be back. Don't shoot me with that damn thing," I added, pointing to the machine gun. I started back through the woods. Flashes of what happened during the attack kept going off in my mind. What happened to Carollo, Katana, Zeichner, and the others I had seen fall? It would be after the war before I learned about Katana and Zeichner.

Zeichner lay in the snow for what seemed like hours as the main attack swept past him and into the woods. The cold and the shock of his wound made his body shake. He noticed a staggered line of men approach him. As they passed, they yelled encouragement to the men lying in the snow—those who were still alive. The last of B Company was moving past. A shot rang out and an infantryman collapsed, holding his head.

A medic hustled across the field to look for wounded. The B Company soldier who had been shot in the head was moving around and moaning. The medic, also from B Company, hurried over to him. He tried to get the wounded man on his feet but couldn't. "Wait a minute, I'll help you," Zeichner called out. His voice startled the medic; he had probably thought Zeichner was dead. Zeichner slowly got to his feet, went over, and draped the wounded man's right arm over his shoulder.

With the medic on the other side, the three lonely figures crossed the field to the road and started back down to the village.

They didn't hear the shell, just a deafening roar. Zeichner came down on the road. Although stunned, he instinctively used his elbows to pull his body into a ditch. Several other shells exploded in even intervals down the road, as if they were walking into town. Shrapnel, thick as bees, buzzed inches over his head.

Ahead Zeichner saw the B Company man in the same ditch. Shell fragments had severed one of his legs. Just beyond him, the medic lay dazed but miraculously unhurt. The medic rose slowly and started to place a tourniquet on the man's stump. Zeichner looked down at his own body and saw the heel of his boot tucked next to his buttocks. His boot could only be there because his foot or leg was no longer attached.

The medic hurriedly finished with the B Company man and looked quickly at Zeichner. He took out a morphine syrette and stuck it into Zeichner's arm.

"I'm getting the hell out of here," the medic said excitedly.

"What about me? What about my leg?" Zeichner cried out.

"Oh, hell, you've stopped bleeding, anyway," the medic said. He turned and crawled wildly down the ditch toward the village.

As darkness settled over the road, Zeichner lay in the ditch. He heard the noise of an engine. A few minutes later, a medical jeep pulled to a halt on the road. The driver and another man jumped off and went over to the B Company infantryman. They gently lifted him and laid him on a stretcher bolted to the back of the jeep. They picked up Zeichner, laid him across the hood of the jeep, and secured his body.

Zeichner felt the morphine wearing off. After about a hundred yards of this, the pain from the jostling became intense. Zeichner pleaded with the driver to take him off the jeep and leave him alongside the road. The driver yelled for him to hang on a little longer.

After what seemed like an eternity, Zeichner found himself inside a large tent in the battalion aid station. An orderly gave him another shot of morphine. As he passed under the influence of the drug, Zeichner felt an overwhelming need to get rid of his equipment. He wasn't going to be in this war anymore.

Katana still lay in the ditch, waiting to be evacuated. The numbness from the shock of being wounded began to wear off and the pain intensified despite the morphine. A litter jeep came slowly around a curve. Two bearers ran over, unhooked a litter from the jeep, and brought it back to Katana. They lifted him on, picked up the litter, and made their way over the icy road to the jeep. As they were about to hook the litter back on the jeep, Katana motioned for one of the litter bearers to come over.

"Could you put the stretcher back down on the road and pull down my pants?" he asked the aid man in embarrassment. "I've really got to take a crap."

"Can't you just crap in your pants? They'll wash you up in the aid station anyhow," the aid man said with some annoyance.

"I don't want to go in there stinking," Katana replied. The litter bearer looked at the dirty, unshaven infantryman's bloodstained OD pants and overcoat. With a sigh, he motioned for the other litter bearer to help him. They lowered the stretcher to the road and pulled down Katana's pants. They moved him to the edge of the stretcher and looked away.

"Okay," Katana said, when he had finished. The litter bearers hoisted him back on the jeep.

As they hooked the litter on the jeep, Katana noticed one of the litter bearers eyeing his boots. "I lost my left boot yesterday. Had to take a civilian's shoe from one of those houses in Remagne," the litter bearer explained as he shifted his gaze back and forth from Katana's boots to his face.

"What size you wear?" Katana asked. He grimaced with pain.

"Eight and a half," the man answered expectantly.

"Take mine. I'm not going to need it anymore," Katana offered.

The litter bearer eagerly unlaced the boot on the sergeant's wounded left leg. When he pulled the boot off, a wave of pain engulfed Katana, who passed out.

Katana regained consciousness to a blurred picture of men treating wounded soldiers, muffled screams, and someone bending over him. He strained to hear the words. Oh, hell, he thought, a priest is giving me last rites. He passed out again.

CHAPTER 8

Not Many of Us Left

I **left Gullet in the woods** and cautiously approached the road that ran north from Remagne, less concerned about Germans than about a GI who might be jumpy from nerves or fatigue. I spotted a small knot of soldiers huddled over a small fire on the opposite side of the road. I walked up to the group and recognized Little, Petrosky, Brewer, and Grieco.

"What's with the fire?" I asked, wary that German artillery might have it zeroed in.

"The lieutenant said it was okay," one of the riflemen answered. "The Germans pulled back. A and B Companies moved through us a little while ago."

"Good," I responded. "Someone else can take on the Krauts for a while. Frank, would you look at my hand?" I started to remove my glove to show the wound to Grieco, but the blood had frozen the fabric to my middle finger.

"Here," Grieco offered. He took out a scalpel to cut open the bloody glove.

"You're lucky it's so cold," Grieco said, pulling off the glove. "Best thing that could happen. It stopped the bleeding." He sprinkled sulfa on the wound and carefully wrapped the finger. "You should get a Purple

Heart for this, but you'll have to go to the aid station, and it's not a very good place to be right now. They're still bringing in the wounded."

"How's Carollo?" I asked Grieco.

"Hurt bad, but he's alive."

"Katana?"

"Hit several times."

"Burden, Zeichner?"

"I didn't see them. Cormack and Laird were killed. Jaroz, Barr, and Coluccio were wounded."

"What about Red Blum?"

"He's all right. Helped take some of the wounded back and stayed while they were being treated. The company took a real hit. Not many of us left."

"Well, I better get back," I said, but I was reluctant to leave what little warmth I could absorb from the meager fire. "Gullet is by himself in there."

"Aren't you going to the aid station?" Grieco asked.

"I don't think I could handle it," I answered slowly as I turned toward the woods. "Besides, I can't leave Paul in there alone."

"Be careful," Grieco called out.

"Thanks. You, too, Frank."

Despite the assurances that the woods were free of Germans, Gullet and I slept fitfully that night. We relieved each other on watch, but the slightest sound brought both guard and sleeper to immediate alert. I forced myself to think about being home. I tried not to think about dead and wounded comrades, or that this had been the worst day of my life. I wasn't very successful. Why hadn't Carollo warned me about the hazards of riding on a tank during an attack? Was he still lying out there in the snow? Why had I been so lucky, coming out of it with only a slight wound on my finger? How many men were left in the company?

I awoke with a start. Gullet was shaking me. I heard Black, who was now acting platoon sergeant, call our names. It was almost daylight. Flurries of snow created weird shadows in the dim half-light.

"Have anything to eat?" Black asked.

"Got a couple K-ration boxes left," I answered sleepily.

Black handed me two more. "Got to eat 'em cold. No fires. We pull out in ten minutes."

"You mean out, as in out of the *line*?" I asked hopefully.

"No, there's a highway crossroad about a half mile away," Black said. "We gotta move up and help the rest of the battalion hold it. The Germans want it back."

The remnants of C Company moved out of the woods past the stone farmhouse and formed along a narrow road that ran off to the right of the woods. The snow on the road had been churned by tank tracks. The sight of the tracks made me shiver.

The little column of infantrymen moved wearily along the road. Just before it crossed the larger highway and continued to the north of the village of Gerimont, the column dispersed to the left, crossed the two-lane highway, and entered the Hais de Tillet Woods. It was more like a forest. Heavy firing could be heard from somewhere in the vast expanse of woods.

Gullet and I dug our .30-caliber in between two trees. The field of fire wasn't too bad. There wasn't much underbrush, nor were there many lower branches on the trees. The rest of the company dug in on both sides of the road north of the highway.

Stec carefully approached the machine-gun position in a low crouch. "I'm going out to relieve Black on outpost," he said. "One of you is supposed to relieve me in an hour. One on, two off. Just the three of us."

"How many of us are left?" Gullet asked.

"Six on this side of the road, maybe six more on the other side," Stec said. "Sergeant Pearson, Captain Wilkins, Lieutenant DiNola, the cooks, Breen, Watson, Rehkop, Dippold, and a couple of others are back at the company CP."

"That's *it*? That's the company?" I blurted out. "Hell, there are more people back at the CP than we have here on the line," I said to no one in particular.

"Right. Don't leave me out there to freeze." Stec trudged off through the snow to relieve Black. A few minutes later, Black returned and, without saying a word to us, disappeared among the trees as he headed back toward the CP.

"Black would appreciate guard duty more if he slept out here in a foxhole rather than the CP. Stec, too," Gullet observed sarcastically.

Gullet, Stec, and I alternated on outpost duty throughout the day and into the night. Black never returned and Stec went to the CP after each of his tours. When not standing outpost, Gullet and I took turns trying to sleep in the mind-numbing cold, huddling under our blankets, nibbling on D bars, and puffing on cigarettes. I didn't really smoke, but it put a little warmth under the blankets.

Periodically, we heard the metallic clanking of armored vehicles north of the crossroads. That night the cold was intense and the wind was so severe that it was almost impossible to stand the full hour on outpost. We discussed how futile it was to be there. The Germans didn't know our strength or they would have attacked hours ago. What could one .30-caliber machine gun and a few Ml rifles do against Tiger tanks? The bazooka teams had been killed or wounded on New Year's Day. There were no mortars. We hadn't seen any BAR men and hadn't noticed anyone carrying rifle grenades. The company was badly depleted after the hard fighting in the Saar Basin and the New Year's Day battle, its losses compounded by numerous cases of frozen feet and trench foot. Rumor had it that several high-ranking officers had been relieved of command because of the high rate of trench foot.

Morning brought little change in the cold, but the Germans dropped some artillery shells. One shell landed next to the foxhole of a rifleman, scattering shrapnel among the trees. "I can't hear! I can't hear!" he screamed as he jumped from the cover of his foxhole, holding his ears. He disappeared into the forest.

"You know that kid is only sixteen years old?" Gullet mused.

"If he had it to do over again, I bet he wished he was home chasing girls right now," I answered. We saw him again several days later when our convoy moved through the rear area. He had been reassigned to battalion headquarters.

The day wore on, but the cold never relented. Snowflakes drifting among the trees created shadowy figures and imaginary enemies. The rumble of tanks continued in the distance, but the road remained clear. Heavy gunfire erupted from time to time on both of our flanks. Nevertheless, no direct attack was made on our position. How easy it would be, I thought. I knew the Germans would eventually attack and that Gullet and I would fire the .30-caliber until the end. After the sixteen-year-old rifleman ran screaming into the forest, we resolved to never run away, no matter what.

I pulled the two gloves from my left hand. The wound on my middle finger was a brilliant red, but at least it was healing. Still, I felt an overwhelming sense of foreboding. The sulfa powder and the subzero weather had taken care of the physical pain, but they hadn't helped any with the emotional pain of New Year's Day.

C Company's position did not change over the next several days, except now it found itself in 1st Battalion reserve. The rest of the battalion attacked and captured Gerimont Station, less than two miles southeast of Tillet, on January 2, 1945. Within the next three days, the same battalion moved over and advanced about two hundred yards into the Hais de Tillet Woods southwest of Tillet.

The fighting had swept past us, and the main highway that ran through our positions was clear of Germans. Finally, trucks appeared from the mist and the few remaining combat troops in C Company pulled themselves aboard.

We traveled only a short distance, but the protection of the canvas truck cover was welcome against the cold wind and snow. We unloaded in a wooded area along a typical narrow, tree-lined road. We filed along the road toward a rather large brick building surrounded by an eight-foot brick wall. We were between the villages of Tillet and Gerimont.

"Looks like a prison," Gullet said.

First Sergeant Pearson appeared from a small house across the road from the larger building, which turned out to be a convent. "Black, put the machine gun somewhere along the convent wall. Don't be obvious; there are still a lot of Germans in that town over there." Pearson pointed in the direction of Tillet.

Gullet and I followed Black toward the entrance of the convent. A stone wall about two feet high paralleled the road. Immediately to the right of the entrance, a GI knelt behind the wall, facing a field that bordered the village. I glanced at the GI. He appeared to be praying, but a trickle of frozen blood was on his temple. His eyes were directed on the town below. My stomach knotted when I realized that his eyes were fixed in death. I stopped. "Come on, Gene," Gullet whispered. "He's gone. We can't help."

Black turned around. "You pick a position. You'll be relieved in an hour."

We set up the .30-caliber and then huddled under our blankets. "Only four of us left in the platoon," Gullet said. "I guess Black and Stec will do the relieving. Either one of them ever fire the gun?" he asked.

"Not that I know of," I replied.

As it turned out, two riflemen, Brewer and Ed Dymkowski, relieved us. Gullet and I took the machine gun with us. There was no way that we would entrust the .30-caliber to riflemen.

We returned to a small house across from the convent. The warmth that greeted us when we entered was a welcome respite. We hadn't been inside a house since Christmas. How long had that been? Neither of us knew what day it was, but Christmas seemed a very long time in the past.

Extreme care had to be taken, because the battle for Tillet, about a half kilometer away, was still raging. Snipers apparently had a good view of the convent, and one or two men had to be evacuated with minor wounds.

Gullet and I decided to strip and clean the .30-caliber. There hadn't been any opportunity since Christmas, when Carollo had done it. We disassembled and cleaned the parts quickly. We had only stripped the gun once before, because ammunition bearers weren't supposed to touch the gun—at least that's what we were told. But casualties had left Paul and me as the gunners.

We thought we had laid the parts in proper order for reassembly, but we couldn't get everything to fit properly. Stec and Black, who knew less than we did, stopped to watch. Pearson came into the room with a quizzical look. "If this weren't so serious, it would be comical," he growled. "Try that gizmo. Now this thing." It worked. Gullet and I were humiliated. Pearson laughed. "That was a good guess."

Black and Stec broke into laughter. Gullet and I exchanged looks. I never had a problem stripping the gun after that.

Fresh snow covered everything the next morning. I came back from guard duty and ate a K ration. I watched as more snow fell, and found myself wondering if I could make ice cream with a chocolate D bar and snow. I shaved as much D bar as I could into my canteen cup. D bars were hard as rocks. I then went outside and found some clean snow, mixed it with the shavings until it was mush. It tasted awful, but I ate it anyway. Two hours later, I had the GIs.

Because of my illness, Black went out with Gullet to stand guard. About an hour later, the company received orders to pack up and move back to the trucks. We picked up our gear and trudged the two hundred yards to the trucks, which were parked among a stand of trees at a bend in the road that passed in front of the convent. I followed slowly in the hope I wouldn't aggravate my stomach.

When I arrived at the trucks, I looked for Gullet. He and Black weren't there. "Hey, Steve, have you seen Gullet and Black?" I asked Stec.

"Didn't they come back from guard duty?" Stec replied.

"I didn't see then. I'll go back after them."

"You better not. The trucks will be leaving soon," Stec responded.

"I'm not leaving Gullet," I said matter-of-factly. I immediately turned back down the road. Gullet was from my hometown. He might be in trouble. I had to find him. About halfway back to the convent, two figures appeared from behind the stone wall of the convent, Gullet and Black.

As they neared, Black asked, "Where're you going?" He sounded irritated.

"Looking for you two. Paul has our gun, and you never gave me my mail." I wasn't sure why I said that. I didn't even know that I had any mail. I hadn't intended to anger Black, but it was obvious that I had said the wrong thing.

Black ripped open his heavy overcoat, sorted through some envelopes, and handed me two of them. "Here," he snapped. I was surprised by his sudden anger toward me.

We boarded the trucks, proceeded back past the convent, and turned away from Tillet toward Gerimont. Destroyed American and German vehicles littered the roadside. The road was partially cleared, but the convoy occasionally had to detour off the roadway to get around tanks and trucks. The ice, mud, and broken machinery of war could not conceal the fallen combatants whose frozen arms, legs, and heads protruded from the jumbled mess.

The trucks soon pulled into Gerimont, which had been destroyed in the battle for its possession. Fresh snow was already covering the shambles of war.

I stared at the dead soldiers who littered the village. They appeared to be only Germans. Either medics or Graves Registration teams had acted quickly to remove the Americans. I was surprised by my lack of emotion. Their deaths meant nothing to me. I was alive. I intended to stay that way.

CHAPTER 9
Replacements

After four days of hard fighting, the Germans still commanded the high ground in the Hais de Tillet Wood. The Panzer Lehr Division repulsed all assaults by the 347th Regiment on Tillet, which anchored the German left flank. The regiment now was being readied to move into division reserve, where the men could look forward to hot meals and some rest.

The 345th Regiment relieved the 347th on January 7, 1945, due to the large number of casualties we had suffered.

C Company pulled back to a small farmhouse near Gerimont. Gullet complained of having pain in his legs and feet. He thought it was caused when he and Black were last on outpost duty near Tillet. German soldiers had discovered their position and opened fire, pinning both men down in cramped positions, from which they couldn't move for almost two hours. Finally, Gullet managed to fire the machine gun long enough for them to retreat to a safer position.

Grieco examined Gullet and determined that he had frozen feet and trench foot, a common affliction in the wet snow and cold of the Ardennes. Changing socks didn't always prevent trench foot, regardless of regulations. Gullet was evacuated.

I felt very alone. The entire machine-gun section, except for me, was

104

gone. As for the rest of the platoon, Stec and Sergeant Black were always at the company command post with 1st Sergeant Pearson. Brewer and Little were okay. Blum had never returned from the aid station on New Year's Day. There were fewer than a dozen riflemen left, altogether.

Not long after Gullet left, I was shaving a D bar for a cup of chocolate while speaking with one of the riflemen, who was heating some coffee. I never drank coffee unless I had doughnuts to dunk. Suddenly, the D bar broke and my pocketknife jabbed into the palm of my left hand. As wounds went, it was rather minor, but painful. The rifleman sprinkled sulfa on the cut and bandaged my hand. I finished the hot chocolate.

That evening, we were told to board the trucks to change positions. I placed the .30-caliber in the truck and grasped the tailgate chain with my left hand to pull myself aboard. I forgot my wound. The cut tore, which sent a shooting pain up my arm. I muffled a half scream, and Brewer pulled me over the tailgate. Black asked, "What the hell's wrong with you?"

I told him what had happened as I found a seat. The pain became worse with each jolt of the truck. "Black, I better see a medic when we stop. My hand really hurts."

Black did not respond.

The truck convoy proceeded through the forested countryside, stopping in Remagne, the village from which the company had launched its New Year's Day attack. The tailgate dropped and I slid out to the snow-covered street. "Black, I'm going to find Grieco and have him look at my hand."

"The hell you are. Take the gun and set up a position at the edge of town," Black ordered.

"You go to hell. I'm seeing a medic."

Another voice cut in, "What's going on here? Garrison, what's wrong?" It was Lieutenant DiNola. I hadn't seen him since New Year's Day.

"I cut my hand and need a medic. Black won't let me go."

"Let me see it," DiNola said.

"I can't remove my glove. The blood's frozen to it."

"You spend the night at the CP," the lieutenant said. "Have a medic look at it. Black, you and Stec take the machine gun." DiNola turned and walked away.

I entered the CP before Black could say anything. I found Grieco, who cut off the glove and cleaned the cut. "You making a habit of this?" the medic asked. "Next time you might lose the whole hand. You tore it pretty good. You can't do anything here. Take a couple of days off and get a bath."

I left for the division hospital the next morning. The examining medic thought it was funny when I told him how I had cut my hand. "Why didn't you use cocoa? My mom always sends me a box. Want a cup?" The medic made us each a cup of cocoa.

I took a bath, got some clean clothes, and had a good night's sleep. The next morning, a major removed the bandage. "Hear you like hot chocolate," the officer laughed. "Some people have received the Purple Heart for less than this. Your hand looks fine. Don't carry anything with it for a few days and it will heal."

I was discharged the next day and sent back to my unit, which was still in Remagne. As I entered the company billet, Black greeted me gruffly. "Here, take this machine gun; we have to go on patrol." Black handed me the gun.

"Did you guys put the war on hold until I got back?" I responded, trying to introduce a little humor.

Black ignored me and plunged through the snow toward the ever-present woods. Lieutenant DiNola waited in the shadows with Brewer, Little, and Petrosky, who made up the rest of the patrol. I shouldered the machine gun with its cutoff belt of ammunition and fell in line. To my surprise, Black was carrying a box of machine-gun ammo. By the time we entered the woods it was dark, but the heavy cover of white snow made the dark figures of the patrol stand out like silhouettes in a shooting gallery.

The patrol's objective was to make contact with or sight the enemy. There were no paths of any kind in the woods. The thigh-high drifts made it impossible for the lead man to make a trail through the snow for long. We alternated as often as necessary. When it was my turn, I refused to relinquish the machine gun, although it was awkward and I could not maintain the pace when tramping down the snow.

DiNola finally decided that we had gone far enough and ordered the patrol to reverse course, following our path back to the village. We arrived exhausted. I felt sympathy for Lieutenant DiNola, who still had to report to the CP. I put down the machine gun, slumped to the floor of the farmhouse, and was asleep in minutes.

Later that same day the company received its first replacements—not many, but enough to boost morale. Two men, Robert Dudley and Tony Hubbard, fresh out of basic training, were assigned to the machine-gun section. The 4th Platoon now consisted of Black as platoon sergeant, Stec as runner, me as gunner, and Dudley and Hubbard as ammo bearers. I had only been in combat for about a month, but I considered myself a veteran, and I felt a responsibility to teach the new men the ropes and keep them from unnecessary harm. On the other hand, I recognized that a machine-gun crew working in such proximity would lead to friendships. I had lost enough friends.

The rifle squads also received several replacements, most of them older transfers from other units, especially the Army Air Forces. There were some ill feelings toward these new men, because they brought previous rank with them yet had no experience in the infantry. Company strength by this time had increased to a total of forty men, still far below its authorized capacity of 187 men and officers.

The day after the first replacements arrived, Major Chapman was relieved of command and transferred to the 3d Battalion. Lieutenant Colonel Robert B. Cobb was assigned as the new 1st Battalion commander.

Cobb was a veteran of combat in North Africa and Sicily with the 9th Infantry Division. He was a no-nonsense, take-charge officer who immediately made his presence felt. Private First Class Dick Cunningham, a company runner, gave the 4th Platoon the lowdown on the new CO. Cobb had gathered all of the company runners together and personally introduced himself. He then asked each of them to take him to the company CPs. Cobb checked every company's positions and grilled the COs about their strength, morale, and problems with trench foot. He also demanded an assessment of the company's tactical situation.

When he finished at one company command post, he nearly ran to the next CP, leaving the next runner hard-pressed to keep up.

"He really impressed me," Cunningham told us. "Chapman never did anything like that. I think Cobb's going to shake things up."

On January 9, the 1st Battalion moved from Remagne to the village of Vesqueville, east of St. Hubert, a town on the main highway to Bastogne. C Company was designated to clear the woods surrounding Vesqueville and other small villages that dotted the area. Although fighting in thick woods can be a nightmare, this assignment seemed to be a blessing. The Germans—their numbers thin from the savage fighting—were concentrating their forces in several key villages near the main highway on the right flank of the Hais de Tillet Woods. The regiment's other two battalions were engaged in constant firefights to wrestle those villages from the Germans and turn the flank. Company C was left to engage in skirmishes from farmhouse to farmhouse, usually with small enemy outpost units.

The weather had not improved. The temperature constantly hovered around zero, and it snowed daily. The company had just swept the wooded area around a hamlet, encountering no resistance. The machine-gun squad rested in front of a farmhouse with a lean-to barn and pile of manure stacked at one end of the house. I didn't like the field of fire for the machine gun, so I moved about twenty feet toward a wooden fence and repositioned the gun.

"Hey, Garrison, come over here a minute," Dudley shouted, standing in the doorway of the farmhouse with a canteen cup in his hand. I scanned the entire area to be sure no Germans were in sight, and then I walked slowly to the house. Dudley and Hubbard were both drinking milk. A farmer filled my canteen cup. It was the first real milk that we had had since Stateside. I glanced into the farmhouse. The interior consisted of only one room with a table, some chairs, and a bed in the corner next to a chest of drawers. A blond girl about ten years of age scampered up a ladder to the loft. A woman sat next to the table.

I moved my gaze away from the house and was startled to see Black and Lieutenant Colonel Cobb standing by the gun, looking intently into the woods. I finished my milk but never moved from the doorway.

Cobb turned from the gun, saying, "Good position. Where else do you have men?"

"Over there, sir," Black replied. Both men walked away.

Dudley, Hubbard, and I dug a respectable foxhole for the gun, then alternated guard duty every two hours. More snow fell and it turned colder. The wind whipped through the tree branches, which in turn emitted eerie noises and created imaginary, shadowy figures. I pulled the gun back to the farmhouse and set up under a corner of the lean-to.

The riflemen on outpost duty alternated every hour. It was remarkable that they could last that long in their frozen foxholes.

It warmed slightly with daylight. Fires fueled by K-ration boxes were started on the back side of the farmhouse, so we could warm the small cans of scrambled eggs or chopped ham.

Everyone hoped that the company would stay in place, but it wasn't to be. We moved out about noon, along a path through the snow into the woods. Our scouts had found no German troops in the immediate area. Deep snowdrifts caused the company to take numerous rest stops. After working up a sweat, the pauses were cruel. The bitter wind speeds up evaporation of perspiration and saps body heat.

Daylight turns to dusk quickly in the Ardennes winter. The bright snow cover was dulled by more snow flurries. The column of men slowly followed behind the scouts, who kept to the woods and avoided clearings. The trees gradually spread farther apart and the terrain became irregular as it sloped downward to a narrow river that blocked our route of advance. The column halted while a scout patrol crossed the river and disappeared into the darkening shadows. I set up the machine gun to offer covering fire if required.

Minutes passed like hours. A lone figure appeared, recrossed the river, and huddled quickly with an officer. Soon, the whole company was fording the river. It was shallow at the crossing point, but the current was swift and the water was freezing.

I felt grateful that my combat boots resisted the icy water, but I was soon immersed up to my knees. Immediately upon emerging from the water, I could feel my O.D. trousers freeze and become stiff.

The men slipped and stumbled up the riverbank and into the underbrush of the woods. With each stop, I wondered if I could start again, but I knew there was no choice—either walk or freeze.

The company reached the edge of the woods and found a road covered with a layer of virgin snow. A barn stood out immediately in front of us, and the men filed in, discovering, to their surprise, that someone had started a fire in an old potbellied stove. The warmth was life saving.

Few words were exchanged as the men lined up along the wall, loosened their blankets and stretched out on the hay-covered floor. Some stayed awake long enough to change socks in an effort to prevent trench foot; others did not. Perhaps they were too tired; perhaps they were thinking of the men who had been evacuated with trench foot or frozen feet and who had never returned to the company. There was a narrow line between duty and self-preservation.

The next morning brought warm oatmeal and hot coffee. The cooks had gotten close enough so that the company jeep drivers, Panther and Blanchard, could bring the large aluminum containers to the forward units.

I ate my oatmeal and took a swallow of the hot coffee. I was so cold it didn't matter now that there were no doughnuts to dunk. I removed my gloves and wrapped my fingers around the canteen cup, allowing the hot metal to warm my hands. The wounds on my finger and palm, though still red, had already healed. It was only a few seconds before the cup cooled and I slipped my hands back into the double pair of gloves.

The jeep drivers also brought three more replacements for the machine-gun section. Lyle Jacobs was from the Air Corps, while Rodney Jacobus and Jesse Knight arrived directly from infantry basic training.

Jacobs, a buck sergeant, was placed in charge of the 1st Squad, which included just Hubbard and myself. It was also announced that

Stec had been promoted to sergeant and had taken over the 2d Squad—Dudley, Knight and Jacobus. Supply Sergeant Breen had finally obtained a second machine gun.

I felt a hard knot of disappointment rise in my abdomen on learning of Stec's promotion. With Gullet gone, I was the only one left in either machine-gun squad with combat experience. It was one thing for a non-commissioned officer from the Air Corps to be assigned as a squad leader; at least he had led men. Stec was a platoon runner, not a machine gunner. But he hung around the company CP with Platoon Sergeant Black. I suppressed any angry words, greeted Jacobs, and introduced him to Hubbard and Dudley, both of whom were rather quiet. I also swallowed my resentment and congratulated Stec.

The next evening brought another surprise; Jack Crooks returned, wearing his steel helmet with a bullet hole dead center in front. He also was still wearing the same slight smile. "Hey, where's the hole in your head?" I called out.

"It healed already," Jack responded. "Here, look at this," Crooks handed me an expended bullet. "It was between my helmet and my liner. It's a small caliber. I'm lucky it wasn't larger. Where is everyone?"

I was startled by the question, then remembered that Crooks was hit early on New Year's Day. We spent some time bringing each other up to date. Crooks knew about most of those who were wounded on New Year's Day; he had seen some of them in the hospital. He hadn't heard about Kelly's death and didn't know what had happened with Carollo after he was wounded. I told him about Gullet's evacuation. Kelly, Carollo, Gullet, Crooks, D'Arpino, and me; that's the original squad.

"Lieutenant Baxter was in the same ambulance on the way back to the division hospital," Crooks said. "He got hit in the left cheek."

"That's too bad," I replied sympathetically. "He was a nice-lookin' guy. Do you think it will leave much of a scar?"

"Gene, I'm talking about his ass, not his face," Crooks said.

Everyone within earshot roared with laughter.

We were quiet for a while. "Here's the machine gun," I said, breaking the silence.

"What?" Crooks replied.

"You were first gunner when you left, you should return to the same position," I said. "I know I would want to. Besides, that damn thing is heavy."

We both laughed. "What do you think, Sergeant?" Crooks asked Jacobs.

"It's between you two. Keep me out of it," Jacobs answered. I placed the gun across Crooks' lap. "I'll carry it once in a while."

"Thanks." Crooks rubbed his hand the length of the gun in silence. Suddenly, he said, "How did Stec get promoted? He was a runner."

I glanced at Jacobs and Hubbard. "I guess Black and Pearson like him!"

Crooks placed the gun in position and adjusted his angular frame in his foxhole. He looked at me for several seconds. Finally, his face broke into his lopsided smile. "Oh, well, at least we know what it takes to be promoted."

We both chuckled and settled down with our own thoughts.

The company spent the next few days in almost constant movement from one position to another, still assigned primarily to sweeping the forests and high ground with occasional mop-up operations in some of the villages. The cold and snow were relentless. K rations were the norm, although the mess truck or the company jeeps brought hot food whenever possible.

I respected the jeep drivers, Norm Panther and Carl Blanchard, and their assistants, Bill Knight and Hilliard Williams. They shuttled supplies and food to the front-line troops constantly, and removed dead and wounded men from the field of battle, often under fire. Bill Knight had been one of the first replacements to join the company between Christmas and New Year's Day. He was several years older than the other drivers and had been in the service for about three years. I had established a good relationship with both Panther and Blanchard at Fort Jackson. It had carried over into combat.

The weather in mid-January remained extremely cold. Company C kept moving forward. It kept snowing, and the wind blew the snow into nearly impassable drifts. The sheer physical exertion of plowing through the deep snow required the company to constantly alternate the three rifle platoons leading the advance. The machine-gun section of the 4th Platoon and a D Company platoon equipped with .30-caliber water-cooled medium machine guns, which was attached to C Company, supported the advance. Despite the snow, the machine-gun squads could set up their weapons quickly and provide covering fire.

After an hour or so of plodding through the snow, the call came back for the 1st Machine-Gun Squad to go forward. Jacobs growled, "Must not be much of a problem if they only need one machine gun."

"They know that our squad can handle whatever it is," Crooks quipped.

We pushed our way past the riflemen and came upon a steep embankment that bordered a narrow road. We slid down the icy slope and were met by Lieutenant DiNola. "Troops are coming down the road," he said. "We haven't made contact yet, but the scouts think they're British. Set up your gun to cover the road, just to be safe. Don't make it too obvious. We don't need a firefight with a bunch of Tommies."

In about five minutes, a scout stepped from the woods and gave an all-clear signal. Soldiers rounded the curve in the road, marching in two columns, one on either side, with each column of soldiers wearing different uniforms. I recognized the helmets. Those on the far side were Brits, and the nearest column was either French or Belgian.

"Damn. Look at those guys," Crooks said.

Both columns of men wore clean, neat combat uniforms, and all were heavily armed. The nearest column turned out to be French. Every soldier had a belt or two of ammunition over his shoulder, and each man was armed with an automatic weapon. They looked very intimidating to the filthy, unshaven, under-armed American GIs.

We later learned that these units—the 4th French Parachute Regiment, the British Derbyshire Yeomanry Blackwatch Regiment, and the 5th Cameron Highlanders of the 1st Highland Division—were attached to the British First Army, and that C Company was the first 87th unit to make contact with the Brits.

We also heard that same day that the company was scheduled to pull out of the line. Rumor had it that we were going to Luxembourg. I figured it couldn't be any worse than where we were.

Later that day, DiNola approached the machine-gun squad and addressed Crooks and me by name. "Just wanted to let you guys know that I've been transferred to Battalion."

"That's good," I said.

"We'll see." DiNola shrugged. "You keep your heads and asses down. I didn't do very well taking care of the platoon."

"Wasn't your fault, Lieutenant," Crooks said, trying to be reassuring. "You were just following orders like we were."

"Well, we're staying here for the night. Better dig in."

Early the next morning, we enjoyed our first hot breakfast in a week. The jeep drivers, Panther and Blanchard, and the cooks pulled up to the bivouac area before daylight, hauling steaming cans of oatmeal and coffee. The cooks served the platoons in order, which meant the 4th Platoon was last, and by that time the order had already come down to move out.

My stomach was rumbling. It was 0500, and I was hungry. Supplies were supposed to have reached the front-line troops the day before, but they didn't arrive and the evening meal had consisted of half rations.

"I'm going to the mess line," I announced defiantly.

"We're ready to move out," Jake said.

"I'll catch up. I'll be damned if I'm going to miss breakfast. You should come also," I said. I left before Jake could object.

I made my way through the remainder of the company, saying hello to those few I knew from Fort Jackson. I approached the chow line and, luckily, there was a break. "Hey, Forsythe. Have anything left?"

Forsythe smiled, filled my mess kit with oatmeal, and gave me some bread in the other half of the kit. Another cook poured coffee into my canteen cup. I stepped to one side and started wolfing down the oatmeal. Just as I finished, the rest of the section arrived.

I fell into line as they passed. "Hey, Forsythe, have anything left?" I repeated.

Forsythe grinned, "Only one serving to a person," he said as he filled half of my mess kit.

"Thanks. See you later," I said.

"No thirds, Gene," Forsythe warned with a twinkle in his eyes.

I laughed as I fell in line behind Crooks and trudged through the snowy forest. It was nice to be on good terms with a cook.

After breakfast, we boarded trucks to join a convoy of jeeps and tanks headed away from the front lines. Unlike the ride into Belgium from France, the ride out of Belgium to Luxembourg was made in style. The men of C Company traveled in trucks covered with canvas to shield them from the snow and wind.

Except for an occasional relief stop, the convoy never slowed. The weather was overcast, which was good, because it kept German aircraft out of the sky. Most of the men slept, but when awake, they were unusually quiet. No one wanted to speculate on what was in store.

CHAPTER 10

Stealing a Welcome Respite

The convoy carrying C Company toiled over snow and ice-covered roads as it rolled south through Arlon and then east into Luxembourg. The overcast skies had darkened, and dusk was changing to night. "Hey, there's a large city coming up," called Crooks, who was taking his turn manning the .50-caliber machine gun mounted behind the truck cab. "The sign says Luxembourg City."

Everyone tugged at the canvas covering until we had an opening to see. The city skyline was visible, and within a few minutes the convoy was traveling along wide, tree-lined streets. There were no lights, and the streets were vacant. It seemed as if the only activity in the entire city was the convoy.

The trucks passed a block-long fence constructed of brick and wrought iron that paralleled the street. Perhaps a hundred yards behind the fence was a large building, two or three stories high. Dark shadows gave the building a very majestic appearance. At least to the young American soldiers, it appeared majestic.

"I wonder if that's the Luxembourg Castle?" Crooks asked.

"It's big enough," Jacobs responded.

"Isn't it Hohenzollern or Hapsburg, or something?" I asked.

"They're in Austria and Bavaria," Crooks said.

Beyond this brief exchange, most of us watched in silence as the convoy moved slowly through the Luxembourg capital, which bore no visible signs of fighting. Soon the city was a silhouette behind us that slowly disappeared from view.

Total darkness overcame the convoy as it continued its journey. The bouncing motion of the trucks didn't prevent the travel-weary men from drifting into sleep.

The 87th Infantry Division replaced the 4th Infantry Division south of Echternach, Luxembourg, facing the Sauer River. Our 1st Battalion was placed in reserve in the villages of Osweiler and Dickweiler, to which no one had any objection. This sector was relatively quiet, a welcome respite from the constant fighting and frozen foxholes west of Bastogne. Although the temperature was still very cold and there were several inches of snow blanketing the ground, at least the men occasionally were billeted in houses and sheltered from the elements. Most of the action consisted of aggressive patrolling by both sides across the river. Patrols were sent out almost every night. The machine-gun section usually wasn't required to participate.

Osweiler was a small village, even for Luxembourg, perhaps two-dozen buildings in all. The villagers had retreated to their basements after three weeks of living in the woods. It was surprising that so many had survived. They had been sandwiched between two armies, had little food or shelter from the harsh winter weather, and had lived in constant fear amid the ever-shifting battle lines.

The 4th Platoon moved into a small stone house at the edge of the village. The house had been vacated and, from the general appearance, had been used by German troops.

I noticed several new faces in the rifle platoons and that a few replacements had been assigned to the 60mm mortar section. The machine-gun squads weren't assigned any new men. I made no attempt to become acquainted with any of the new soldiers in the company.

Shortly after we had settled in, Dudley poked his head into the small room occupied by the 1st Squad. "Crooks. Garrison. Come in here."

We silently followed Dudley into the small kitchen, where he reached through a hole in the chimney wall and extracted the remnants of a smoked ham. On the table lay seven shriveled potatoes.

"If we can find a pan, maybe we can have some hash," Dudley said.

"Are you going to try to eat that ham? It looks like it's left over from last winter!" I laughed.

"You don't have to eat any," Dudley said. "Jack and I can share it."

I ignored Dudley's comment. He rummaged behind the old, potbellied stove. "Here's a pan. We can use K-ration boxes for the fire."

Crooks washed the potatoes and cut them into small pieces while Dudley worked on the ham. The ham was mostly skin, but there was a small portion of dark, smoked meat attached to the uppermost part. I broke apart the K-ration boxes, stuffed the pieces into the stove, and set them on fire. Dudley scraped the cut-up ham and potatoes into the pan and placed it over the heat radiating from the stove. As the ham started to heat, the odor became nauseating. Crooks and Dudley hovered over the pan until the contents were hot and slipping about in the ham grease. Dudley divided the hash into our three mess kits, and everyone tasted the home-cooked meal.

I couldn't swallow the ham—the rancid smell made my stomach turn—but I managed to eat a couple bites of potato. Dudley and Crooks busily scooped up large spoonfuls of their shares. "How does it taste?" I inquired.

"I've had better," Crooks replied between bites.

"Don't you want yours?" Dudley asked.

"I feel a little sick. Here, you guys share mine." I divided my portion between the two and left them to their feast. Two hours later I had the GIs.

My stomach was still upset in the morning. Crooks and Dudley thought it was hilarious. I received no sympathy from Jacobs or Hubbard, who had not been invited to participate in the feast, although both of them laughed at the idea that anyone would attempt to eat anything that smelled so bad. The odor still hung in the kitchen.

Luckily for my queasy stomach, the company stayed in the village another day.

* * *

While Crooks, Dudley, and I were preparing our ham dinner, jeep drivers Panther, Blanchard, and Williams had been involved in a different pursuit.

One of their jeeps was minus a windshield. Earlier, Panther had noticed a Signal Corps jeep, complete with windshield, parked behind a 6×6 truck about a block from the C Company CP. It had been parked in one spot long enough that it had caught Panther's eye. The company drivers decided that a front-line infantry company jeep needed a windshield more than a Signal Corps jeep. With typical GI ingenuity, the jeep drivers planned a midnight requisition.

It was cloudy and bitter cold that night. A combat patrol was out in search of some Germans to take prisoner for interrogation. Part of the company was on alert, waiting for the patrol to return; the rest caught some sleep. Panther, Blanchard, and Williams took advantage of the diversion to make their way undetected to their target. They reached the Signal Corps jeep, unscrewed two wing nuts, and removed the bolts that held the windshield. But as they lifted the windshield, they discovered that an electrical wire ran from the wipers to the battery. The horn suddenly blared, which interrupted the quiet and jeopardized their larceny. They desperately yanked the windshield again, which disconnected the battery wire and silenced the horn. They ran away with their prize and hid in the shadows until they were sure they wouldn't be discovered. Knowing that it would be too obvious to place the windshield on their jeep, they hid it in a barn and covered it with straw.

The next morning, the Signal Corps drivers came around in search of the windshield. Panther told them to search away, and pointed out that they also had a missing windshield. He suggested that another company that had moved out that morning was the likely culprit.

Despite a thorough search, the Signal Corps drivers didn't discover the windshield. One of the drivers declared: "Damned good thing I didn't catch them. I would have shot them."

Panther could barely resist asking if they had heard the horn last night. The Signal Corps company left the area later that day, and the C Company drivers installed their new windshield.

The battalion had been patrolling the area along and across the Sauer River. Several prisoners had been taken, German soldiers who had decided that their chances were better in a prisoner-of-war camp than on the battlefield. Company casualties had been minimal, with no deaths.

Until now, the machine-gun section and the rest of the 4th Platoon had escaped the nightly forays into enemy lines. Today, our number was called. Battalion wanted a rare daylight patrol to check out reports that a German patrol had crossed the river and established an outpost in a farmhouse near the west bank.

Lieutenant John Hammond, the patrol leader, selected enough volunteers to make a combat patrol. Hammond had recently joined the company to replace DiNola as executive officer. The 4th Platoon still didn't have a platoon officer. Black was platoon sergeant and acting platoon leader. (Although I didn't get along well with Black, I had to admit that Black did his job.)

The twelve-man patrol moved out through the snow squall toward the wooded bluffs that dominated the riverbank. Movement was slow to allow the scouts plenty of time to safely reconnoiter. "First Squad, come with me," Black called in a hoarse whisper. Jacobs's squad quickly followed him to the front of the column at the edge of the trees. Below, in a narrow valley, stood a farmhouse with straw and manure piled against the far wall of the dwelling.

Hammond surveyed the farmhouse with his field glasses. "Jake," he said to Jacobs, "give us covering fire if we need it. I'm taking the rest of the patrol to check that house. From some of the litter lying around, it appears that some Krauts are either here or have just left."

The patrol left the cover of the woods and started down into the valley. As Crooks was positioning the machine gun, the front door of the house slowly opened and a white cloth was thrust into view. In a few seconds, an elderly farmer emerged, waving a white cloth high above his head and shouting something in French. A woman and two children followed him into the farmyard. They were bundled from head to toe to ward off the cold weather.

The patrol quickly surrounded the farmhouse. After determining it was safe, Hammond waved for our squad to join them. The lieutenant posted flanking guards while everyone else crowded into the building. Inside was a kitchen and pantry, a small sitting room, and a bedroom on the first floor. A ladder led to the loft, which was one large bedroom. Two more women were discovered in the loft, each with a small child. Communicating in English, French, German, and sign language, the patrol learned from the family that the Germans had left within the hour. One of their scouts had spotted the American patrol before it reached the wood. The officer in charge had ordered his men to immediately leave and make their way back across the river.

Hammond placed the loft off-limits and directed the family to stay there. Only the old man was allowed to come down if they required something.

Several patrol members found a potato bin in the pantry, and a limited supply of other food. The men hadn't eaten anything since breakfast K rations, so there was a rush to get potatoes. A pan with boiling water was already on the stove. Hammond realized that the potatoes and the other meager contents in the pantry were the only food the farmers had to eat. He directed that most of the potatoes and any other food taken be returned to the pantry. "Cut the remaining potatoes into smaller pieces and eat them with whatever K rations you have. Make sure every man has an equal share. We should receive more rations tomorrow. These people don't have anything else to eat."

While the potatoes were boiling, I decided to explore the adjacent barn. Farmers built their barns next to the house for the warmth generated by the livestock and the manure. I opened the door and stepped into the barn. I noticed three milk cows and, at the far end of the barn, two Belgian work horses. Finding the horses surprised me, because the Germans usually took horses for their own purposes. I surmised that the Germans had left in such a hurry that they either forgot the horses or figured they couldn't get the animals and themselves safely across the river.

I had spent a lot of time on a farm as a kid, so I appreciated cows. As I rubbed the nearest cow's head and ears, I discovered that she needed milking. I extracted my canteen cup and knelt to milk her. I had the cup about half full when the farmer opened the door and saw me.

I never understood the torrent of words flung at me, but I knew the farmer was upset, and I knew why. I held my hand up, palm forward, in a gesture of peace. I then pulled out my last D bar and offered it to him. It seemed to work; he became quiet and stepped aside so I could re-enter the house without further incident. I had no fear of the farmer, but I was on good terms with Lieutenant Hammond and didn't want to get into any kind of trouble.

As I entered the kitchen, I glanced back at the farmer, who had a milk bucket and was kneeling next to the cow. I felt relieved but a little ashamed for taking the milk.

"Hey, Gene, better get your potato before Jack wants seconds," Jacobs called to me. Crooks glanced at Jacobs and smiled, but he said nothing as he continued to eat. Jacobs seldom needled anyone.

I sipped the warm milk and took a bite of the potato. I hadn't eaten since my K-ration breakfast, so it tasted awfully good. I took another sip of milk. Everyone was busy eating. I swirled the milk in his cup. "Here, Jack," I offered. "Take some of this warm milk and pass it around." Jack tasted the milk and passed it to Hubbard. I concentrated on my potato. Dudley tapped me on the arm. "Here, there's a swallow left. Thanks."

On January 24, the 87th Division and the men of C Company left the relative quiet and comfort of Luxembourg to be thrown into the pursuit of the German armed forces. Another wet, freezing convoy ride through the Ardennes took us southeast of St. Vith, near the Our River, to join the Third Army's drive to push the enemy out of the Bulge.

The 1st Battalion was in reserve, but the men were still engaged in combat and reconnaissance patrols. Tanks and tank destroyers were attached to the battalion, but C Company was assigned the task of clearing the high ground around villages, so we couldn't take advantage of the armor support.

For more than a week, C Company and the rest of the 1st Battalion advanced through deep snow and inclement weather, chasing the enemy across the German border to the Siegfried Line, from whence they had come on December 16. Although casualties were light, the harsh conditions and constant fighting took a physical toll on the men. In early February, the division paused to catch its breath before we were to take part in the final assault to breach the Siegfried Line.

PART IV

THE SIEGFRIED LINE

CHAPTER 11
Sick Call

Hubbard and I were on outpost duty in a German-dug, machine-gun emplacement on the point of a small sloping hill that dropped gently into a large meadow fringed by a dense growth of pine trees. Some of the trees extended into the meadow, pointing like a finger toward the gun position. It was a perfect location.

The Germans were masters at positioning their guns. The emplacement had the complete visibility of a 180-degree arc. The only danger point was the finger of trees, which had enough cover to hide a sniper who could pick off anyone in the front of the bunker. Nevertheless, there were sufficient open spaces in the woods to enable the machine gunners, if they stayed alert, to detect any movement.

The bunker was over six feet in height and measured about six feet wide and eight feet long. Hubbard lay asleep on a ledge that crossed the back wall. One of the advantages the machine-gun squad had over riflemen was that two men were always assigned to the gun, making short catnaps possible. As I watched my gun mate sleep, I thought back to a comment that Gullet had made at Fort Jackson, when he suggested there were advantages of being part of a two-man machine-gun crew.

When a rifleman, on the other hand, was on guard duty, he was alone—about as alone as a person could be.

I shifted about and leaned heavily against the cold dirt. I could stand upright and rest my elbows on the front edge of the bunker. The cold metal of the machine gun was somehow reassuring, and I knew that any enemy transgression in that point of trees could be dealt with quickly.

The bunker was located near the German border town of Losheim. C Company and the rest of the 1st Battalion, 347th Infantry, took Losheim on February 4, 1945, after brief but heavy fighting. Its capture concluded C Company's weeklong drive out of Belgium into Germany. Moving east, the company had taken the Belgian villages of Heum, Schonberg, Adler, and Manderfeld from the retreating Germans, and had crossed the Our River. Now, along with the rest of the 87th Division, C Company was marking time to prepare for the eventual attack through the Siegfried Line.

As I stood in the bunker alone with my thoughts, I allowed my body to absorb the heat from a sun made warmer by a winter thaw. The warmth and quiet gave me a serene feeling. My eyes drifted to the rifleman positioned at the edge of the trees on my right. I didn't recognize him, which wasn't unusual. I didn't know many of the replacements, and most of the company was now comprised of new men. Schneller, the rifleman on my left, was barely visible, but I could make out a slight movement, so I knew that he was awake. Schneller was one of the few veterans and also one of the few in the company who could speak some German. His parents were Austrian.

I gazed over the pasture in front of the bunker. Five or six dead and badly bloated milk cows lay in the field. I couldn't help thinking about how many beef roasts had gone to waste.

The heat from the sun grew warmer and made me drowsy. I shook my head to stay awake and keep focused. I glanced at the watch loaned to me by Platoon Sergeant Black for use on guard duty. It was ten minutes before I should awaken Hubbard. My eyelids became heavy again. Sleep was luring me with ease. Suddenly, I jerked wide awake, and what I saw made a tight knot in my stomach. About thirty yards in front of the emplacement stood Lieutenant Colonel Cobb, the battalion CO. With him were Lieutenant Hammond and Sergeant Black. Cobb stared at the bunker while Black pointed in the direction of Schneller's position. Looking that way, I saw that the rifleman to the right was standing. My God, I thought in panic, they must have walked right past me. I've been *asleep*. Falling asleep in a front-line position is a court-martial offense. I looked at my watch. Only five minutes had passed. "Tony," I called softly. "Get up here, quick." Hubbard sleepily swung his body off the ledge and lurched forward as I explained our situation. Cobb turned again and looked at Schneller's position.

Hubbard whispered: "They didn't notice; they think we've been watching them all of the time."

Black turned and approached the bunker. I casually said: "What's going on, Sarge?"

"The colonel is just checking our positions," the sergeant said. "He congratulated the Krauts on their gun placements."

"Maybe he could convince some of the POWs to dig holes for us," I returned.

"Sure. Your relief will be out in a few minutes." Black turned to follow the two officers up the hill.

Hubbard sighed. I rested my head on the stock of the machine gun. "It's about time we had a little luck. That sun just put me to sleep."

"Right. Here comes our relief now. Let's get the hell out of here."

Hubbard and I hurried through the pasture, avoiding another dead cow, to a narrow road that led to a nearby village. As we passed the house that served as the company CP, the door opened. "Hey, buddy, you still here?" My glance followed the sound of the words. The GI with the wide smile standing in the doorway suddenly made the day and the war seem brighter.

Tony D'Arpino was back! My close friend had recovered from wounds he had sustained outside Obergailbach nearly two months ago.

"Haven't you won this damned war yet? I can't trust you guys to do anything." D'Arpino's smile was even wider.

"Didn't want you to miss out on anything," I laughed, as we shook hands. I introduced the two Tonys—D'Arpino and Hubbard—as we made our way to the house on the edge of the village in which the machine-gun section was quartered. The entire 4th Platoon was billeted on the second floor of the house, part of which was above an attached stable that sheltered half a dozen live cows. Actually, part of it was the haymow, and the hay made rather soft beds, especially compared to the frozen foxholes.

Our chatter as we entered the house awakened Crooks. "Tony," he greeted D'Arpino. "Looks like you gained a little weight."

"You know how it is. Wine, women, song, and lots of food. Where is everyone?"

"This is it," Crooks answered slowly.

D'Arpino's exuberance quickly dissipated as Crooks and I related the events that had overtaken us after Tony had been wounded. Bialk, Cole, Sullivan, and Kelly were dead; DeVine, Carollo, and Katana were wounded. Gullet had been evacuated with trench foot. No one remained from the entire mortar section. "Jeesh, a replacement and a runner as squad leaders," D'Arpino responded.

I watched D'Arpino store his gear. I was glad to have him back, but I also had mixed emotions. In the hospital, Tony was safe; back on the lines, he was in danger. D'Arpino and I had hit it off from the instant we met at Fort Jackson. Tony kept things loose with his jocular personality, and he held everything in perspective. I thought, What if D'Arpino is hit again or killed? I didn't know how or if I could deal with that. I didn't expect to see another close friend, Gullet, again.

As the day wore on, most of the men in the house dozed, wrote letters, or engaged in quiet conversation. Jesse Knight complained to me about not feeling good. Knight was married and had a baby he had never seen. He had a fear that he would never see his child, and needed constant reassurance that he would live through the war.

I wondered why some of the replacements talked to me about their aches and pains and personal problems. Must be that I was the most outspoken member of the section was all I could figure. On occasion,

I would refer them to Jacobs, for whom I had developed considerable respect.

Knight's face was flushed, and he obviously didn't feel well. I remembered that Knight hadn't eaten at breakfast.

"Chow time," Black said as he entered the room. "Half of each squad go now and the rest as soon as they return. Don't waste a lot of time. You know Fry; he might decide to close the kitchen."

The first men to get up were those on duty in a couple of hours. Hubbard, D'Arpino, Knight, and I didn't attempt to join them.

"Hey, Sarge, how about asking a medic to come look at Jesse," I asked Black. "He looks awful."

"Hell, no!" Black snapped. "All you guys do is bitch!" He turned and stamped down the steps.

"What caused that? I thought I was nice for a change," I muttered. I looked over at Knight and said, "I'll go for a medic, Jesse."

"Forget it, Gene. You'll just get into more trouble with Black," Knight said.

"Yeah, some days he does something nice and other days all he does is yell at me," I observed. "At least he doesn't yell at anyone else. That's something."

A few minutes later, Frank Grieco, the medic, entered the room. "Hear we have someone feeling bad."

"Jesse doesn't look too good," I said. "Did Black tell you?"

"No. Jacobs said something," Grieco said. The medic examined Knight. "I don't see anything wrong, Jesse. It's wishful thinking on your part. Try not to think of your family so much; it just makes things that much worse. You'll make it."

Grieco's words of reassurance didn't take. Knight curled up again, resting his head on his knees in silence.

Grieco looked at me. "Your face is awfully flushed. Let me check your temperature."

"I'm okay," I answered.

"He has a case of 'Blackitis,'" D'Arpino chuckled.

Grieco laughed as he stuck a thermometer into my mouth. "That's what I thought," Grieco said as he read the thermometer. "You report to the battalion aid station. You might have pneumonia."

I felt misgivings about reporting for sick call. Getting off the front line was great, but I felt sorry for Knight. "I feel all right."

"The aid station is about two blocks down the street. It's marked. Don't argue."

"What about Knight?"

"Sorry, I can't send him if I don't feel he's sick. Now go. I'll tell the CP."

I gathered my belongings. "You all be careful," I called to the other platoon members. "Tell Jake and Jack where I've gone. Sorry, Jesse."

"You tried, Gene," Knight said despondently.

"Hey, suppose I could go with you?" D'Arpino asked.

"No way," Grieco said.

"Why not?" I asked.

"Because he isn't sick, that's why," Grieco shot back.

"See you guys later," I said, as everyone laughed at the verbal interchange. For once Hubbard lost his smile as I disappeared through the doorway.

The medic at the battalion aid station glanced up as I walked into the small room. I was a little surprised at being tired after such a short walk. "What's wrong with you?" the medic asked. His tone implied that he thought I was goldbricking.

The less-than-subtle comment put me immediately on the defensive. "Frank Grieco thinks I have pneumonia."

The medic took my temperature, looked at my throat, and felt my forehead. His attitude quickly changed. "I think Frank is right. Your temperature is a hundred and one degrees. Maybe they can get rid of it back at the division hospital before it gets too bad." He walked into another room and soon returned with a jeep driver. "He'll take you back to the division hospital," the medic said as he handed me some papers.

The division hospital was in what appeared to be a converted schoolhouse in a town some distance behind the lines. It was filled with ailing GIs afflicted with minor wounds, trench foot, or viruses. I was given some medication and clean clothing, then directed toward the shower room. Despite my illness, I lingered as long as I could under the hot spray, allowing the water to cascade off my head and down my body. I closed my eyes and let the heat from the steam put me into a brief stupor.

As I returned from the shower, I passed a medical orderly munching on a Hershey bar. He nodded to me and asked if there was anything I would like. "Haven't had one of those since I left Fort Jackson," I answered, gesturing toward the candy bar.

"Really? We get boxes of them. I'll get ya some. I know the companies get 'em all the time."

"They probably never get past the command post and the mess hall," I said.

The orderly gave me three candy bars and showed me to a cot in the middle of a large room that was crowded with recuperating soldiers. It took me only a few minutes to determine why the battalion aid station medic was suspicious. From overheard conversations, it was clear that a good number of goldbrickers were in residence. Discussions revolved around such topics as sex, methods of avoiding any work, and how to fake injuries. Two of the soldiers were especially obnoxious, discussing how they raped girls while on leave. I decided that they were pretty stupid and tried to ignore them.

The next day, following a good night's sleep, I felt much better. After two nights, I had taken all I could stand, in spite of the comforts of clean sheets, showers, and hot food. I was tired of the shirkers and felt guilty about being away from my squad; I requested a return to my unit. A doctor signed the order, but I had to spend a third night before being discharged.

It was midafternoon when a medical jeep dropped me off at the company command post. I opened the door and entered. The only person present was Walt Dippold, the company clerk.

"Garrison, you back? Rehkop has some mail for you."

"Yeah, I'm back. Sign me in, or whatever you have to do. Is my squad still in the same place?"

"I think so," Dippold said somewhat hesitantly. "Let me get your mail. I'll tell Rehkop I gave it to you."

The company clerk handed me three letters, two from my mother and one from my grandmother, and a package, which I hoped was filled with cookies and candy pecan logs. The entire machine-gun section usually shared my treasures from home.

I headed toward the 4th Platoon billet. As I entered the room, I saw Jacobs, Crooks, and Hubbard sitting with their backs to the wall. Before they could comment, I said, "You guys could have at least taken one more town without me."

"Ah, look who's talking," Jacobs responded.

"Yeah, who's been sleeping in a nice soft bed with pretty nurses taking care of him?" Crooks cut in.

"I don't know. Who?" I replied as I sat down next to Hubbard.

"Where's D'Arpino?" I asked apprehensively after looking quickly around the room.

"Out with Byrnes, trying to find some chicken eggs," Crooks said. "Who got the package?"

I ignored him. I was just glad to hear that Tony was safe. Walt Byrnes was a replacement assigned to the mortar section. I thought it unusual that Walt Byrnes had replaced John Byrnes, who had been killed on December 16. There was also a Charles Byrnes, who had been killed on New Year's Day. John and Charles had been in the mortar section, and both were with the unit at Fort Jackson.

Walt Byrnes had a really hard time adjusting to K rations. Every time he tried to eat one, he came down with a quick case of the GIs. Forsythe, the assistant cook, tried to get Byrnes some mess-hall food that he could digest, but the head cook, Fry, with his lack of charm and empathy, chased Walt away from the mess tent whenever he spotted him. Therefore, Walt used his natural GI scavenger instinct, and no German pantry or barn was safe. Once, he actually caught an egg as it was being laid.

I carefully unwrapped my package while paying no attention to Jacobs and Crooks. Hubbard leaned forward: "You need any help with that string?"

"Maybe," I replied as I slowly cut the strings around the package, removed the wrapper, then cut the tape holding shut the cardboard box. I folded down the box flaps and saw toothpaste, toothbrush, soap, shaving cream, and razor blades. Then I came to the good stuff. There were cookies—sugar, oatmeal, two with some traces of chocolate icing, which my four-year-old sister had made (a note from my mother said my sister had eaten the rest of the cookies while packing the box); two pecan logs; four Milky Ways; and some other assorted pieces of candy my dad had tossed into the box.

Jacobs cased the contents of the box and tried to make amends. "Maybe he didn't have a soft bed," he said to Crooks.

"Yeah, he probably had to walk back," Crooks added.

I took a cookie and a Milky Way for myself, passed the box to Hubbard first—as a reward for being respectful—and he passed it to Jacobs, then to Crooks, and back to me. Later, I broke down the box, dividing the remaining contents with my squad mates. I set aside a few things for the company jeep drivers, Panther and Blanchard. It paid to keep them happy. Sometimes I shared with the other machine-gun squad, but not this time.

As the squad enjoyed the treasures from home, Sergeant Black entered the room. "I didn't know you were back, Garrison," he said without pausing for an answer. "We need two volunteers for a patrol tonight."

Jacobs and Crooks spoke up in unison: "I went last night!"

Black looked at Hubbard and me. "You don't have to go. There are several others who haven't gone for a while."

Hubbard and I exchanged glances. "I'll go," I said after a pause. "How about you, Tony?"

"Yeah, I'll go, but I'll probably be sorry."

"Be ready right after chow," Black continued. "Lieutenant Lidster is leading the patrol. There's supposed to be a pillbox that's giving us trouble. Lidster went up in an L-4 [a light observation plane] today and supposedly knows the way. A couple of ordnance guys are going along to blow it. You better get some sleep."

Jacobs and Crooks left with Black. Hubbard and I stretched out under our blankets to get some sleep. It promised to be a long night.

That evening, on the way to the makeshift mess hall, Crooks asked me: "Did you hear about Blum and LeBate?"

"No."

"They were in our patrol last night and when we made contact with the Germans, LeBate was hit real bad. We had to pull back. When Blum realized LeBate wasn't with us, he went back after him. LeBate was dead. Blum got his dog tags, but then he got hit right in the kneecap. He emptied his grease gun, and the Germans decided to leave. We got Blum out, but we had to leave LeBate. Another patrol picked him up this morning."

"How bad is Blum's knee?"

"Don't know. It appeared to be a small-caliber bullet wound. We put splints on it so he couldn't bend it. The medics took him to the aid station right away."

I walked on to the mess hall in silence. It wasn't the kind of news I wanted to hear right before a patrol. One after the other, my friends were being killed or wounded. I wondered when it would be my turn.

Darkness had long since descended when Lieutenant Lidster, who had recovered from his wound on New Year's Day, gathered his patrol outside the mess hall. It was large for a night patrol—forty-five men. They must expect trouble, I thought.

Looking over the knot of men, for once I saw some familiar faces among the riflemen. It brought a smile to my lips as I ticked off the names in my mind: Jaroz, Yanacheck, Dymkowski, Brewer, Michon, Petrosky, Little, and Szymanski. I even knew two replacements, Jim Cheatwood and Bob Jones, who were in the 3d Platoon.

"Line up in order according to your platoon, First, Second, Third,

Fourth," Lidster instructed. "That way, when we're out there, you can check on each other. Be sure you know the man in front of you. Garrison, who else is with you from the Fourth?"

"Tony Hubbard," I replied.

"You two bring up the rear. Everyone keep just enough distance so you can see the man in front of you. Our objective is to blow the pillbox. No firefight if we can avoid it. If we don't make contact, it's my call as to how long we stay out. Let's go. No unnecessary talking."

The patrol filed through the small village and into an adjoining pasture. On this patrol, I carried a carbine issued to me by Watson, the company armorer. I disliked the carbine because of the flip-flop sights used for distance. The wrong one always seemed to be up. Well, I thought, at least the cold had let up a little.

The patrol stopped frequently as Lidster checked for the landmarks he had noted earlier that day from the L-4 observation plane. I recalled a conversation I had had with Bob Jones while the patrol members were assembling. Jones had commented: "Hell, Lidster reconnoitered the area this morning in an L-4, but I'll bet he still gets lost."

During one particularly lengthy stop along a fence line, I started to wave Hubbard forward when I heard him softly calling to me.

"Gene, what's going on?"

"Nothing, I hope," I replied in a loud whisper. "See, there's Jones ahead of us."

"Let's go check with him," Hubbard suggested.

We moved forward carefully.

"Hell, Gene, that's not Jones," Hubbard blurted out. "That's a fence post."

"Oh, no," I sighed. "Let's go. They can't be too far away."

We hurried along the fence line and found Jones about fifty yards farther along, next to another post. He hadn't realized that Hubbard and I had fallen behind. He was too busy trying to see the man in front of him.

The patrol moved forward again, closing the gap slightly between members. Fear of losing contact now overrode caution. We moved around the top of a small hill, being careful not to break the skyline. Below was a narrow road that paralleled a dense wood. We passed the woods and then a large field. Beyond that was another large woods that extended on both sides of the road. The patrol had to enter the woods or proceed on the road.

Lidster didn't like the situation. It was too easy for the Germans to mine the road and boobytrap the woods. The pillbox was farther down the road, and he knew that there were German troops flanking the pillbox. His orders were to knock out the pillbox if he could do so without substantial loss. He decided to end the patrol. He doubled back along the line of men, looking openly relieved that there had been no contact. His patrol would return with no casualties. The men were scattered along the hillside, barely able to see one other and slightly relaxed now that we were headed back. The patrol recrossed the pasture, and was almost to the woods when one of the riflemen slipped and fell heavily to the ground. He cursed, and someone involuntarily asked if he was hurt.

A German burp gun opened fire from the woods. Lidster screamed, "Move out—run! Stay in contact!"

Hubbard stumbled and went down. "Tony!" I grasped his arm and pulled him to his feet, thinking he had been hit.

"I'm all right. I just slipped," Hubbard shouted.

Additional fire erupted from the woods. The darkness was thick with whining bullets. Mortar rounds fell on the hillside. The direction of the incoming fire was random; it never concentrated in one area for more than a few seconds. The Germans could not see the patrol, so they were just raking the hillside, hoping to get lucky.

The patrol raced around the curve of the hill and at last gained protection from the gunfire. Lidster regrouped the patrol as the men gasped for breath. "Give me a report. Is anyone missing or hurt?"

The men looked around and quickly established that everyone was present and no one had been wounded.

"I'll bet a Kraut guard went to sleep, or we would have been caught going by that woods the first time," Jones commented. "I'd like to hear Lidster's explanation to Captain Wilkins as to why we didn't blow that pillbox."

The patrol continued back to the village with a lot less urgency as the German shelling and gunfire subsided.

CHAPTER 12
A Letter Home

The **1st Battalion** went into regimental reserve but stayed on the front line on the same wooded slope it had occupied for several days. Its job was to provide flanking protection as the other two battalions attempted to breach the Siegfried Line near Ormont, Germany. Although we were still harassed by sporadic enemy shelling, the men of C Company tried to make the most of our brief reprieve.

An impromptu craps game among the weapons platoon men broke out on an Army blanket with two K-ration boxes to stop the dice. Dudley, Jacobus, a couple of mortar men, and I wagered military-issue franc notes. I won about twenty dollars before First Sergeant Pearson wandered by and suggested we stop before an officer spotted our activity. Just then, Lieutenant Hammond walked up to check on the men. He glanced at the game but continued with his rounds. The dice quickly disappeared and the group dispersed.

Bothered by an infection in my left eyebrow, I sought out Frank Grieco, who was dug in farther up the wooded slope. I plopped down beside the medic's foxhole. "Haven't worked on you for a while," Grieco laughed. "What's wrong?"

I showed him the infection. Following a brief inspection, Grieco looked in his medic bag. He pulled out a small scalpel, and with a swift stroke, lanced the sore and applied medication.

"That should take care of it. Wash and shave once in a while and this type of thing won't happen," Grieco chuckled.

"Thought about it, but I don't want to be conspicuous," I said. We both laughed, and I returned to my foxhole.

Not being on the move every day gave the men a chance to scour the local countryside for fresh food. One evening, D'Arpino and Byrnes, the inveterate scrounger, were looking for eggs. They entered a ram-shackle barn that had been overlooked by other foraging soldiers and found several chicken nests. They quickly roamed from nest to nest, scooped out every egg they could find, and hurried back to their fox-holes.

Byrnes poured water from his canteen into an aluminum cup and placed the eggs inside. He arranged some rocks in a small circle around pieces of a K-ration box and a pile of twigs, which he set afire. He placed the cup on the fire, and soon the water was boiling. D'Arpino left for a few minutes, and returned to find Byrnes already eating some eggs. Byrnes offered him the remaining eggs, which D'Arpino took to his foxhole, relishing a meal that didn't come in a cardboard box. Much to his chagrin, he discovered that all but one of the eggs was fake, made out of light wood and placed in the nest to induce the hens to lay. D'Arpino accepted the practical joke rather well, but everyone knew that he would get even sooner or later.

The weather was a miserable mixture of snow, sleet, and rain—and it was always cold. These damp conditions made the cold even more penetrat-ing inasmuch as our uniforms were often wet. The countryside was a patchwork of colors: white snow interspersed with swaths of muddy brown earth set against the dark background of woods and a pewter-gray sky. Throw in the constant specter of death and it was a desolate, demoralizing portrait that we faced every day.

The machine-gun squads were dug in at the edge of a dense wood. The pine boughs were low to the ground and furnished a false sense of security as they waved gently in the slight breeze. To our left was a shrub-filled fencerow that led to another dense wood about two hundred yards away. Jacobs said he had been told that the Germans were there. Real or imaginary noises could be heard from the wood—metallic sounds, like tanks positioning to fire.

I stared across the open field and tried to focus on anything within the wood. I thought of New Year's Day and Carollo and Burden and Kelly and Coluccio and Zeichner and Katana.

"Gene, what's wrong?" Crooks asked.

I jumped at the sound of my name. I looked at Crooks, and the apprehension must have been in my eyes.

"This isn't New Year's Day. It's just another woods," Crooks murmured.

"How did you know?" I asked.

Crooks tapped his helmet and the bullet hole it had sustained on January 1. "This hole never lets me forget," he replied.

I changed my position behind the gun slightly. Somehow I felt a little better knowing I wasn't alone in my memories.

Orders came down from Regiment for the 1st Battalion to join the attack on the Siegfried Line. C Company was sent to occupy a town north of Ormont. The rolling countryside north of Ormont was part of a thick belt of concrete pillboxes placed to command roads and valleys running through the formidable defensive fortifications. The pillboxes were located so that each could give supporting fire to the others. Long rows of inverted, triangle-shaped cement blocks spaced every few feet and sealed by rolls of barbed wire ran for hundreds of yards. They blocked roads, intersections, and flat ground. The blocks, we learned, were called dragon's teeth. Any armored vehicle that attempted to go over these tank traps would either be hung up or expose its vulnerable underbelly to German antitank fire.

The Siegfried Line. Just the name disturbed me. While in high school,

I remembered seeing movie newsreels showing posturing German storm troopers at the West Wall. The huge pillboxes still looked as invincible as I remembered from the film.

In expectation that murderous fire would erupt at any second from the pillboxes and entrenched positions, we moved in rushes. A group of two or three ran forward and dropped in concealment to cover the next group. I decided to use one of the dragon's teeth for protection as I leapfrogged my way through the fortifications. They were only about three feet high. When I rose to aim my weapon, I discovered I wasn't concealed anymore. The next time I stopped, I just flung myself on the ground.

As C Company advanced, not a shot came from the vaunted West Wall, no interlocking streams of machine-gun fire decimated our ranks. The pillboxes, we discovered, were unmanned. In this surreal setting, I hoped that the Germans would decide to bring the war to an end by either surrendering or simply going home.

The whole day proved uneventful. The battalion took the village without a fight. The Germans had chosen this time to withdraw. The game of cat and mouse continued, but who was the cat?

The 2d Machine-Gun Squad was assigned to cover C Company's advance, while our squad moved up front with Lieutenant Hammond. The objective was to clear the wooded area leading to a village that guarded part of the West Wall. The scouts entered the woods very slowly, followed by riflemen and the 1st Machine-Gun Squad. Every man kept a sharp eye for trip wires that could detonate mines called bouncing betties. These antipersonnel mines would spring about three feet in the air before exploding; they could inflict hideous wounds to a man's torso.

We saw fresh vehicle tracks and footprints on a dirt road that wound through the trees. Hammond turned to Jacobs. "Sergeant, position your gun here and give us covering fire if necessary. We'll check the woods on the other side of the road." The lieutenant and a rifle squad crossed the road and disappeared into the woods.

The machine-gun squad set up to cover the opposite woods as well as the road. D'Arpino watched the riflemen disappear and then looked at the tracks in the muddy road and said, "I hope they don't stop until they get home."

The Germans harassed us with shelling and sniper fire rather than put up a full-fledged fight. We found booby traps in the woods, but they caused no injuries. The major damage occurred on the roads, where land mines had been buried. Fortunately, C Company was spared casualties. Numerous Germans surrendered, but none of them were SS troopers, who were rumored to be among the regular Wehrmacht troops manning the area's defenses.

The company riflemen returned, stumbling down the heavily wooded hillside. The machine-gun squads slid down a slight embankment to a narrow road to join them. An icy blast of wind hit us as we left the protection of the woods. The wind cut through our overcoats and layers of clothing. Two pairs of long underwear, two pairs of trousers, two shirts, and a field jacket under a heavy overcoat could not keep out the cold. We were soon shivering, almost uncontrollably. The last gray light of dusk faded quickly.

Gunfire erupted somewhere in front of us. "First Machine-Gun Squad to the front," came an order shouted from the deepening darkness. "Machine gun! Machine gun!"

"Let's go," Jacobs shouted. We started at a trot, half crouching from habit.

The snow had been packed into ice by the passing troops. Crooks, who was carrying the gun on his shoulder, suddenly lost his footing on an icy log and crashed to the ground.

"Jack, are you all right?" I yelled. D'Arpino and I rushed to Crooks' side as he struggled to rise.

"I'm okay," Crooks replied, but his face belied his answer. He hurried to catch Jacobs.

The gunfire stopped as abruptly as it had started. The squad spotted Lieutenant Hammond standing in front of a huge pillbox silhouetted in a backdrop of snow. "The Krauts must have decided it was too cold to fight," he said. "Everyone in the pillboxes, except for some guards. One hour on, one hour off. It's too cold to stay out any longer. Let's get with it."

I couldn't stop shivering. I looked at Crooks, who appeared to be under control. I swallowed my pride. "Jack, could you take the first hour? I'm freezing."

"You beat me to it. Go ahead, but be sure it's just one hour. It's cold out here."

D'Arpino, Hubbard, and I made our way to the pillbox. Jacobs stayed with Crooks. The pillbox was cold and rusty, and it had puddles of water on the floor. Metal cots hung from the walls, held in place by chains. We removed our ammo belts, unfolded our blankets, and crawled into the cots.

Danny Mendelsohn, who was assigned to the company CP, came in with an armload of abandoned German blankets. "Here, you'll need these. Hope they aren't infested with lice. Who needs to get up in an hour?"

"Make it fifty minutes," I answered, "and wake these guys up in two hours." I completely ignored the comment about lice. I really didn't care.

Later. I struggled to awaken. Someone was shaking my shoulder and calling my name. It was Mendelsohn.

"Is my hour up?" I groggily asked.

"You said fifty minutes," Mendelsohn said.

"Oh." I thought of Crooks, drew myself to my feet, put my helmet in place, and threw my GI blanket over my head. D'Arpino and Hubbard were sleeping soundly. As I left the pillbox, I saw several German POWs in an adjoining room. I muttered, "Put the bastards outside in the cold."

I found Crooks and Jacobs huddled together in a clump of bushes next to the roadside embankment. "You were supposed to be back in an hour," Crooks said through chattering teeth. "It's been two hours."

"No it hasn't," I replied defensively. "Ask Mendelsohn."

"Who's on guard with you?" Jacobs asked.

"I don't know. Nobody ever told me. Guess no one is."

"I'll stay until someone else comes," Jacobs offered.

"Jake, you can't stay. You'll freeze," Crooks chattered. "Come on." Jacobs started to argue, but he could hardly speak. He followed Crooks to the pillbox.

I took my place behind the machine gun. I was already cold, miserable, and wishing I was back under the scant warmth of the lice-infested blanket. Hubbard showed up in about twenty minutes with news that didn't make my mood any better. "We're supposed to stay for two hours. D'Arpino's feet are swollen real bad. Can't get his shoes on." It was almost impossible to keep your feet dry, because of slogging through mud or snow, or wading half-frozen streams. These conditions resulted in numerous cases of trench foot.

The wind blew huge clouds of snow and caused nearby pine branches to wave, creating eerie sounds. Somehow we made it through the cold that numbed body, mind, and spirit. Two riflemen relieved us a short time later with instructions to remove the machine gun to the pillbox. Lieutenant Hammond had decided not to risk more troops to frostbite.

The next morning, Tony D'Arpino was evacuated with frozen feet. As I watched him prepare to leave, chatting with everyone about soft beds, clean sheets, and soft girls, I felt uneasy. It brought back memories of Gullet, who had been evacuated for trench foot after New Year's Day. I wanted them both to return to the unit, but while they were in the hospital they were safe. I wondered how much longer I would survive.

Turnover in the front-line units was high. Dozens of men had been evacuated for trench foot, frozen feet, or both. Disquieting stories circulated about amputations, that, whether fact or rumor, caused some of the troops to be a little more conscientious about changing socks and keeping their feet dry. Others, however, felt that the possibility of losing a foot was better than the possibility of losing a life. Then there were the self-inflicted wounds, usually a shot in the foot or through the fleshy part of the lower leg. These desperate acts, hard to prove, were guaranteed to get a soldier off the line.

I forced myself to stop thinking about losing my buddies and entered the ongoing conversation about D'Arpino and his previous hospital antics.

C Company was relieved the following day and sent to occupy a small nearby village.

"Garrison, you and Hubbard find the mess truck and pick up two cases of C rations," Sergeant Black said. His voice reflected his exhaustion. "We'll be in that house on the right fork of the road."

Hubbard and I made our way toward a line of trucks parked in the shelter of a long, two-story stone building. We found Forsythe, the assistant cook, and collected our C rations. The box of cans was as heavy as the machine gun.

We found the house that Black had mentioned and set the two cases in the center of the front room. As we sought a place to sit among the rest of the platoon members, I called to Black, "I'll take a can of pork and beans."

Black exploded, "You'll take whatever you get, damn it! You bitch about everything. You're no better than anybody else!"

I looked up in surprise. It had been an offhand remark, but Black and I didn't seem to need a valid reason to vent our anger and frustration at one another. "I went after them. I should get my choice."

I slumped against the wall, wishing I had never said anything. "Here!" I heard Black yell.

A can of C rations flew across the room at me. I caught it on my chest. It was pork and beans. I mumbled, "Thanks," and tried to melt into the wall.

Someone laughed and the mood changed. We were all busy opening the C-ration cans. The pork and beans were cold but had an excellent flavor.

The 4th Platoon was located in the same house as the company CP. Jacobs' squad was in a room at the top of the steps. Extra blankets provided from Supply made the room quite comfortable. Anything out of the damp cold would have been comfortable.

We cleaned our weapons, played cards, or talked quietly about home. I fell asleep, only to be roused as Crooks entered the room. I sensed immediately that something was wrong. There was no lopsided smile. Jack was hunched over slightly and he wouldn't meet my gaze.

Crooks murmured, "Carollo didn't make it."

"What? I don't believe it."

"It's true."

"Who told you?"

"Pearson."

I left the room and stumbled down the steps to the CP. I pushed aside the blanket that served as a blackout cover and entered.

"What can I do for you?" Pearson drawled.

I noticed Captain Wilkins and Lieutenant Hammond in the background. "Is it true about Carollo? Did he die?" I stammered.

"Yeah, it's true," Pearson answered.

"When?"

"Second of January. We were just notified."

"Thanks." I dropped the blanket back in place and returned to my room. I had always looked up to Carollo, who had been the squad's first gunner. He was different, the cocky, rugged cowboy from Wyoming. After all the death I had witnessed, I felt overwhelmed that yet another squad member had died. In the back of my mind, I had held out hope that Carollo had survived.

I fell upon my blankets as warm tears ran down my cheeks. Hubbard rose to an elbow, got up, and left the room. I turned to face the wall, pulling the blankets to partially cover my face.

Crooks was sitting in a corner with his knees pulled up under his chin. He stood, walked across the room, and placed a hand on my shoulder. "It's okay, Gene. I didn't come back to the room for an hour after I heard." As Crooks left the room, I saw Pearson peering through an opening in the blankets that covered the door to the CP.

Crooks later returned with the latest rumor: The platoon was going to attack the next morning. The immense, almost suffocating sense of foreboding felt even heavier to me. I sat up, took a small writing pad

and a pencil from my gasbag—long ago converted into a knapsack—
and wrote a letter home:

Dear Mom, Dad, and Barbs,

*How's the half-pint? Is she still getting into your perfume? Hope
everything and everyone is doing well. I bet Dad has his fishing trip
already planned. Hope he can get enough gasoline coupons. Has
Paul's mom heard from him yet? His feet were really bad.*

*Nothing much has changed here. The snow has let up but it is
still really cold, especially when the wind blows. I'm fine. Had an
infection on my eyebrow lanced because it was so sore. I need
some of Mom's soap so I can wash my face more often.*

*I've had this strange feeling for several days now. The slightest sound
seems to scare me. I see things that really aren't there. Too many of my
friends are gone. I'm afraid I might goof up and get someone killed. I
think it might be my turn. I hope it's just a wound that will send me
home, but I might not be that lucky. A lot of guys haven't been.*

*I guess I can say anything in this letter; if it's ever mailed, the
censor will cut most of it out. If it is mailed, you'll know I didn't
make it. I hope you never receive it. I know I'm rambling. I guess
I'm saying good-bye for the final time. I'm giving this to one of my
jeep drivers, Norm Panther. He will mail it if necessary.*

*Tell Grandma and everyone that I think of them often. Thank
Uncle Herbert for trying to get me out of the service to work on
the farm. That would have been nice.*

I love you. Give Barbs a hug and kiss for me.

Your son,
Gene

The morning dawned cold over the Siegfried Line; the sky was dark gray.
C Company was greeted with a hot breakfast, consisting of scrambled

eggs, Spam, bread, and coffee. Crooks wangled a second piece of Spam from Forsythe and commented to no one in particular as we headed back to our billet, "Too much food. Now I know we must be going on an attack today."

Breakfast was barely finished when Black showed up and called the 4th Platoon to assemble. "Pack up. We leave in ten minutes. Move it. Jake, your squad goes up front with Lieutenant Hammond!"

"Crooks, Garrison, Hubbard, let's get with it," Jacobs ordered.

Crooks stuffed the last bite of Spam into his mouth and grumbled, "I knew it."

As the men formed, I sought out Panther. "Norm," I called. "Will you hold this letter for me?"

"Sure. What is it?" Panther inquired.

"A letter home, just in case I don't make it."

"Oh?" Panther looked surprised. "Sure, but nothing's going to happen to you." He took the letter, stuffed it into the breast pocket of his field jacket, and continued to load supplies onto his jeep.

I paused, then slowly returned to the squad, which was forming for its march to the jump-off point. I wasn't reassured by Panther's words.

As the platoon moved out, small frozen droplets of rain beat down in a rhythmic tune upon my steel helmet. The ragged line of men passed the body of a GI alongside the road. I noticed that mud had oozed around the helmet and had begun to edge its way into the jagged hole above the chinstrap. A swollen hand, protruding from the greasy cuff of a field jacket, was stretched toward the helmet. A blanket covered the rest of the body, but a gust of wind had pulled it from the bloody face. Sightless eyes seemed to watch the soldiers pass in silent mockery.

The line of troops passed slowly, some of us still wearing overcoats while others were dressed in field jackets. A rifleman stooped over the dead GI to straighten the blanket and place the helmet over the dead man's face.

The steady drizzle of rain was slowly turning the fields into quagmires. Sporadic gunfire echoed through the forests as small pockets of Germans were discovered. With each step I thought that I would be unable to take another. My boots sank inches deep into the plowed meadow, and each time the mud tried to hold my foot. The sucking sound my feet made as they popped loose seemed to beckon me to lie down and rest. The slime slowly caved into my footsteps and obliterated my passing.

I shifted the machine gun to my other shoulder and immediately felt the strain. I uttered a groan as I looked at the weary figure ahead. Why didn't he stop? Why didn't they all stop? If they did, I could lie down and sleep, right in the freezing mud.

PART V
MOSELLE RIVER

CHAPTER 13

Chaney Demonstrates His Marksmanship

Winter reluctantly loosened its miserable grip on the war-torn countryside along the western fringe of Nazi Germany in early March. Snow and sleet gave way to rain; frozen, snow-packed fields had melted to thick, gooey mud. Bursts of sunlight were becoming more frequent, their warmth more radiant. And the grudgingly improving weather dragged with it a renewed hope for survival for the young soldiers of C Company.

After we passed through the Siegfried Line and secured the town of Allendorf, Germany, the men of C Company boarded trucks for an assembly area just west of the Moselle River. Rumors indicated that other divisions had pinched the 87th out of the line. The company trucked along roads that wound through hilly terrain carpeted with thick pine forests.

The trucks halted in a wooded area west of the Moselle River town of Winningen, several miles south of where the river flows into the Rhine at Koblenz. The men dismounted and immediately established outposts. Patrols worked toward the steep bluffs overlooking Winningen and the river. The 4th Platoon, exempted from patrol duty, dug positions and waited for the evening meal.

* * *

Late in the afternoon of March 15, Lieutenant Colonel Cobb reconnoitered crossing sites in Winningen. He found a site at the end of a street that led from the main road down to the riverbank, a route retreating Germans had used to ferry troops across the river. Figuring the Germans had this location zeroed in on their artillery maps, he selected instead a site farther south. Upon returning to his CP, Cobb learned from Regiment that the crossing had been moved up to midnight.

The northward-flowing Moselle made a sharp S loop before continuing northeast for another ten miles to join the Rhine at Koblenz. Winningen stood in the second turn of the S. The 1st Battalion was to cross at Winningen and advance to the southeast. The 2d and 3d battalions of the 347th Infantry were to cross the river at Kobern, five miles below Winningen, just before the S loop, and advance east to hook up with the 1st Battalion. The regiment then was to clean enemy forces out of the triangular area between the Moselle and the Rhine.

Hubbard and I sat in our newly dug machine-gun position, contemplating the dense woods that surrounded us like a dark cloak. Scattered around in seemingly haphazard fashion were other foxholes marked by the freshly dug rings of earth around them. A soldier came by to announce that a hot meal was being served. We made our way silently through the woods. As we approached the chow line, a familiar voice called out from among the trees.

"Gene, you still here? Look at my shoulder. See how it's shrunk." I turned to the voice. Pat Coluccio, my old Camp Croft friend, who had been wounded on New Year's Day, stood there with a grin on his face, pointing to his shoulder.

"When did you get back?" I asked.

"A week ago, and I'm ready to go back to the hospital again. A guy could get hurt up here," Coluccio answered. He told me how he got wounded on New Year's Day.

"There's no one shooting at us—what more do you want? Fry even has a hot meal for us."

"His hot meal is another reason to go back," Coluccio retorted with a laugh.

"Keep your head down," I said as I turned to catch up with Hubbard.

"You, too, Gene," Coluccio called back before he disappeared into the trees.

After we ate, Crooks and I cleaned and checked the machine gun, shaved, changed socks, and relaxed. More replacements had arrived. One of them was Clifton Chaney, an Air Corps staff sergeant who had been assigned as the machine-gun section leader, with Jacobs and Stec as squad leaders. Crooks and I took note that our new section leader had no combat experience, but we had no say about the situation. Replacements had to be assigned somewhere.

Sergeant Black approached the platoon's positions. "Everybody, front and center. We all get to learn how to paddle a boat."

"Should I bring my water wings?" Barr quipped.

The company filed into a wooded area off a road lined with trucks from an engineer unit. Nearby were a half-dozen flat-bottom rubber boats. About the length of a quarter-ton truck, each boat was designed to carry about twelve men and contained six paddles. We spent the rest of the afternoon learning the techniques of carrying and paddling the boats and disembarking in an assault formation.

Staff Sergeant Chaney appeared as darkness crept between the huge pine trees. "We need two men for outpost duty. Two hours on. Need to go about thirty yards to the edge of that small clearing. First Squad's turn. Who goes, Jake?"

"Garrison and Hubbard," Jacobs replied without hesitation.

"What did we do?" I asked.

"Nothing. That's why you're going," Jacobs answered.

"Oh. Don't forget us," I responded sarcastically.

The two of us walked through the woods to the edge of the clearing. We picked appropriate spots about thirty feet apart and dug shallow holes in the root-infested ground. "You stay awake, now, Tony," I admonished after the hole was finished.

"I'm not even in my hole yet," Hubbard answered. "Besides, you're the one who will go to sleep."

We called each other's names every few minutes until we eventually drifted into sleep. The forest was pitch-black and eerily silent.

I awakened with a start. Something was very wrong. Warm, hot air was blowing against my face. A shrill scream immediately next to my head pierced the stillness. There was a snorting sound and the rustling of pine needles and underbrush. My heart beat wildly as I grabbed my .45. Amid my panic, I suddenly realized what was happening. I recognized the intruder by its squeal as a wild boar.

"What was that?" Hubbard yelled as he was yanked from his sleep.

"A wild boar," I replied, still breathing heavily from the surprise.

"Are there more of them?"

"Maybe, but I probably scared this one as badly as he scared me. I bet we get some relief in a hurry," I said.

"Good. I was tired of listening to you snore anyway."

"If you were awake, why didn't you answer when I called you?"

We laughed and settled back to await relief, but we no longer had a problem staying awake.

"Garrison! Hubbard! Where are you?" Jacobs' shrill voice penetrated the darkness. "Wake up and answer me."

"Give the password," I challenged.

"I'll give the password with the end of my carbine. You guys have a nice nap?"

"Not with those wild pigs out here. Did you hear them squeal?" I asked.

"I never know when to believe you, Garrison," Jacobs snorted.

Hubbard responded quickly, "Honest, Jake, it's true. The boar tried to get into Gene's foxhole."

"A pig. That figures. Come on. We're moving out. Almost left you two."

Pine needles that covered the forest floor muffled the sound of our footsteps. As I followed Hubbard and Jacobs through the woods, I felt an intense need to relieve myself, but there was no time.

We rejoined the platoon just as it was pulling out. The men bumped each other and grumbled quietly as we made our way to a forester's path and then to a narrow dirt road.

Soon we entered a small town and approached a knot of military trucks and jeeps. At first, we thought the platoon was going to be trucked somewhere else, but we continued walking along a cobblestone street past the vehicles. The street sloped downhill and then leveled off as it crossed a wider, bisecting street, and then it dipped downward again. At the bottom, the troops stopped and began to bunch up.

"Machine-gun section, over here," Chaney loudly whispered. "Each squad in a different boat. Jake, your squad is with me."

At least now we know where we're going, I thought. Everyone knew: We're going to cross the Moselle River. This must be it, unless they intended us to practice loading while the boats were in the water. My intestines were giving me fits, but there was no time and no place to stop.

In the pre-dawn darkness and quiet, the sound of the river lapping against the shore and sloshing against the boats seemed loud enough to wake up the Germans on the other side. Men loaded quickly and silently into the boats. Soon it was the 1st Squad's turn. As fast as a boat loaded, the engineers pushed off into the blackness. Lieutenant Colonel Cobb rode over with the first wave of Company C.

We slipped our paddles into the dark water and tried to coordinate our strokes. In spite of the fact we had practiced only once—and that was on dry ground in the middle of a forest—we maneuvered the boat across the Moselle with surprising ease.

As I pushed the paddle over and over again into the ink-dark water, my stomach felt like it was tied in knots. I didn't know whether it was fear or because I needed to take a crap. Concern over my stomach helped me take my mind off what might lay in store on the other side of the river—or if we would make it across at all. The silence was impenetrable. In my mind, every tiny sound was magnified, and I was certain that every German on the other side of the Moselle knew we were out on the river. Any second, flares would light up the sky and tracers would track them down like a carnival shooting gallery.

Not a shot was fired.

The boats reached the opposite shore and we unloaded on the stone-block wall along the river's edge. The platoon moved quietly across a narrow dirt road and huddled at the foot of a steep, terraced grape vineyard. Lieutenant Camilo Caporali, the new 1st Platoon leader, appeared from the darkness: "Everyone start up the hill. Be careful of grapevines and be quiet as possible. Regroup at the top. There should be a road that parallels the river. Turn right and wait for me."

Caporali started to climb the first stone wall to a terrace, stopped, and called out in a hushed tone, "You squad leaders, be sure no ammo bearer is carrying no more than one box of ammo. You can't climb these walls with both hands full."

Caporali turned to Hubbard, who stood next to him, and said, "Give me one of those boxes." Hubbard handed a metal ammo box to the lieutenant, who tucked it under his arm and resumed climbing.

I cradled my box under my left arm and followed Jacobs and Crooks up the steep slope. Hubbard was right behind me.

The openness of the Moselle Valley allowed sufficient nighttime illumination to see a short distance, enough to find handholds on the stone walls and grapevines. We kept low to avoid exposing our silhouettes against the skyline in case some German sentry was awake at the top of the vineyard. We inched our way up the steep slope, careful not to make a sound, fearful that gunfire would erupt with every muffled cough or the scrape of boot against a rock.

"Look out below," Caporali suddenly called. The men froze. A box of machine-gun ammunition clattered down the slope. I saw Crooks move quickly to his right. The box now had a clear path straight at my head, which I buried in a grapevine. I heard Hubbard utter an unintelligible word as the box plummeted past. Each bounce was as loud as a hammer on an anvil. Then silence. We waited breathlessly, but no gunfire split the darkness.

Everyone started to climb again, but with even more urgency. The rifle platoons slowly reached the crest of the vineyard and moved downstream along a dirt road. Lieutenant Caporali paused long enough to apologize to Hubbard and the rest of the 4th Platoon for dropping the ammo box. Luckily, it seemed to have eyes and had missed everyone.

I labored the last few yards before I reached the road. I stopped there to relieve myself. "Tony, hold up. I have to take a crap. Wait for me, will you?"

"What? Okay, but hurry," Hubbard answered nervously.

I hurried, but I suddenly started to laugh. "Can you see me?" I whispered to Hubbard.

"What? No," Hubbard replied. "Why?"

"With my bare rear hanging out, I feel like I'm waving a white flag."

Hubbard laughed. I finished and we hurried to rejoin the squad.

For about the next half hour, the 4th Platoon moved cautiously across the ridgeline, stopping only long enough for the forward scouts to explore the roadway and surrounding terrain, before we advanced farther. We finally left the road and made our way up a wooded hillside. The rifle platoons, meanwhile, stayed on the road until they came to an intersecting road that led east. The intersection was our immediate objective.

Sporadic gunfire erupted along the high ground above the river valley as Germans were discovered and flushed from their positions. Bright orange tracers briefly stitched a pattern through the darkness. C Company took defensive positions along the hillside in case the enemy decided to mount a counterattack.

Heavy firing broke out between the company's position and the Moselle. The 2d and 3d battalions were crossing the river at Kobern, a mile north of Winningen. Apparently, they weren't as lucky as C Company. Support troops and supplies were being ferried across along the same route taken by C Company. It sounded like they also were in trouble.

A large combat patrol led by Lieutenant Colonel Cobb started out to silence some of the German gun emplacements. As the 4th Platoon remained in position to await orders, daylight edged its way across the eastern horizon. The outline of trees on the opposite side of the Moselle gradually became visible as the dawn threw its pale light over the tops of the river valley. The sound of battle abated but lost none of its deadly peril.

"Look," exclaimed Barr. "Isn't that someone across the river? There, in front of the trees. He's walking along the road."

"That's a Kraut," Chaney cut in. "Look at the shape of his helmet. He acts like nothing's going on. I'll bet they don't know that we're even over here."

Discovery of this lone, unsuspecting German soldier elicited comments from everyone in the squad.

"I bet I can hit that guy from here," Chaney bragged. "Then he'll know there's a war on."

"That's eight hundred yards, at least. You can't hit him from here," Jacobs challenged.

"Don't be too sure," Barr replied. "Chaney here is a North Carolina squirrel hunter, you know."

From a sitting position, Chaney raised his rifle and took aim. The whole squad watched the German's every step, transfixed in anticipation. It seemed like minutes rolled by before Chaney squeezed off the shot. The soldier spun around and dropped to the ground. The German rose on one leg, grabbed the other, then fell to a sitting position. He slowly dragged himself toward cover.

One of the recent replacements shouted, "Shoot him again, Chaney!"

"He's a man, dammit," Chaney growled. "He isn't any danger to us. He's out of action. Don't anyone *dare* fire at him!"

Chaney's comments drew some surprised looks from the squad members, because even though he was a section leader, he had had no combat experience before joining the 87th. He was low-key when it came to combat decisions, deferring to the combat-hardened wisdom of Jacobs and Stec. Chaney was the target of a lot of jibes, but he got along rather well with everyone except Dudley. For some reason, sparks flew between them at the slightest provocation.

Following Chaney's marksmanship exhibition, everyone settled back and waited. The rattle of an engine could be heard near the crossroad, signaling the approach of a lone vehicle. Crooks pointed the machine gun at the road below; I held the belt of ammunition, my adrenaline flowing, just like before a basketball game.

A German command car came into view, traveling full speed toward the Moselle with soldiers half sitting, half standing on the running board. Others filled the seats inside. Several riflemen and a BAR man stepped from the trees and yelled, "Haltz! Haltz!" but the command car didn't slow down. Instead, a soldier on the running board, hanging onto the car with one hand, used his free hand to wildly fire a grease gun. It didn't deter the BAR man, who fired a burst at the car. The riflemen also opened fire. The gunfire was extremely effective. The impact of the bullets toppled the men on the running board, the windshield disappeared in a shattering of glass, and the driver slumped sideways. The car careened off the road and plowed into a group of small pine trees. A few of the riflemen rushed the car. Several shots rang out, and then there was silence.

All occupants of the German command car were officers. They apparently had been drinking in a nearby town and were trying to get back to their units stationed on the bank of the Moselle. It was fortunate that they were not with their troops, who undoubtedly would have been more alert and made the crossing nasty.

As full daylight expanded, C Company climbed out of its positions near the crossroad and headed toward the next objective, leaving the crumpled staff car and the bodies of dead German officers behind.

The 1st Battalion completed the initial phase of the assault crossing of the Moselle with few casualties. We had surprised the German defenders, killed or wounded sixty, and captured another one hundred and sixty. The 2d and 3d battalions, crossing at Kobern, encountered more resistance.

C Company and the rest of the 1st Battalion continued to mop up retreating Germans while we waited for the other two battalions to clean out their sectors of the Moselle and move to us. We received harassing fire most of the day, until all of the German gun emplacements were destroyed. Major General Troy Middleton, VIII Corps commander, visited the 87th Division headquarters and complimented the 87th on the smooth completion of its mission.

With the Moselle conquered, the regiment's three battalions prepared for the advance to the Rhine. Attack plans called for the 1st Battalion to move north of the town of Waldesch and rush to the Rhine at Rhens. A and B companies swept across the territory between the Moselle and Rhine rivers, capturing several small towns, bypassing pockets of resistance, and pushing toward the river town of Rhens. C Company followed with the assignment of clearing out bypassed Germans.

The 4th Platoon was bringing up the rear of C Company; the machine-gun section was in front with the mortar squads protecting the flanks. Behind C Company was D Company, the heavy weapons company, composed of water-cooled .30-caliber medium machine guns and 81mm mortars. This order of battle was common procedure for all three line companies. If a rifle squad or platoon became engaged in a heavy firefight and required more firepower, one or both of the machine-gun squads from the weapons platoon was dispatched immediately.

The responsibility of maintaining contact between these units belonged to the company and battalion runners. Their mission often exposed them to enemy fire. The runners had at least one advantage over the other infantrymen, though: They usually slept at the command post, which was almost always in a house or some other protected spot.

First Lieutenant Henry O. Wise had taken over as temporary commander of C Company from Captain Wilkins. Wise, a regimental headquarters officer, had approached Lieutenant Colonel Cobb during the Siegfried Line action and requested a transfer to his battalion. Appreciating Wise's moxie, Cobb told the lieutenant he would do his best to honor the request.

Distant shelling and small-arms fire were audible as C Company moved through the heavily wooded terrain between the two rivers. For the first few hours, we advanced without meeting any resistance. That changed quickly with a burst of fire from a German burp gun, answered immediately by American rifle and BAR fire.

"Machine guns, front and center! Move it!" Sergeant Black yelled as he pumped his arm up and down in the infantry sign language to move forward. Jacobs and Stec led their squads forward at a trot. We moved through a squad of kneeling riflemen toward Lieutenant Hammond—the company executive officer—and several noncoms.

The firefight was brief and deadly. Fifteen Wehrmacht soldiers who had evaded A and B companies decided to ambush a squad from C Company that was setting up a bivouac area in a large meadow.

Wise's runner, Chuck Yanacheck, noticed a boot sticking out from behind a tree. He informed Wise, who called to his BAR man, Dick Coble, and the three of them went to investigate. As they neared the spot Yanacheck had pointed out, a slug hit Coble's helmet, creasing the steel and bruising his forehead. He fired several short bursts from his BAR as the three fought their way from tree to tree through incoming fire.

Coble spied a German coming toward them along a ravine and shot at him just as the enemy soldier fired a Panzerfaust in his direction. The explosive recoil of the handheld antitank rocket launcher raised the German about four feet in the air, and a ball of fire sped by Coble's head. The concussion burst his eardrums. Three more Germans were killed and six were captured in the firefight. Coble later was awarded a Silver Star and Yanacheck received a Bronze Star for their actions. Coble was sent back to the battalion aid station for treatment of his damaged ears. After being examined, he was given two aspirin and ordered back to the line.

With the sudden engagement over, Lieutenant Wise gave instructions to establish defensive positions on the perimeter of the woods. He also ordered patrols to sweep the area for any bypassed German units.

The 4th Platoon pulled back into the fringe of the woods and Jacobs placed his machine-gun squad to cover the road. Stec's squad covered the open meadow and the firebreak where Yanacheck had discovered the Germans.

It was late afternoon, and most of the troops were preparing little fires using the K-ration boxes and twigs. The Spam-like meat in the K rations tasted a lot better warmed. The men relaxed, confident that German stragglers had been eliminated.

Sergeant Barr entered the machine-gun squad's positions. "Who wants to check out that hill on the other side of the clearing?" he asked. "Someone says you can see a little town that's supposed to be on the Rhine River."

"Hubbard and I will cover the gun. You guys can go," Jacobs answered as he nodded toward Crooks and me.

"Why not?" I said. "Might be worth the view. Besides, it'll probably be as close as we'll get to a town tonight," I added. I was resigned to spending another night in a cold, damp foxhole.

Although the area was secure, Barr, Crooks, and I skirted the meadow—snipers could be anywhere—as we cautiously advanced toward the hill. We noticed that the trees were scarred from shrapnel. The knob had taken a direct hit from an artillery barrage. We parted some underbrush and discovered a foxhole containing two dead Germans. Three more Wehrmacht soldiers lay nearby, also dead. Pasty gray skin made their faces look unreal. There were no weapons, or anything else of military value, around the corpses. Someone had effectively scoured the area after the shrapnel had done its deadly work.

Crooks poked around the area, trying to find a vantage point to see the village.

I couldn't take my eyes off the dead Wehrmacht soldiers. I wondered if they had families. I had never gotten used to seeing dead American soldiers. It turned my stomach and sparked a premonition of my own death. I would have to close my eyes, wipe the scene from my memory, and move on to the next objective.

But the sight of dead Germans aroused no emotion in me. They were inanimate objects, like a tree trunk or a crumpled farmhouse. I could divorce myself from the reality of seeing a dead enemy and concentrate on the present, the living, the immediate future. Now, staring at the corpses clad in field-gray winter uniforms, I pondered those feelings, especially since I was of recent German heritage. It bothered me that I was concerned about whether these dead men had families. I couldn't allow myself to have feelings for the enemy. Such feelings could have deadly consequences. Then I saw a photo lying on the ground next to one of the dead Germans—a handsome soldier with his wife and two small children. I tore my gaze away from the photograph and called to Crooks and Barr, "We better get back." I turned abruptly and left without a look back to see if they were following.

I returned to my foxhole and had started to write a letter home when I was interrupted by a familiar voice—Tony D'Arpino.

"Why are you guys goofing off?" D'Arpino jibed. "First Sergeant Pearson wants you front and center so you can learn how to paddle a boat out of this forest."

"Well, look who's back," Jacobs said in a voice that revealed his obvious pleasure over the unexpected arrival.

"Tony!" I shouted. "I thought you would be in Paris trying to make a nurse by now."

"I don't have time for that kind of stuff," D'Arpino said as he crouched next to my foxhole. "We have a river to cross and a war to win. Besides, they sent me to Luxembourg City, not Paris."

To our amusement, D'Arpino uttered some unkind words to describe the ethnic heritage of the doctor who had returned him to the line. He also affirmed that Pearson really did want the 4th Platoon to report for boat training. The laughter petered out, and the men rose to trudge off to find Pearson. As tongues of fading daylight flickered through the trees, the platoon practiced loading and disembarking from rectangular metal boats, far different from ones used to cross the Moselle. Fortunately, we couldn't know that the Rhine would be nothing like the Moselle.

That evening, as we were eating our K rations, D'Arpino told of an incident that Bob Jones, a replacement in the 3d Platoon who had been evacuated with trench foot, recounted to him in the hospital.

While in the replacement depot before joining the 87th, Jones had been issued a pair of shoepacs, a replacement for combat boots designed to keep feet warm and dry. But the particular pair issued to Jones leaked, which eventually contributed to his trench foot. Lieutenant Colonel Cobb, who frequently checked the aid station to keep a handle on types of wounds and causes of injuries, came by and noticed that Jones had trench foot. Cobb asked Jones why he had not changed his socks to keep his feet dry.

Jones, who apparently was not in a good mood because of his feet, answered, "When you're issued boots that leak, it doesn't do much good to put on dry socks." Jones's reply must have been so spontaneous that Cobb considered it an accurate observation and did not continue the conversation. Many officers would have slapped an insubordination charge against Jones, but Cobb was not "just any officer." His men were used to seeing him, usually with a junior officer, in the midst of many actions.

The next morning, fog obscured much of the Rhine Valley, giving it an ominous look. During intermittent breaks in the mist, boats could be seen ferrying Germans to the east bank.

C Company moved off the high ground above the river valley and overran a few Germans manning rear-guard positions on its way down into the evacuated town of Rhens. The men took shelter in the houses in the center of town and outposts were set up in a riverfront hotel, the main post office building, and an observation tower. Word spread that C Company would once again spearhead a river crossing.

No one was allowed to frequent any street, building, or area that was visible to the Germans on the far bank. The Americans knew the Germans were on the east bank, and the Germans knew the Americans were in Rhens and other west-bank cities. For now, each side was content to leave the other alone.

PART VI

THE RHINE

CHAPTER 14

Like Ducks on a Pond

Soldiers of the 1st Battalion, 347th Regiment, settled into houses and buildings in Rhens. Before us, the legendary Rhine River ran wide and swift to the north, an intimidating obstacle. Rhens had an eerie, surreal feeling. There were no civilians to be seen. There wasn't any evidence of German troops, either. No fire was coming from across the river, yet the enemy must have known the American soldiers were among the houses. Had the Germans made a military or moral decision not to destroy the picturesque river town? Maybe they weren't on the east bank at all?

Movement in view of the river was forbidden during daylight. There was no sense tempting fate. Nevertheless, curiosity or the possibility of finding souvenirs—better known to GIs as loot—led many members of the company to investigate surrounding buildings. Everyone was warned of booby traps, which deterred some. Those who did go foraging were especially careful. Fortunately, there were no casualties.

D'Arpino, Grieco, and I decided that a school building might be the best place to avoid trouble. The three-story corner building was constructed of stone. The basement had been a storage room but now was completely empty. The top floor, visible from across the Rhine, restricted exploration to the ground level. Grieco found a black, shiny top hat and placed it on his head. A bus driver's cap was the next find, and then some sort of insignia, which we decided was probably a badge for a crossing guard. I came across a box of German stamps, most of which portrayed Adolph Hitler's picture. I boxed them and later had Rehkop, the mail clerk, send them to my mother.

Someone discovered a Leica camera and a lot of film. Almost every member of the 4th Platoon eventually had his picture taken with the camera, many of them wearing the top hat.

More replacements arrived during the next two days to fill the company's depleted ranks, actually making some squads overstrength. Extra hands were always welcome to carry ammunition and share sentry work.

It had been several days since the Moselle, and everyone was on edge with the knowledge that a Rhine crossing was coming soon. In a strange way, we were looking forward to it; we had been lulled into a false confidence with the ease by which the company had crossed the Moselle.

After the first quiet day in Rhens, the Germans started to lob occasional artillery fire across the river onto the outskirts of the town. Careless exposure to the river during the day drew a sniper's bullet. At night, American reconnaissance patrols sneaked across the river to map landing sites and pinpoint enemy positions. But, mostly, the men of C Company and the rest of the 1st Battalion took advantage of several days of static defense to rest, enjoy hot meals, and drink plenty of confiscated beer and wine.

The order came for the 4th Platoon to assemble in the playground behind the school building. It was dusk on March 24, 1945, and the last troops had just returned from chow. That made four days in a row that we had hot food, an unusually long stretch during combat.

When the last of the platoon reached the assembly point, 1st Sergeant Pearson addressed the company. "Men, we're crossing the Rhine just after midnight. Don't expect it to be as easy as the Moselle. For your information, Captain Wilkins has been sent on leave. Lieutenant Wise is the acting company commander. We have a new 4th Platoon leader, Lieutenant . . . [Someone coughed, and I didn't catch his name.]

He has a few words for you. Good luck and God bless on the crossing."
Pearson melted into the background and a young officer replaced him.

The officer displayed no sign of rank—no insignia on his helmet, no
gold bars on his shoulders. He wore an OD jacket and combat boots.
"Men, I've just been assigned to the 87th. This isn't the time to make a
speech. After we've crossed the Rhine, there will be time to get acquainted, so good luck, and I'll see you tomorrow." With that, the lieutenant and Pearson headed back toward the CP.

"Wonder how long it'll take him to screw things up?" D'Arpino
grinned.

"Maybe you can keep him out of our way, Black?" Jacobs said.

"I've already been told to watch him," Black responded. "Hell, I
didn't even catch his name."

We never saw the officer again.

We drifted back to the billets to catch some shut-eye. The time to
H-hour was short. "Hey, buddy, wake up." D'Arpino's voice penetrated
my sleep. "Time to take a boat ride." D'Arpino hurried on to help Jacobs awaken the squad. "Get everything together. We have to assemble
in the street in twenty minutes."

Grumbling and swearing, we collected our gear and answered the
wake-up call. We assembled quietly again on the playground. Noncoms
spat out curt instructions. Like an uncoiling snake, the column of men
left the assembly point and started down a narrow, cobblestone street.
They passed dark, lifeless houses; the only sound came from clanking
equipment and boots scuffling over the stone pavement. A railroad overpass built in the form of an arch over the street loomed out of the darkness. We walked by clusters of trucks and other vehicles from the engineer
battalion responsible for amphibious operations. After the cobblestone
street passed beneath the overpass, it gently sloped down to the river's
edge. Water lapped at the shoreline. The dank smell of mud and river
odors greeted our nostrils. Muffled voices gave instructions and shadowy figures directed us to our assigned boats.

The machine-gun and mortar squads were separated to decrease the
possibility of losing more than one squad with a direct hit on a single
assault boat.

"Hey, Jake, where are you going? This is our boat," Crooks called out to Jacobs.

"I know. I've been assigned as leader for the 2d Squad. Stec is on leave in Paris."

"Man, that's a crock," D'Arpino snorted. "First he gets to be a sergeant, and now he gets to go to Paris. What did we do wrong?"

"We got in the Army, that's what we did wrong," I answered.

We quietly and efficiently climbed into steel assault boats. The craft looked like small ungainly scows; they were rectangular in shape, square at both ends, and the sides were about three feet high. We knelt in our boats, six to a side, our heads and most of our torsos exposed above the gunwales. An engineer whose job was to bring the boat back across the river sat in the front. One by one, the boats slipped away from the shoreline and were swallowed up by the darkness, leaving each of us to his own thoughts.

I didn't pray, but I fervently hoped the crossing would be as safe as the Moselle. I tried to suffocate the anxiety in my mind by concentrating on maintaining a rhythmic paddling, staying in unison with Hubbard in front of me. I hoped Hubbard was doing the same.

We struggled against the relentless river current to keep our boats on course. Every sound seemed amplified—the ripples of the water on the hull, the paddles swishing downward into the darkness. Surely the Germans heard us. Halfway across, hope soared that we would make it undetected.

Then a dreaded sound broke the night. The *pop* and *shssss* of a flare turned the darkness into an eerie blue daylight. It ripped hope from our hearts and replaced it with fear. I recognized the sound and drove the paddle into the water as if I alone could propel the assault boat to the distant shore.

The deep throbbing sound of 20mm guns suddenly echoed across the river, sending orange balls of death to seek targets among the advancing boats. The metallic thud of bullets striking the hulls was terrifying. The unfolding scene wrenched my thoughts back to one of my uncles firing at mallard ducks on a pond during one of our last hunting trips. After the second or third shot, the remaining mallards skimmed along the still water, rose quickly into the air, and scattered in every direction so rapidly that no more shots could be fired. Dinner had been secured, though.

Fly ducks, fly! Get off the water!

I dipped my paddle downward and deeper into the river. With each stroke, I felt more naked as each lift of my arm exposed my side. Hurry! Cover my side before a 20mm shell tears me apart. How stupid. What protection is my arm against a high-velocity antiaircraft weapon? But I covered my side anyway; I had no other way to hide. Fly! Fly, birds. Fly!

A nearby explosion snapped me back to reality. I focused on D'Arpino and Hubbard, who knelt immediately in front of me. I noticed that both were furiously paddling. Before the flares and the 20mm fire, they had shared a paddle. Now, D'Arpino was paddling with his carbine. Everyone was desperate to get off the river.

The metallic thuds of bullets grew more frequent. A scream pierced the gunfire, and the boat right in front of us lurched to one side. For the brief second it was visible, I saw no occupants; then the current whipped the boat sideways to reveal a lone figure holding on to the side, halfway submerged in the water. Then the boat was gone, swallowed by the darkness. The endless paddling continued.

More flares, smaller this time, illuminated the river in their artificial sunlight. The bursts of light and trailing streamers would have been beautiful under other circumstances. Here on the Rhine, they only brought additional gunfire. Mercifully these flares faded quickly, and darkness descended again across the river. The gunfire ebbed and flowed. Tracer bullets etched brilliant, looping lines across the black-shrouded river gorge. Soldiers struggled to maintain direction of the boats even as they were buffeted by the swift current. Men continued to die or fall wounded. When someone went down, there was no one to take his place on that side of the boat. This combination of imbalance and the swift current pulled boats off course. One boat, careening out of control, nearly rammed our craft. Then another helpless victim of the current just missed us.

Gunfire from the black cliffs towering above us on the opposite shore suddenly intensified and grew louder, creating a cacophony of death: 20mm cannon shells hissed overhead; artillery whistled into ear-splitting explosions; mortar shells fluttered down, spreading their deadly shrapnel; bullets buzzed around like angry bees.

The boats in the lead bunched together like a family clinging to one another for protection as they approached the shoreline. They bumped against a stone levee at the water's edge. Shadowy figures jumped out, turned, and extended their hands to help other men ashore. The shoreline, murky in the darkness and below the field of enemy fire, offered a temporary haven.

Miraculously, our assault boat reached the riverbank, one of only a few unscathed by enemy fire. Only two C Company assault boats were totally lost in the Rhine crossing. One by one, the men climbed out onto the top of the levee, each one helping the man behind him. Crooks, D'Arpino, Hubbard, and I huddled together behind a stone wall, searching for access to the next level on the bank. In the confusion and darkness, it was impossible to tell where the others had gone. The ground vibrated from shells exploding directly in front of us.

"Friendly fire! Friendly fire!" Lieutenant Caporali's shrill voice rose out of the shadows and above the din.

"How the hell does he know?" D'Arpino muttered. "It could be Russians as far as he knows."

As if Caporali overheard D'Arpino, he continued, "Our big guns are scheduled to give us covering fire. There should be only a couple more rounds, and they'll stop."

The earth trembled with additional explosions, and then the artillery fire stopped, just as Caporali had predicted. "Well, I'll be damned," D'Arpino exclaimed.

The small-arms fire, the throbbing beat of the 20mm guns, and the occasional shrill bursts of mortar fire seemed almost acceptable in the absence of the heavy artillery explosions.

Jacobs emerged from the shadows. "Everyone okay?" he asked, without waiting for answers. "Lieutenant Wise wants a machine-gun squad to take that castle. A lot of fire is coming from that direction. Crooks, you take the squad. Have you seen Dudley? I saw him right after we left the boat but haven't seen him since."

"Haven't seen him," Crooks said. "You have any suggestions on how to get to the castle?"

"Yeah, carefully. Try to avoid any firefights, but if you have to, shoot your way in. It's just you guys. You won't have any riflemen to cover you. Don't do anything stupid, understand? Good luck." Jacobs disappeared into the shadows.

Somewhere in the darkness, I heard Caporali as he tried to assemble the rifle squads, but the crackle of small-arms fire and the heavier thumping of the 20mm guns snatched away his words. Mortar rounds burst within the landing site, but not in any discernable pattern.

"Well, we may as well go," Crooks said, as if off on a Sunday errand. He hoisted the .30-caliber machine gun onto his right shoulder and made his way up the crumbling rock wall. The rest of us scrambled after him, staying as low as possible. We reached the top of the wall, crossed a narrow road, and then stumbled over a series of railroad tracks and wires installed along the rails about eighteen inches above the ground. The wires were part of the railroad switching system. As the squad crossed the rail yard, switching signals, lampposts, and freight cars suddenly loomed out of the darkness, treacherous obstacles to our journey. Small-arms fire crisscrossed the rail yard at random intervals. Every fourth or fifth round was a tracer, giving everyone a frightful visual of the bullets that were seeking us out. The Germans couldn't see their targets in the blackness, but their firing pattern was effective. Shouts of "Medic!" and cries from the wounded penetrated the night air.

Moving in short rushes, our squad reached the other side of the rail yard. Ahead were several darkened buildings, good hiding places for snipers. We gave the buildings a wide berth, throwing cautionary glances at the ominous structures as we circled away. We headed for the protection of some woods and avoided roads or paths as we started up the steep side of the river canyon. We breathed heavily as we worked our way slowly upward, gradually moving away from the gunfire, which was to our right, along a deep ravine. Sweating from our exertion and the damp air, we laboriously picked our way up the hill. We discovered a narrow path that wound back and forth up the incline and decided to take the trail to make better time, even though it might mean a chance encounter with a German gun position.

It was nearly daybreak when we reached the bluff and stopped in a patch of woods held together with a medium covering of undergrowth. Peering through the trees, we saw the castle framed against the first streaks of daylight in the eastern sky. It wasn't a large castle, just one stone-block turret surrounded by several other stone buildings that served as the castle walls. The tops of the walls and the turret had irregularly spaced firing parapets. It was designed and built for medieval combat and survival.

D'Arpino and Hubbard moved cautiously to check out a small clearing in front of the castle. Crooks and I covered them with the machine gun. Suddenly, an unidentified American rifleman stepped from the protective undergrowth and took a prone position in the open clearing. Immediately, a sniper squeezed off some shots that kicked up dirt around the soldier. The rifleman froze, not firing his weapon, not moving.

"Take cover! Move before you get killed," D'Arpino shouted at the soldier.

The rest of us also screamed at the rifleman, exhorting him to move to safety, but to no avail. The unseen sniper kept his victim pinned down. Observing the pattern of the shots, Crooks noted that the firing was coming from above. He lifted the machine gun barrel up, placed it on my shoulder, and fired short bursts at any opening or conceivable place that might conceal a sniper. One of his targets was a church tower across a small river, which flowed by the side of the castle before it joined the Rhine.

D'Arpino and Hubbard scurried from the shelter of the undergrowth and grasped the rifleman by each arm, and half walked, half carried him to safety behind a tree. Crooks stopped firing. So did the sniper. Either the German didn't like the odds, or a bullet had found its mark.

"Well, now what?" D'Arpino asked.

"Guess we better see if anyone else is up here," Crooks said.

With our weapons ready to fire, we slowly and carefully searched the area surrounding the castle. There were footprints, crushed cigarettes, and other signs that troops had been in the area, but they had either left or were in the castle.

The squad returned to the front of the castle. From this vantage point, we could look down on a village located at the junction of the Rhine and the small river that flowed behind the castle. A church steeple, the same one Crooks had sprayed earlier, towered over the village.

"Look," I exclaimed, "that boat. Are they German?"

I pointed to a rowboat containing four men as it crossed the smaller river. Crooks again placed the machine gun over my shoulder for more accurate fire and aimed at the boat.

"Are they German?" Hubbard repeated.

"Probably," D'Arpino answered.

"Maybe we should fire a warning burst in front of them," I suggested.

"Look at the helmets," Crooks interrupted. "They look GI."

"Wait a minute! Isn't that Jacobs?" I asked.

"Yes!" Crooks and Hubbard responded in unison.

"Shoot 'em, anyway, Jack," D'Arpino chuckled. "You could make sergeant."

Everyone burst into laughter for the first time since we had boarded the assault boats hours earlier. We watched the boat until it docked. Its occupants scampered ashore and disappeared into the village.

"Where's that rifleman?" Crooks suddenly asked as he glanced around the clearing.

He had vanished. None of us had recognized the soldier, and we never saw him again. More than likely, he was a replacement. We turned our attention back to the castle.

We crouched down among the trees on the edge of the clearing to discuss the best approach to the castle. We saw no visible ground-level doors or windows. In front of us, a narrow road bordered by stone walls rose steeply upward before it curved toward the main part of the castle. Our only choice was to follow the road. Crooks and D'Arpino crossed to the left side of the road while Hubbard and I hugged the wall on the right. We had advanced only a few yards when Crooks called out, "Look here!"

He pointed to a German Walther P-38 pistol that lay next to the wall in front of him. After several minutes of probing, feeling, and searching for booby traps, he picked up the prize and stashed it in his pocket.

"Come on, Jack, let's flip for it!" D'Arpino chided.

"Yeah, this is a squad effort," I added.

Crooks, with a faint grin, answered quickly, "Sorry fellows. Finders keepers," and continued along the road.

As we followed the curve of the road, we saw a large, dark oak double door, rounded at the top. The door enchanted me. I visualized a medieval knight charging out on his huge black horse. Maybe a white horse. But it was a German castle, I reminded myself, so it *had* to be a black horse.

To the right of the large door was a smaller entrance also dark in color. Both doors appeared to be firmly closed; there were no handles or doorknobs.

"Now what?" I asked. "How do we open the door?"

"We could just knock," D'Arpino offered cheerfully. He cautiously approached the door, staying to one side, out of direct line of fire in case someone suddenly opened the door and started shooting. Standing sideways to the door, D'Arpino swung the butt end of his carbine out in front of him and used it to knock three times.

The seconds ticked slowly by. We waited, our eyes glued to the door, weapons at the ready. Very slowly, the door opened to reveal an elderly German woman. Fear was etched on her gnarled face as she uttered several words in German, none of which I understood.

Crooks replied in his high-school German. The old woman visibly relaxed, although her gaze remained riveted on the machine gun cradled in Crooks's arms.

"Jack, I think she's afraid of the gun," I said. "Maybe I should go in first and leave my pistol in its holster. If I hit the floor, start shooting."

I moved toward the door. The woman stepped aside, and I carefully walked through the doorway, closely followed by the other squad mem-

GENE GARRISON

Gene Garrison (top) home on leave in Middletown, Ohio, after basic training in July 1944. The same sitting (lower image), with his family: his little sister, Barbara; his mother, Nora; and his father, Donald.

GENE GARRISON

Gene Garrison in Munich, Germany, as a member of the Army of Occupation, October 1945.

An antitank gun crew of the 87th Infantry Division battles the cold weather while guarding against foraying tanks from the Panzer Lehr Division during fighting west of Bastogne.

A tank destroyer rumbles along an Ardennes road, going to support the fighting west of Bastogne.

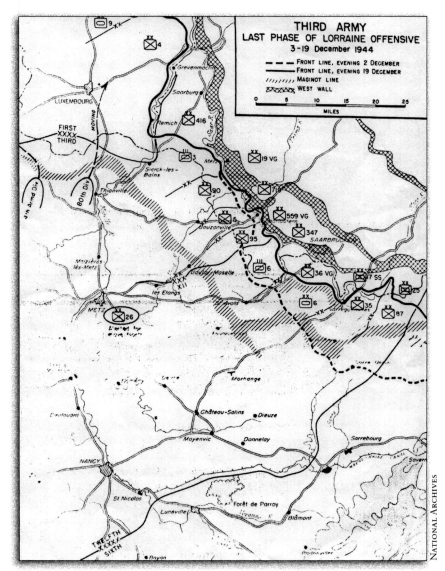

This contemporary map shows the deployment of the 87th Division along the German border from December 13–18, 1944. This was the last push of Patton's Third Army to breach the Siegfried Line before it was rushed north and committed into the Battle of the Bulge.

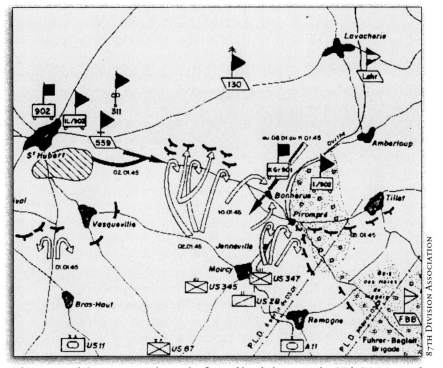

This captured German map shows the flow of battle between the 87th Division and the Panzer Lehr division west of Bastogne during the Battle of the Bulge.

General George Patton arrives at 87th Division headquarters on December 30, 1944, at the start of VIII Corps' attack west of Bastogne.

Soldiers of the 347th Infantry take a break from the fighting near St. Hubert, Belgium, to line up for chow.

An 87th Division convoy crawls along a narrow, snow-packed road northeast of St. Vith, Belgium—the division's thrust to force the Germans out of the Bulge and back to the Siegfried Line.

German soldiers surrender to the 87th after heavy fighting in the Bulge.

C Company attacked across this ground on January 1, 1945, to penetrate the woods and cut the Bastogne–St. Hubert highway two hundred yards beyond. The farmhouse (bottom image) is located on the far side of the woods seen in the center background. The company suffered more casualties in this fight than any other during the war.

The farmhouse as seen from inside the woods. German tanks parked on the far side devastated the first reinforced reconnaissance patrol. The light-colored brick on the right lower portion of the house is where a bazooka shell exploded after missing a tank.

GIs of the 347th Regiment pass through St. Hubert, Belgium, in January 1945. St. Hubert was used by Panzer Lehr as a staging area during the Battle of the Bulge.

Soldiers admire a sign erected after taking Losheim, Germany, from the enemy. Located near the Belgium border, Losheim was one of the jumping-off points for the Sixth SS Panzer Army at the outset of the Ardennes counteroffensive.

Boats used in the assault crossing of the Rhine line the east bank as 87th Division soldiers push the Germans out of the river gorge.

A pontoon boat (foreground) used in the assault crossing of the Rhine and an LCI line the east bank, as 87th Division soldiers push the Germans out of the river gorge.

Tanks hurry across a pontoon bridge to support the 87th Division, fighting to hold off German counterattacks on the east side of the Rhine River.

The town of Rhens, Germany, where the 347th Regiment made its assault crossing of the Rhine on March 25, 1945. The 1st Battalion, 347th won a Presidential Unit Citation for withstanding German counterattacks against its beachhead on the eastern shore bluffs seen in the background.

Lahneck Castle, at the junction of the Rhine and Lahn rivers. Garrison's machine-gun squad "captured" it on March 25, 1945.

87th Division soldiers take on German snipers from behind a Sherman tank during the dash across Germany.

GIs mount up as an 87th task force gets ready to roll through Germany.

Men of the 87th Division at Rhens on the Rhine, March 1945. Back row (left to right): D'Arpino, Hare, Petersly, Stec, Dudley. Front row (left to right): May, Garrison, Crooks, Hubbard, J. Knight

Men of the 87th Division at Rhens on the Rhine, March 1945. Left to right: Petersly, Garrison, Crooks, Hubbard, D'Arpino, Lyle Jacobs (kneeling).

Men of the 87th Division at Rhens on the Rhine, March 1945. Left to right: Jack Crooks, Eugene Black (top hat), Gene Garrison (German helmet), Graig Wise (Nazi flag).

This sign was erected by order of Lt. Col. Robert Cobb to greet 1st Battalion soldiers on the morning of May 5, 1945. It was the best news they could have received.

Gene and Juanita Garrison at the September 2002 reunion in Hampton, Virginia.

Some of the "boys" at the September 2002 reunion in Hampton, Virginia. Left to right: Robert Jones, Walter Byrnes, Thomas Katana, Anthony D'Arpino, Robert Fulton, Norman Panther and Gene Garrison.

bers. We observed three more elderly people in a small rectangular room, which looked like a combination kitchen and sitting room. On a narrow cot to the left of the door lay a German soldier, his gray face drenched in feverish perspiration.

The elderly Germans were eager to talk. They jabbered away until Crooks motioned for them to slow down. The civilians identified themselves as caretakers of the castle. They told Crooks that other German soldiers, some of whom had occupied the castle, had left the ill soldier by the entry door that morning. These soldiers departed shortly before Crooks had started firing the machine gun at the sniper. The woman who had opened the door revealed to Crooks that she had discovered a pistol on the ill soldier. She had taken it from him and thrown it out the door; this was the pistol Crooks had found on the road. She also mentioned she had a cousin living in Cincinnati.

The talkative caretakers assured us that there was no one else in the castle. We decided to leave Hubbard with them while the rest of us found out for ourselves. D'Arpino, Crooks, and I cautiously entered the inside of the turret, which appeared to be the main hall. A stone stairway bounded by an iron railing curled to the top of the tower, where the open parapets were visible. The stairs didn't look safe and there was no indication they had been used or that anyone had stayed in that part of the castle.

Open doorways led to adjoining rooms on the lower floor. We carefully looked into each room. We had no desire to trip a booby trap. Every room was empty. Anything of value had long since been removed.

Satisfied there weren't any enemy soldiers lurking about, the three of us returned to the kitchen and the Germans. "We better get back outside," Crooks said. "Don't want someone trying to shoot their way in here."

"You're beginning to sound like a sergeant, Jack," D'Arpino laughed.

We filed out of the small castle door and followed the narrow road back to the clearing in which the sniper had pinned down the unknown rifleman. After searching the area again, we positioned the machine gun to cover the approaches to the castle, which overlooked a portion of the village below. Then we waited for the rest of the company to catch up with us.

After we had captured the castle and rejoined the company, we spent the remainder of the day rooting out Germans along the heights above the Rhine. The initial confusion after we hit the Rhine shoreline was short-lived due to the valiant efforts of Lieutenant Colonel Cobb, Lieutenant Wise, Lieutenant Caporali, and some of the other officers and noncoms. Parts of the 1st Battalion crossed the Rhine during the day and helped take the high ground above Oberlahnstein, the initial battalion objective. After we spent most of the day guarding the castle, the 1st Machine-Gun Squad rejoined C Company in its fight to eliminate German gun emplacements that were creating hell on the river.

Death of an Officer

With darkness came the threat of a German counterattack. The rifle platoons were strung out somewhere in front of the 4th Platoon. Crooks lay behind the machine gun with his hands wrapped tightly around its handle, and his face contorted from tension. Next to him, I had my hands under a belt of ammunition that unfolded from the ammunition box to the feeding chamber on the gun. D'Arpino and Hubbard were a few feet behind us, their carbines pointed to the front. Our only concealment was the high, dead grass that had grown up through the wires along an old farm fence that had long outlived its usefulness. About fifty yards up the hillside above us, a German 20mm antiaircraft gun sent its deadly message to the river beachhead below. The ground under us vibrated with the rapid *frump-frump* of the gun's discharge. The Germans didn't know how close C Company had penetrated to their position as they continued to concentrate their fire several feet over the prone Americans.

"I hope to hell they don't see us," I muttered to Crooks as I obsessively watched the frightening orange tracers fly over our heads.

"Me, too," Crooks answered. "We don't have much protection here."

"Are you going to fire if someone gives an order?"

"Don't know. Hopefully, they aren't that crazy."

D'Arpino crawled closer. "Jack, let's get out of here. We're dead if the Germans see us."

Just then a GI a few yards to Crooks's right whispered: "Move out." The order rippled along the line of men.

We rose from the ground in a staggered line and silently crept forward, our perilous route taking us through the scattered enemy positions. We came to another fencerow crowded with small trees and thick undergrowth; it paralleled a shallow ravine. The company followed the ravine uphill until we were above the 20mm emplacement, which still spewed its deadly projectiles on the Rhine.

Lieutenant Wise, Sergeant Yanachek, and Sergeant Chester Casasanta left the cover of the ravine to find a way to eliminate the 20mm position.

"First Squad, follow me," growled Sergeant Jacobs, who had rejoined the 1st Squad after briefly leading the 2d Machine-Gun Squad. Jacobs led the squad through the underbrush and into an open field. As we broke into the open, I watched the 20mm gun, which was still firing toward the river, its tracer bullets still lighting up the dark night.

As the squad crossed a small plateau that dipped slightly downward in an arc away from the ravine, gunfire erupted in front of us. It sent everyone diving to the ground. The darkness and the contour of the terrain prevented us from seeing what was happening ahead. Suddenly, Yanachek and Casasanta rushed over the crest of the plateau. "Get down! Get down," Yanachek screamed.

"Wise is dead! If he isn't dead, he was captured." Yanachek's words tumbled out in short, anguished bursts. "The 20mm opened up on us! The lieutenant jumped into a foxhole! There were Krauts in the hole! They shot him coming in! I've got to report!" With that, Yanachek was gone. Casasanta followed closely behind.

I realized that the 20mm was no longer firing at the beachhead and that the Germans must be able to see us silhouetted against the skyline. Tracers suddenly followed the crest of the plateau, throwing chunks of dirt through the air, methodically working toward the ravine.

"Get back!" Jacobs shouted. "Get back! Hit the dirt!"

It was a needless command. Everyone already was hugging the

ground, squirming backward as fast as possible. Dirt and pieces of sod splattered against my helmet as I pushed farther out of the line of fire.

The only casualty in the brief firefight had been Lieutenant Wise. Losing our CO was a major blow to the men. Although he had commanded C Company for just two weeks, Wise had earned a great deal of respect from his soldiers for his leadership. He led by example, and that built confidence in his decisions. Wise was awarded a posthumous Silver Star for his actions in the Rhine River crossing and for his steady leadership in repulsing the German counterattacks that followed.

After the 1st Machine-Gun Squad scrambled back from the enemy fire, Jacobs quietly gathered the men around him. "We'll stay here for the time being."

"Too bad about Wise," Crooks murmured.

"Yeah," D'Arpino answered. "He knew his job, and he did it. I know Yanachek really liked him. Said he was the best."

"Better get some sleep, fellows," Jacobs inserted. "We can't bring him back."

The platoon watched apprehensively as the first streaks of daylight peeked through the barren trees. Would the Germans continue the fight, or would they surrender? The question was soon answered. Two Wehrmacht soldiers walked parallel to the ravine toward the machine-gun position, obviously unaware of its existence. Each of them carried a potato-masher grenade in his left hand, holding it down as if trying to conceal it behind their legs.

Cries of "Hande Hoch!" came from a squad of riflemen dug in along the edge of the ravine just beyond the machine gun. The Germans ignored the order as they drew back their arms to throw the grenades. The action was fatal; a fusillade of shots cut them down. Their grenades exploded harmlessly in the field.

Mortar fire, called in by Lieutenant Caporali, dropped down on the 20mm emplacement and German infantry foxholes. A near hit on the 20mm convinced the crewmen that their war was over. Enemy soldiers, their hands held high, rose to surrender. Singly and in small groups, they moved cautiously toward the Americans. Their surrender led to the recovery of Lieutenant Wise's body.

The 1st Battalion was dug in on the high ground along the upper portion of a steep ravine. A sizable enemy force occupied the other side of the ravine and the woods beyond. German gunners periodically reminded the Americans of their presence with bursts of machine-gun fire and by lobbing mortar shells on our position. B and C companies were on the line, with D Company's heavy weapons in support and A Company in reserve.

C Company's second day on the east bank of the Rhine was nearing an end. Darkness settled in rapidly, enveloping the depths of the ravine first, and slowly pushing shadows up the sides. I watched a forward artillery spotter work his way down the side of the ravine and conceal himself close to the enemy. I didn't envy him his job. It took a lot of courage to call artillery fire from so far forward.

D'Arpino and Hubbard were dug in below Crooks and me. Jacobs was off to the right. Danny Mendelsohn, who was usually assigned to C Company headquarters, sprawled in a foxhole above and directly behind Crooks and me. Mendelsohn fired his carbine at any sound, no matter how slight or imagined.

"Someone's down there," Mendelsohn cried as he nervously squeezed off three shots in rapid succession. His shots prompted several mortarmen to the immediate right of Jacobs to join the firing.

"Gene, Jack, you see anything?" D'Arpino asked.

"No, and neither does Danny," I called back. "But he should be keeping any Krauts down there pretty loose. Let him shoot away, but let's keep our heads down."

"I sure wouldn't want to be that artillery observer," Crooks added.

Mendelsohn fired again, and again the mortarmen joined him. "I tell you, someone is moving down there," he shouted.

"Dammit, Danny!" Jacobs yelled. "You're going to kill one of us! Stop firing!"

"But something is there," Mendelsohn protested.

"Maybe there is, but remember, you have a machine gun and a bunch of other people down here to help out," Jacobs said in a more soothing voice. "If the Germans attack, they have to get through us before they get to you, so relax."

One of the mortarmen laughed. "That's Barr," Crooks chuckled.

More laughter rippled along the foxhole line as men released a little tension, then quiet slowly returned.

Someone snored. "Wake up down there," a voice growled. "No one sleeps tonight. Keep each other awake, or you'll find a German in your foxhole."

D'Arpino called out encouragement. "That's it, Sarge. Give 'em hell!"

"Who was it, Tony?" Crooks inquired.

"I don't know, but it had to be a sergeant to say all that."

Restrained laughter again drifted over from the foxholes and trailed off into silence. I noticed that Hubbard and D'Arpino had quickly fallen asleep.

"Jack? You awake?" I asked Crooks.

"Barely."

"Go to sleep. I'll wake you in about an hour." There was no answer. Jack was already asleep.

I struggled to stay awake. In my exhaustion, time ceased to have a distinction. Had twenty minutes gone by, or two hours?

"Jack, wake up." I nudged Crooks' inert body. "It's your turn."

"I just closed my eyes," Crooks grumbled. But he sat up and groped for the machine gun.

I sank down in the corner of the foxhole and vaguely heard that someone was calling my name. Why?

"Gene! Wake up! Wake up! There's an attack!" It was Crooks. "There's gunfire on our right flank!"

I scrambled out of my sleep and leaned against the foxhole wall, listening intently. Mendelsohn fired two quick shots. Someone shouted, "Hold your fire!" There was no incoming fire from the woods on the other side of the ravine. B Company was bearing the brunt of the attack, supported by D Company's water-cooled .30-caliber machine guns. Mortar rounds exploded sporadically. The battle sounds trailed off into complete silence. "Stay alert down there; they may be changing directions." It was the same commanding voice in the darkness as before. I still didn't recognize the voice.

Crooks drifted off to sleep, and I pulled myself to a sitting position on the side of the foxhole. I fought sleep and kept changing positions, determined not to awaken Crooks.

"You think we're going to get an attack?"

The sudden question startled me. I turned to find someone standing less than three feet from me, yet I hadn't heard the sound of his approach. I knew I had been awake, but if that were true, no one could have gotten close to me.

"Don't know; hope not," I answered. "You'll get shot wandering around. Mendelsohn is trigger-happy."

"Who's Mendelsohn?"

The question made me instantly wary. I slowly drew my .45. Everyone knew Mendelsohn. On the other hand, would a German react in such a manner?

"Where's your position?"

"'Bout a hundred feet to the left of here. I'm stuck out there alone."

"Who's your squad leader?"

"Thomas. He's over there somewhere. They just put me in his squad before we crossed the Rhine. Guess I'd better get back. I'm awake now."

"Yeah, you do that. Stay down," I said, relaxed and now wide-awake. The surprise visitor had to be a replacement who didn't know any better than to walk around at night among a bunch of nervous GIs.

Another firefight broke out on our right flank. The Germans were attacking again. Why didn't they hit Company C? The sounds of battle made for a long, tense night, but not nearly as long as it was for B Company.

Shortly before dawn, A Company relieved the battered B Company and spearheaded an attack to clear the Germans beyond the Rhine River. Much to their surprise and relief, the enemy had completely withdrawn. The battalion followed in hot pursuit.

The 1st Battalion was awarded the Presidential Unit Citation—only the second unit in the 87th Division to receive such a distinction—for its assault crossing of the Rhine and repulsing constant enemy counter-attacks to preserve the bridgehead for the rest of the 347th Regiment.

Our battalion advanced rapidly along the slope of a long valley, which channeled toward the Rhine River. Artillery fire rumbled on our right flank; otherwise quiet reigned in the battalion's immediate sector. The day was warm and sunny, and if one could forget the overall circumstances, it was rather pleasant to walk along the scenic hillside.

I closely followed Crooks, carting my single ammo box in case shooting erupted. Crooks carried the machine gun behind his head with his arms wrapped around either end. A cutoff ammo belt with about forty-five rounds dangled from the breech, a standard practice used by both machine-gun squads since early in the Bulge. We attached one end of a belly strap from a horse harness on the barrel of the machine gun and the other on the stock. This made a sling that was worn on the gunner's shoulder. It ensured instant firepower and saved valuable seconds in a firefight until the assistant gunner could supply additional ammunition.

A roar in the sky above interrupted the morning's serenity.

"What's that noise?" D'Arpino asked in surprise.

The entire line of men twisted and turned to scan the horizon. An airplane broke the crest of the hill and swooped along the column of soldiers, then a second, third, fourth, and fifth. The planes were American P-51 fighters, distinguished by their squared-off wings. But something didn't look right. One of the planes was different. The soldiers at first watched the planes apprehensively, but as soon as we realized the planes were American, we cheered and started to wave. Our jubilance was short-lived. The aircraft circled to make another pass. The first four planes made their passes and started to circle again. However, the fifth plane, perhaps a P-47, pulled out of its dive and fired wide along the entire column.

"What the hell is he doing?" Crooks yelled.

At this time, some of the forward troops broke for the safety of a wooded area ahead. As the last plane started to pull up, I heard the familiar thumping noise of a German 20mm gun in the woods to our front. The plane circled again and made its run, the second plane strafed the column, the third and fourth planes made clean passes, and the fifth plane sent a stream of bullets down the line of men. I had to control my impulse to run. How could this happen? Was I going to be killed by our own planes after everything I'd gone through? Where are the identification panels? Get them out!

The scene was strange. Panic seized some of the men, who ran madly toward the woods. Others stood around or continued to walk, still looking over their shoulders as if this really couldn't be happening. But with each pass the German 20mm fired a few shots, which fueled the incentive of the pilots to make more passes.

As we entered the woods, we scattered in search of some sort of shelter. I threw myself behind a tree and hugged the ground.

The planes came low for one more strafing run. Then it was over.

I was as scared as I had ever been. The thought of our own planes killing me shook me badly. I felt helpless. I started to get up when I realized the tree in front of me was no more than three inches in diameter. Next to me was a rather large pine. The irony of the situation helped to settle my nerves.

"Are they gone?" Hubbard asked.

"Hope so," I said. "Where are Jack and Tony?"

"There they are." Hubbard pointed to a couple of trees about twenty yards away.

"How did we get so far away?"

"They can't run as fast as we can," Hubbard said with a weak grin.

Several minutes passed before the company reassembled with orders to stay put. Several men from the battalion had been wounded in the strafing. The 1st Squad gathered at the edge of the woods. As the company waited for further orders, most of the conversation turned to the strafing by the American warplanes.

"What a hell of a note that was," Crooks lashed out angrily. "Our own planes. You can't shoot back. If you run, they think you're Germans, and that damn Kraut 20mm sure didn't help anything." No one replied. What else could be said?

Jacobs said he heard that a reserve unit had taken too long to get the identification panels forward and displayed before the planes attacked. After the panels were down, the planes had circled once more, then left.

"Were they P-51s?" Crooks asked.

"Think so, but I heard that one of the planes had Brit markings," Jacobs said.

"I knew there was something different about that one plane," I commented.

"Yeah, me, too," D'Arpino laughed. "They were probably getting back at us for dating English girls."

D'Arpino's laugh quickly infected everyone, but after a few minutes we lapsed back into silence, each lost in his own thoughts as to what had happened, or what might be in store for us the next day.

The two machine-gun squads bivouacked together that evening. We took turns asking Stec about his leave in Paris. His most interesting story was about combat boots. Before he left, Stec was issued new boots to replace the cruddy ones worn down in combat. Stec wore size 10 B, but Breen, the supply sergeant, only had a pair of size 12s, which he issued to Stec, while telling him he could trade when he reached Paris. But the quartermaster in Paris wouldn't trade with him.

As Stec walked down a Paris street, a Frenchman leaned out of a second-floor window and asked if he had any cigarettes to trade or sell. Stec didn't smoke, but he did have several packs for trading purposes. He told the Frenchman that he needed size 10 B combat boots. To Stec's surprise, the Frenchman offered to trade a pair of size-10 B boots for two packs of cigarettes and his size-12 boots. How the Frenchman got hold of a pair of GI combat boots, Stec didn't know or care. He got his boots.

Stec started to laugh. "Have you seen Blanchard and his motorcycle? He found it somewhere down by the Rhine. He brought me back to the company on the cycle."

Dudley commented, "Wish I could find one. It's better than riding the trucks."

Stec suddenly turned serious. "Have you heard about Grieco? Frank lost an arm. Everyone in his boat got hit except Ed Szymanski. Their boat went out of control and Ed jumped into the river to guide it ashore, but he had to fight the current for nearly two miles to do it."

The news about Grieco quieted everyone. Frank was well liked. He had treated many of the men at one time or another during combat. A few owed their lives to the medic. His loss left Gilbert as the only company medic.

My thoughts went back to the hellish river crossing. It must have been Szymanski I had seen jumping out of the boat and guiding it ashore.

The 347th Regiment headed east, away from the Rhine gorge, in pursuit of the retreating Germans. The 1st Battalion, with A Company in the lead, filed out of a ravine into a U-shaped valley surrounded by tall hedges and scrub trees. The narrow valley was perhaps only a hundred yards wide on the open end. By the time C Company's 4th Platoon emerged from the ravine, the A Company scouts were hidden from view by the dense hedges.

A church steeple rose out of the morning mist above a hedge line at the closed end of the valley. It was like a scene from a picturesque postcard. My mind wandered back in time to a hunting trip with my father and uncles. I could picture a rooster pheasant breaking cover in front of me.

A BAR's throaty roar, answered by a burp gun, snapped me back to the present. The platoon suddenly found itself in the line of fire from a brief but deadly encounter at the front of the column.

I instantly dove for the ground. I turned my head to see if anyone was hurt, and was surprised to find myself alone. The rest of the squad had veered to the right without my noticing. I was so intent on my safety that I had become separated from the machine gun—a mortal sin.

A bullet plowed into the earth about a foot from my side. Was it a sniper, or just an errant shot?

I heard movement to my rear and immediately covered the area with my .45. My heart was pounding. Lieutenant Colonel Cobb and a battalion headquarters officer emerged from the brush and saw my .45 leveled at them. I instantly lowered the pistol.

Cobb asked briskly, "What's going on up there?"

"A Company must have met some resistance by that church, sir. There may be a sniper . . ." My voice trailed off as Cobb and the captain disappeared along a narrow path.

I felt bad that I had allowed myself to become separated from my squad. I rapidly worked my way through the hedges to find them. I saw them crouched behind some shrubbery and crept quietly in behind them. An all-clear sign was passed along the line, and then the signal to move forward. No one seemed to have missed me, and I wasn't about to say anything.

"Lieutenant Caporali wants a squad to check out that clump of trees and that little thicket at the crest of the hill," Chaney shouted. "Jake! Your squad!"

Jacobs, Crooks, D'Arpino, Hubbard, and I took off at a trot, alternately watching the trees and the thicket. We detected movement in the shadows of several small saplings. The squad hit the ground, ready to fire.

"Don't fire! Don't fire! We're Third Platoon!"

"Who's your squad leader?" Jacobs challenged.

"Thomas," came the reply.

"Hey, John! Is that you?" I yelled.

"Damn right," Thomas answered.

"Thought you went to OCS. How long have you been back?"

"About a month," Thomas replied.

Jacobs interceded, "What's in that clump of bushes?"

"Can't tell," said Thomas.

"Jack, clear the thicket," Jacobs said to Crooks.

Crooks fired a short burst of bullets into the bushes.

"Need anything else, John?" I asked.

Thomas looked at me and smiled. "Smart-ass!"

The two squads moved on, cresting the hill and making sure it was free of enemy soldiers. Jacobs signaled an all-clear to the troops who waited below. The mission of pursuing and destroying Germans continued.

That evening, as Crooks and I dug in our machine gun, Crooks very quietly said, "Gene, you know you got separated from the squad today. It was all right. Both Hubbard and D'Arpino were there, but you were a little too far away when we were strafed this morning, too."

"I know," I replied, guilt creeping in. "I don't know what happened. I think those planes really got to me. I'm sorry."

"Don't worry about it. I just thought I should say something."

"But I should have been closer to you," I said. "You want me to switch with Tony? I will."

"No. You remember when I first came back in January. You didn't have to give me the gun!"

There was a long pause.

"It won't happen again," I finally said.

"I know," Crooks answered softly.

The two of us left it there and continued to dig our position in silence.

PART VII
CENTRAL GERMANY

CHAPTER 16

A Night Patrol and the Mysterious Poles

After the 347th Infantry Regiment consolidated its gains east of the Rhine River, it was held in place as the U.S. Army units on this part of the line paused to catch their breath. Except for standing guard duty and sending out patrols, the GIs cleaned equipment and themselves, and generally relaxed. Our attitude was, "Let someone else fight the war for a while."

"Dig in the best you can. This damned ground is like a rock!" drawled Pearson.

"I can't even get through the roots to find the ground!" answered Black.

"Do the best you can; it's your ass. Double up. Half the holes, and you'll be warmer. Be sure sentries are posted! Have them double up, also. They can keep each other awake!" Pearson made his way through the trees to visit the other platoons.

Black approached the 1st Squad. "Garrison, you and D'Arpino take the first two hours. Crooks and Hubbard next. I'll have someone from the Second Squad relieve you. Dig your holes before you go on watch! Jake, you and I can take whatever time is left. I'll come get you."

Jacobs grunted his assent, and everyone set to the task of digging holes. Getting through the thin crust of dirt took only minutes as both D'Arpino and I hacked away. It was like hitting cement when we reached the roots; it took at least half an hour to carve out a hole about twenty inches deep, two feet wide, and a little over five feet long. Large roots at either end of the hole stopped any further effort.

We took our positions as sentries on a narrow road that doubled as a firebreak. The positions were only about twenty feet from my foxhole. Our tour was uneventful.

Our problem was that the hole was not as large as it should have been, and it wasn't prudent to make any more noise this night.

"We'll have to sleep on our sides," Tony said. "Facing the same direction. We can't stretch out."

We sat on the edge of the hole and then slid in. "Snug fit, isn't it!" I said.

"Yeah, but it is warm!"

Some hours later, I was awakened by Tony's tugging on my shoulder. "Wake up! I have to turn over. My leg keeps cramping. We both have to turn over at the same time."

We turned in unison and started laughing. "If the Germans ever saw this, they would die laughing," chuckled Tony. We were asleep immediately.

Some time later, I awakened. I had to urinate. I moved from the foxhole carefully, without awakening Tony, and crawled several feet from the foxhole and then froze. I could hear or maybe sense movement on the road. There were muffled voices—probably a patrol. But they were not speaking English. Damn, a Kraut patrol. A large one. If the sentries challenge them, all hell will break loose. I had to wake Jack so he would be ready with the machine gun.

The patrol was abreast the sentries. Any second now. Nothing. Hell, they must be asleep. What should I do? My hand was on my .45. Stupid. The patrol moved on and out of sight. I sighed in relief. I urinated and crawled back into the foxhole. Tony never missed me.

I lay there thinking. If I had taken any action, there could have been deaths. If I reported the incident, the sentries and probably I would be in trouble. I closed my eyes and slept. I never mentioned what had happened.

D'Arpino and I were seated on the edge of our foxhole, hurriedly writing letters home, trying to beat the onrushing dusk. What could I say in a letter that was going to be censored by someone in the company command post? Where I was, what I was doing, and usually whom I was doing it with, was all classified. Only through GI ingenuity or personal code words could a front-line soldier occasionally sneak pertinent information past the censor to a loved one back home. Before going overseas, I had written about many of my comrades. If I wanted to relay any information I would make reference to Cousin Paul or Uncle Tony and then would ask questions such as has Tony's leg gotten any better, hoping that my parents would understand. Sometimes it worked, other times it didn't.

As we finished trying to outwit the censor, Jacobs strolled toward the dug-in members of the squad. Hubbard was asleep in his foxhole, his hands clasped across his chest, helmet tilted down over his forehead, gently snoring. Crooks and Barr talked about high school days in their respective towns of Lancaster and Bethlehem, Pennsylvania.

"Garrison. D'Arpino. It's your turn for guard duty tonight," Jacobs said. "Better get some sleep. You're on duty at 0400."

"Come on, Jake. Hubbard's already asleep. Send him," D'Arpino pleaded with mock indignation.

"Okay by me, if you can talk him into it," Jacobs responded as he settled into his hole, which was larger than the one shared by D'Arpino and me.

We looked at each other and laughed. We didn't intend to take advantage of Tony Hubbard. He was so good-natured that he would go on duty even knowing it wasn't his turn. Still chuckling, we prepared our letters to give to Rehkop, the mail clerk, unfolded our blankets, and lay down in our tight-fitting foxhole.

"Don't set the alarm too early," D'Arpino deadpanned.

* * *

A few minutes before 0400, D'Arpino and I headed for the guard post along a road that curved gently up a small hill and past several houses clustered among early-budding shade trees, fallow gardens, and small stockyards. The Germans controlled the top of the hill, although scouting reports indicated that they had no established positions.

As we neared the guard post, I was about to give the password when we heard "Turkey" out of the thick darkness. D'Arpino immediately responded with "Feathers." No one fooled around on passwords; there were too many chances to get shot.

I recognized the voice as that of Jim Cheatwood, a replacement in John Thomas' squad. "Advance very slowly and be recognized," Cheatwood commanded in a hushed tone.

"Is that turkey serious?" D'Arpino asked me.

"You bet I am, smart-ass," Cheatwood replied in a louder voice.

"Hey, Jim," I called.

"Gene? Tony?" Cheatwood queried.

"It's us. You seem a little jumpy tonight," I said.

"Yeah. The Krauts tried to infiltrate through here about an hour ago."

"Hilfe! Bitte! Hilfe!" The eerie, quivering half-moan rose out of the night somewhere farther up the hill.

"Who's that?" D'Arpino whispered.

"A wounded German, I guess," Cheatwood answered matter-of-factly. "Lieutenant Hammond thinks he might be playing possum."

"Shouldn't we go check on him or bring him in as a prisoner?" I suggested. "He sounds like he's in real pain."

"Sure, Gene. Shoot him and risk your ass to bring him in," Cheatwood growled sarcastically. "Listen, Hammond gave strict orders that no one was to go up that hill."

"Okay by us," D'Arpino quickly responded. "Right, Gene?"

I didn't respond. Cheatwood and the other rifleman picked up their gear and faded into the darkness. D'Arpino and I settled into the foxhole.

"Hilfe. Bitte. Hilfe."

It was a long and disturbing two hours. I kept thinking, Maybe he'll die and the maddening noise will stop. What if it was one of us lying in terrible pain in the darkness? What would we want an enemy to do? We knew better than to disobey an order from Lieutenant Hammond, but our instincts told us to do something for the stricken enemy soldier. We calmed ourselves by swapping whispered stories we'd heard about booby-trapped bodies, both Nazi and Allied.

"Hilfe. Bitte. Hilfe."

The German soldier's calls for help became weaker and weaker as he apparently slipped in and out of consciousness.

Brewer and Little relieved us promptly at 0600. It wasn't quite daylight.

"Is that German still alive?" Brewer asked.

"You know about him?" D'Arpino replied.

"Yeah. Hammond is taking a patrol out in a few minutes to check on him. He said you guys better not have gone up on your own, or your asses will be in a sling."

Everyone laughed nervously as D'Arpino and I quickly left. Although we were curious about the fate of the German soldier, the incident was soon forgotten as the 87th Division resumed its pursuit of the German Army.

April brought warm sunshine and pleasant days—provided the Wehrmacht didn't make it uncomfortable. Snow, sleet, and intense cold were things of the past. Nevertheless, when the sun disappeared behind a cloud, the troops were quickly reminded that winter had not completely relinquished its grip. Or, as D'Arpino would say, there was still a nip in the air. The O.D. wool blankets were a requirement at night.

Our heavy woolen overcoats had been returned to Supply Sergeant Breen, and a limited quantity of underwear, socks, and other items of clothing were made available to the soldiers who desired them.

I hadn't shaved or bathed in a couple of weeks and decided I might as well take advantage of the warmer weather to clean up. I emptied a

K-ration box and stuffed the contents into the pockets of my jacket. I then gathered some dried pine needles and tore up the envelopes of several letters from home while keeping the letters to reread. I balanced the helmet against a small rock, filled it with water from my canteen, and distributed the tinder around it. A small but ferocious fire soon surrounded my helmet.

While I waited for the water to warm, I used a small amount of it to clean my teeth. I then sorted out my razor, soap, and washcloth from my converted gas-mask bag. Then I lathered my face with soap, made sure my one razor blade was clean and firmly placed in the army-issue razor, and scraped the soft blond hair from my face.

By then, the water was lukewarm and the fire had burned down to pine needles and some smoldering twigs. I wet the olive drab washcloth and used the soap sparingly to bathe. I started with my face and neck and, shedding my garments one at a time, worked down my body. I put my clothes back on as quickly as possible, using clean items when available. Although the weather was warmer and the sun was shining, I was soon shivering.

I paid special attention to my feet. My toes were white and they tingled, but as I rubbed them they turned pink and felt warm. I felt lucky that they hadn't frozen in Belgium when Paul Gullet had been evacuated with frozen feet and trench foot.

I made sure my feet were dried thoroughly, put on clean socks, and finished dressing. As I was cleaning my helmet, I heard someone call, "Chow time." I replaced all of my toilet gear, made sure the fire was out, and joined the squad to go eat a warm meal.

C Company was dug in along a meandering stream in a sparsely wooded valley. We hadn't encountered a German all day and didn't expect trouble now. But the habit of digging foxholes had become ingrained so deeply that any stop longer than a few miutes brought out the entrenching shovels. The mess truck had not caught up with us, so K rations were the only menu item for the evening fare.

After dinner, Dudley and Jacobus practiced their version of hand-to-hand combat. They were matched equally in size and strength, and they had become close friends since Jacobus had joined the machine-gun section in January.

They unsheathed their trench knives, held them in their right hands with their arms high, and then grasped one another's wrists.

Their struggle was realistic, as was the possibility that one could get hurt. "I wish you wouldn't do that," I said in a slightly subdued voice. I hadn't intended to say anything. It had just slipped out. "It makes me nervous. You might slip and hurt each other."

"We won't hurt each other," Dudley admonished.

"We practice too much," Jacobus added. That part was true. They had their mock battles frequently, whenever breaks in combat would let them.

Almost as if my interruption had broken a spell, the two combatants stopped their struggle, sprawled on the ground, and began reminiscing in hushed tones of previous patrols and encounters.

A single gunshot shattered the relative quiet. The machine-gun squads scrambled to an instant alert. The minutes ticked by in ominous silence. We expected return fire, yet nothing happened. We looked around apprehensively.

Lieutenant Hammond appeared from the rear. "At ease, everyone," he said, breaking the silence. "Just had an accident at the command post. One of the medics got shot in the foot. You men better sack out. We have a long day tomorrow." With that, he strolled away. It was his way of saying, "Don't ask questions."

It was the next day before someone could find Danny Mendelsohn, one of the company runners, to get the scuttlebutt. According to Mendelsohn, one of the medics was cleaning his .45 when it went off, striking him in the foot. Medics were not supposed to be armed, according to the Geneva Convention, but many carried sidearms, anyway. Another version of the incident that floated around indicated that it wasn't an accident. Front-line soldiers greatly respected medics, who took incredible risks, often exposing themselves to enemy fire to treat the wounded and save lives. No one wanted to pass judgment on this medic. We preferred to accept it as an accident.

* * *

Later that morning, the company mounted trucks and moved about twenty miles east to occupy a small town near Limberg.

"Listen up!" Black shouted as he entered the two-story house that would serve as a temporary quarters for the 4th Platoon. "We need three volunteers for a patrol tonight. You guys sort it out and be in front of the CP at 1900 hours." With that, Black turned and disappeared through the doorway.

"Hey, Gene, you want to go? It's been awfully quiet around here today." D'Arpino had that look of a kid with his hand in the cookie jar.

"What do you have in mind?" I replied cautiously.

"They won't go very far," D'Arpino said with a mischievous grin. "There's no moon, and it'll be so dark, they'll be too afraid they might get lost."

The squad members laughed at D'Arpino's assessment. Jacobs spoke up, "I don't think it's a good idea for two men from the same squad to go."

"Ah, c'mon, mother hen. We promise to come back," D'Arpino said.

"Hey, Garrison. If you and D'Arpino go, I'll go," said Clark Holmes, a sergeant from the mortar section.

"There you go, Jake. We're taking another 'mother hen' with us," I laughed.

"It still isn't a good idea," Jacobs insisted.

Holmes interrupted the discussion. "We better go eat now and then get some shut-eye. Forsythe will have something ready."

Jacobs's objections faded with our departure to the makeshift mess hall. Jacobs was rather proud that his squad had not suffered any losses since he had become the squad leader, and that we could take care of ourselves. Still, he preferred that no one in his squad take unnecessary chances. He thought he had a good squad. He wanted to keep it that way.

The patrol members gathered that night by the CP. There were thirteen men, nine from C Company and three men from A Company, plus Lieutenant Lyons, an officer newly assigned to the 1st Platoon. The A Company men were along because they had patrolled the same general area the preceding night.

Lyons laid out the patrol's plan, which was to make contact with the enemy, avoid a firefight, and capture prisoners, if possible. The previous night's patrol had discovered a farmhouse at which several Poles the Nazis had conscripted as slave labor were living. Lyons' orders were to coordinate with them to map out German positions.

Lyons briefed the men about patrol procedures, such as carrying no identifying papers, letters, or diaries; wearing no shiny objects or anything loose that might rattle; securing dog tags under clothing; bringing sufficient ammo; and adhering to a buddy system to keep track of everyone. D'Arpino and I were paired, and Holmes was coupled with Lieutenant Lyons. I was encouraged that Lyons seemed more thorough than some previous patrol leaders.

The thirteen-man patrol departed at about 2000 hours. It took at least half an hour of easy walking on a dirt road before we came to a blacked-out farmhouse. The Poles were waiting for the patrol. Two men and a woman emerged to join Lyons and the men from A Company.

The patrol was directed to remain grouped by the edge of the road, but I noted that several men moved toward the house. Holmes ordered the rest of the squad not to disperse before he disappeared into the darkness. He returned a few minutes later with the errant troops. His choice of words left little doubt about his displeasure with their action.

Lyons reappeared with one of the Poles. The lieutenant approached Holmes, D'Arpino, and me to explain, "This fellow is going with us for a little way to make sure we're headed in the right direction. We'll stop here on the way back. Sergeant Holmes, you and I will take the point. Garrison and D'Arpino, you bring up the rear and keep a count of the patrol. I don't want to lose anyone."

The troops filed out onto the road as D'Arpino and I counted thirteen, plus the Pole. The patrol moved along the road in a textbook staggered column. After about a hundred yards, the Pole doubled back along the line of men and passed D'Arpino and me on his way back to the farmhouse.

The patrol made slow progress, partially because of the darkness and also because Lieutenant Lyons was extremely cautious. The patrol stopped and started several times. Several riflemen looked to the members of the machine-gun section for direction and guidance, probably because of our longevity in the company. Many of the riflemen were recent replacements, and, to them, the .30-caliber machine gun represented a symbol of power and protection.

The patrol had been stopped for a longer time than usual when a rifleman called, "Garrison, D'Arpino. Why the hell are we stopped this time?"

"Don't know," D'Arpino replied. "Come on, Gene, let's go see."

D'Arpino and I cautiously passed the waiting patrol members until we found Lyons, Holmes, and two riflemen standing a few feet from the road at the edge of a wooded area. Towering above them was a German soldier, whom the riflemen had discovered sleeping and taken captive. The man must have been at least six feet, six inches tall.

Lyons turned to Holmes, "Search this guy, and let's get out of here."

Before Holmes could move, a metallic *click-click* sounded clear and sharp in the night air. "Machine gun! Hit it," I shouted.

As I dove for cover, I saw the German soldier push the nearest rifleman away from him and disappear into the darkness. Bullets cut through the underbrush. The German machine gunner seemed unconcerned about hitting his comrade. He probably didn't know that he had been captured.

I hit the ground and rolled as bullets passed inches above me. I quickly moved farther into the open field while I made my way back toward the prearranged meeting point at the intersection of the last crossroad. I heard muffled voices in front of me, but I also sensed someone to my rear. I dropped to the ground with my carbine ready.

Two figures emerged from the shadows—D'Arpino and Holmes. "You guys sure took your time," I said in a hushed tone.

"Gene, we thought you were still back there," D'Arpino answered.

"I made my way back staying off the road. What happened to that big Kraut?"

Holmes chuckled, "For a big man, he disappeared in a hurry. I fired a burst in his direction. He's probably halfway to Berlin."

"Holmes, is that you?" Lieutenant Lyons arrived out of the darkness with the rest of the patrol.

"Yes, sir," Holmes replied. "Garrison and D'Arpino are with me."

"Good. Let's get going. D'Arpino, you and Garrison take a head count before we go."

We counted, I from the front of the forming column to the back, and D'Arpino from the rear forward. "Everyone's here, Lieutenant," D'Arpino said.

"Let's go. Holmes, you take point, Garrison and D'Arpino, bring up the rear again."

A feeling of relief passed through us as we backtracked toward the farmhouse. We moved swiftly along the narrow farm road.

The patrol had accomplished its missions by making contact with the Germans, locating their positions, and almost taking a prisoner. We were very lucky that the enemy machine gun hadn't caused any casualties. D'Arpino and I, the rear guards, stopped occasionally to listen for boots crunching sticks and other ground debris, the rattle of metal hitting metal, or muffled voices—any telltale sounds that might indicate that enemy soldiers were pursuing the patrol. We heard nothing except the normal sounds that the night gives up. It was a good sign.

The return to the farmhouse was uneventful. The men clustered in the barnyard; some sat, but most of us waited impatiently to continue. Lyons and Holmes entered the house, then returned within minutes. Lyons ordered Holmes to group the patrol for departure and then approached D'Arpino and me. "Those Poles were waiting for us. I was supposed to let them know when we returned. Would you guys count the patrol again before we leave?"

We didn't question why the Poles had to be briefed, but went about counting the patrol members. "I count thirteen, what about you, Gene?" D'Arpino asked.

"Right, thirteen," I answered. "Tell Lieutenant Lyons."

The patrol moved out and reached the company area without incident. We reported to the company CP and, as the men entered in single file, D'Arpino and I took another head count. "I only count twelve, Tony," I stated.

"The other guy is taking a leak by the door," D'Arpino said as he jerked his thumb in the direction of the GI.

"I see him. Hey, when you finish, come in the house for debriefing," I instructed the urinating soldier.

The man, who wasn't fully visible in the shadows, answered with a gruff "Okay."

"Don't take too long, I want to sack out," D'Arpino urged.

I laughed as Tony and I entered the building. Lyons dismissed the men and then briefed Lieutenant Hammond on the patrol's activities.

The next morning, Jacobs let us sleep late, but he awakened us in time to catch the end of breakfast. He knew he would never hear the end of it if either of us missed a meal. We were returning from breakfast when Lieutenant Lyons approached us. "How many men did you count in the patrol last night?" he asked.

"Thirteen," D'Arpino answered. "Why?" Lyons was the kind of officer who wasn't a stickler for formality unless another officer was present; he preferred that the men not address him as "sir."

A worried look spread across the lieutenant's face. "A Company reported that one of their men didn't come back last night, and Colonel Cobb is really upset."

D'Arpino laughed. "Baloney. Gene and I counted thirteen when we regrouped, thirteen at the farmhouse, and thirteen when we went in for debriefing."

"In fact, I counted once after we left the farmhouse," I added. "Tony, did you see that guy by the door after we went inside?"

"What guy?" Lyons interjected.

"When we were going into the CP, someone stopped to take a leak. We counted him," D'Arpino answered. "But we don't know if he went inside."

"Who was he?"

"Don't know, didn't really see his face. What happened to A Company's buddy system? Didn't they know someone was missing?"

"The other two guys say they were paired, and the missing man was paired with someone from C Company," Lyons explained. "He was a replacement; they didn't know him. I've checked with all of our men. No one was paired with him. The A Company CO is mad as hell. I'm taking another patrol out tonight to look for him. Battalion seems to think he might be at the farmhouse."

"Then who was by the door? One of the Poles?" D'Arpino quipped.

"Lieutenant, you want us to go with you?" I asked.

"I asked for you two and Holmes, but they want an all–A Company patrol. Thanks, fellows," Lyons replied as he turned to leave.

"If they want an all–A Company patrol, why don't they have an A Company officer as patrol leader?" D'Arpino queried.

Lyons chose not to answer.

"Good luck," D'Arpino and I called out to Lyons in unison.

"Poor guy. He's for sure on Colonel Cobb's list," D'Arpino muttered.

"Yeah, guess so. But who was the guy by the door?" I asked again.

"Maybe he was the big German who decided to go home."

Sergeant Black appeared in the doorframe of the second-floor room and called to me. "You're next in line for a pass." I was elated. I was going to Paris on a three-day pass, travel time not included! Each company was allotted a small number of passes.

Black informed me that I had been on the line longer than anyone else who had not already received a pass. I was to leave in two days. Crooks and D'Arpino enjoyed giving me a hard time about the "mamselles" of Paris. I received more advice from my buddies than my dad had ever thought about giving me.

As I listened to the squad chatter about what they would do if they ever got to Paris, I felt sharp pains in my lower right side. I had suffered from chronic appendicitis since I was about twelve years old, but doctors never considered it serious enough for an operation.

I remembered the first and most serious flare-up. My dad had taken my mother and me on a fishing trip to Wisconsin. The sharp stabs of pain had awakened me in the middle of the night, and we left for home the next morning, shortening their vacation by two days. I knew I must be sick, or my dad would never have left early. In fact, we stopped in Madison to see a doctor and stayed the night at a boarding house in case I required an emergency operation. The lady who owned the house, I remembered, had been very nice and had given me milk and cookies.

Damn it, why hadn't they operated on me in basic training, when the appendicitis had flared up then?

The pains kept getting worse. I winced and rubbed my abdomen. Hubbard volunteered to stand guard duty for me. The battalion was sending out patrols at night, but we were pretty much on our own during the day as long as we stayed in the company area. Crooks, D'Arpino, and Hubbard covered for me. Even Jacobs didn't know I was ill.

Late on the afternoon before I was to leave, I lay curled up on the floor. The pain was becoming worse by the minute. My three companions urged me to see a medic, but I refused. Nothing was going to keep me from Paris. I didn't notice D'Arpino slip silently out of the room.

"Garrison, where does it hurt?" I looked up to see Doc Gilbert. I felt both anger and relief toward this unwanted intervention. The pain was becoming unbearable.

"You're going to the hospital," Gilbert said firmly.

"No! Paris!" I replied through my pain.

"No, you're going to the hospital." I looked up to discover Jacobs standing over me.

"You guys are ganging up on me. I'll be okay in the morning."

Gilbert laughed, "Yeah, and probably without your appendix."

"Sorry, buddy. We don't want you to die from a busted appendix. Get shot on a patrol like everybody else," said D'Arpino, who was trying to joke even as the look on his face reflected concern.

"Look at it this way, you can trade French 'mamselles' for American nurses," Crooks chimed in.

They helped me to my feet and outside to a waiting jeep. "Gene, you just have all sorts of good luck, don't you?" observed Norm Panther, the jeep driver.

I crawled into the backseat of the jeep, taking with me the best wishes of my squad mates. The assistant driver, Bill Knight, tossed me a blanket, and Panther eased the jeep onto the cobblestone street. "Gene, if we hurry, maybe the medics can yank that thing out and you can make it back in time to leave for Paris in the morning," Panther said over his shoulder.

I groaned as the jeep bounced along the cobblestones. I thought of the jeep ride with Panther at Fort Jackson, when the hot coffee had splashed on me. Norm wasn't one to waste time.

It wasn't a long ride, but it felt like Panther hit every bump in the road. Knight and Panther hauled me from the jeep to a large tent housing the battalion aid station. "Good luck, Gene," Panther called out as the medical orderlies lifted me to an examination cot.

Before I could answer, a medic loosened my belt and gently probed my side. The battalion surgeon, Major Leroy Travis, approached the cot and moved the medic to one side. "Well, soldier, what's wrong with you?"

"Appendicitis," I replied.

"How about that. They do their own diagnosis now," Travis growled as he poked his fingers into my tender side.

I gasped and reflexively jerked my right knee upward, within an inch or two of Travis's jaw. The major snapped his head back, and someone behind him said, "This time it appears the soldier was right." The voice belonged to the battalion commander, Lieutenant Colonel Cobb.

"Better get him to the hospital before that bursts," Travis ordered.

"Good idea," Cobb added.

Within minutes, orderlies wheeled me to a waiting ambulance, and I was on my way to the division hospital. The ambulance ride was rough, but not nearly as bad as what I experienced in Panther's jeep. At some point during the trip, exhaustion conquered pain and I fell into a deep sleep.

The movement of the stretcher awakened me as I was being unloaded from the ambulance. I was wheeled through a pair of swinging doors and roughly placed on an examination table.

At that time, I realized that my side no longer hurt. An officer with captain's bars greeted me, "You the one they called about with appendicitis?" he asked.

"Yes, sir," I replied.

The captain immediately started his examination. He frowned as he gently touched the sore area. He pressed and pushed, but I felt no pain. "Thought you were having an appendicitis attack," the captain said, looking perplexed.

"I was," I answered, "but it doesn't hurt anymore."

The captain laughed, "I imagine that the ambulance ride jostled loose whatever was causing the blockage to the appendix. We'll keep you here a day or so to be sure everything is all right."

"No operation?" I asked hopefully.

"No operation," the captain said. "But look at it this way, you can have a bath and a night's sleep in a clean bed."

I laughed ironically at the officer's comment. I was getting the clean sheets, hot meals, and blissful sleep after all. It just wasn't going to be in Paris.

They kept me two nights and sent me back to the company.

Jacobs spotted me ambling into the squad's billet. "What are you doing here?" he asked.

"They wouldn't operate," I replied. "The jeep and ambulance rides bounced me around enough that it cleared up."

"We could have done that much for you," D'Arpino laughed.

"Why are all of you guys here?" I said quizzically. "I thought one of you would be in Paris."

"Dudley went," Crooks said.

I jumped at the chance to rib Crooks. "Well, he was the first replacement before you came back. You wouldn't know what to do in Paris, anyway."

"I'd like the chance. I learn fast," Crooks said with a hint of bitterness.

"Hey, Jack, maybe you'll find a fraulein in Germany somewhere," D'Arpino said to Crooks, causing everyone to laugh.

Finally, Jacobs turned toward me. "It's time for chow. Can you eat?" But I was already on the way.

CHAPTER 17
The War Turns Personal

The 87th Division was poised to take part in the Allied race across Germany. Gone were the methodical advances against one set of defensive positions after the other. It would be a new kind of war, with divisions formed into speedy task forces set to knife through the enemy heartland. In early April, the 1st Battalion, 347th Infantry, received orders to form one of those task forces.

The battalion climbed aboard tanks and tank destroyers (TDs). The TDs were put at the head of the columns because their 90mm guns were more than a match for German tanks, and they were much faster and more maneuverable than the Shermans. But the tank destroyers sacrificed heavy protective armor for their speed and agility.

Our task force headed east in the chilly April morning air. We soon emerged from a heavily wooded area that overlooked a small valley surrounded by low hills and a village at either end. The column slowly stopped. A sister battalion, led by two TDs, proceeded along the right fork of the road, toward the more distant town.

The remaining tank destroyers, along with a half-track and supporting jeeps, headed toward the other village. The troop trucks slowly followed. There was no sign of movement in the village, which was usually not a good sign.

The road curved toward the village and rough terrain blocked the view of the front of the column from the troop trucks. An explosion interrupted the steady drone of the engines. A burst of .50-caliber fire followed the explosion, and then there was nothing but the hum of the engines. The column ground to a stop and then started forward again moments later.

Up the road, a TD sat slightly askew along the right side of the roadway, as if it had been pushed aside. I wondered why it had been left there, as it forced the rest of the column to detour around it. Then I noticed that the turret was scorched black and a tread was off its track. Several tankers were gathered around the TD, along with Lieutenant Colonel Cobb, Lieutenant Hammond, and some other officers I didn't know, probably from Headquarters Company.

As my truck pulled around the tank destroyer, I could see a figure lying facedown in front of the tank. What remained of his clothing indicated he was a tanker. His jacket and shirt had either been burned off or removed by the medics who were hovering over him. His auburn hair was singed, and angry red powder burns covered his face and upper body. He was moving his head and talking to the medics. There were no signs of shrapnel wounds.

Another medic knelt over a crumpled body in the side ditch. A panzerfaust, the German version of a bazooka, was lying next to them. Our truck moved around some bushes and out of sight of the disabled vehicle.

Strangely, no one on the truck commented about the brief, violent encounter until the trucks stopped and the troops were unloading. Barr sauntered over from the mortar squads. "I never wanted to ride on a tank," he said to Crooks. "And after seeing that, I know I never will want to ride inside one."

Panther and Knight pulled their jeep next to us. "Hey, Norm, you know what happened?" D'Arpino queried.

"Yeah. The way I heard," Panther explained, "was that a fourteen- or fifteen-year-old kid waited in those bushes with a bazooka. He let two jeeps and the half-track go by and shot at the tank destroyer. Couldn't very well miss."

"What happened to the kid?" D'Arpino asked.

"Colonel Cobb thinks he planned on hitting the tank destroyer and then surrendering, but he never got his hands up. The .50-caliber gunner on the next vehicle saw him as he rose to fire but couldn't shoot quickly enough to prevent him from firing. He was smart enough to wait for a TD, though."

The arrival of Lieutenant Caporali disrupted the conversation. "You. Second and Fourth platoons, front and center. Follow me, double file. Platoon sergeants to me." Caporali took off along the road toward the village. All conversation ceased as we made ourselves ready for battle.

The platoons entered the village, one column on either side of the road in a staggered formation. The 1st and 3d platoons were stretched out behind in a similar fashion. The road that separated at a Y-intersection was lined with a mixture of homes and small shops.

Caporali gave the arm signal to halt. "Establish a machine-gun position here to cover this street, and the other gun to cover that street," the lieutenant ordered as he waved first to the left and then to the right. "Second Platoon and the mortar squads, let's sweep this street. Sergeant Black, would you send a runner to Lieutenant Shue and have the 1st and 3d platoons go to the right? You machine gun-ners, cover us."

Both machine-gun squads set up in a small courtyard. It offered an excellent view of both streets, and the positions were well protected by a stone building on the left and a waist-high stone wall in front and on the right. Hubbard and I manned our gun to cover Caporali's platoons; Dudley and Jacobus positioned their gun to cover Shue's column.

Darkness was settling over the village, casting treacherous shadows along the street. The riflemen slowly disappeared into the dusk, and distinguishing reality from imagination became a difficult task.

The rest of the machine-gun section disappeared into the stone house. Shortly, D'Arpino emerged with four slices of dark bread covered with jelly. Each of the four gunners eagerly took a slice and made short work of them. Excess jelly on our fingers was licked off and fingers were wiped on our trouser legs. Stec relieved Dudley a few minutes later.

After darkness had engulfed the streets, surveillance was left to sound. The door leading to the house opened slightly. "Garrison," Dudley said in a loud whisper. "Come here."

"Dud, every time you say, 'Come here,' it means trouble," I responded.

"Come here."

I left Hubbard with the gun and went to the door. Dudley handed me a canteen cup partially filled with a sweet-smelling liquid. "Be sure everyone gets some. This is all that's left. This German woman said it's kirsch."

"What woman?" I asked, but Dudley had already disappeared. I sipped gently. It was cherry flavored, alcoholic, and good.

"That's enough, Garrison. Let me taste it," Jacobus called out. He took a swallow. "Cherry brandy," he said matter-of-factly. "I'd rather have bourbon. Here." He handed the cup to Stec.

"Too sweet for me," Stec said, and gave it to Hubbard, who sniffed it and drank some.

Hubbard and I sipped until the cup was empty. Minutes later, I felt slightly light-headed and was glad there was no action in the village. Hubbard kept dozing off next to the machine gun, and each time it was more difficult to awaken him. It was a welcome feeling when Crooks and Jacobs relieved us.

The house consisted of a combination living room, kitchen, dining area, and small bedroom on the first floor, and a sleeping loft on the second floor. A door to the cellar was located in the kitchen. D'Arpino was sitting at the kitchen table, cleaning his carbine. He faced the open door to the cellar.

"I suppose you guys ate all the bread and jam?" I asked.

Hubbard leaned against the kitchen wall and slid to the floor, asleep before he was completely down. He was definitely not a drinker.

"No, Jake told frau housewife to keep her food and hide her booze," D'Arpino replied.

"That sounds like Jake," I laughed. "What happened in here?"

D'Arpino put down his carbine. "Well, when we came inside, there was some fresh bread on the table, but no one was in the house. The only logical place they could be was in the cellar. Jack said something in German that sounded like 'grenade.' This woman started yelling, 'Nein! Nein! Bitte!' Jack told her to come upstairs. Guess her husband decided his war was over and came home without his uniform or gun. She's scared to death that we're going to take him prisoner or kill him. Jack told her to keep him in the cellar and keep out of the way. Her father and mother are down there, too."

D'Arpino's story was interrupted when Stec burst through the front door. "First and Second squads! Let's go! We're moving out now. You guys on the second floor, wake up." He clumped up the steps, making as much noise as possible.

D'Arpino and I lifted Hubbard from the floor and guided him to the courtyard, where we were met by Jacobs and Crooks.

"We're going to support Caporali," Jacobs said. Without further explanation, he turned and jogged down the cobblestone street. The rest of us ran after him. After a couple of blocks, we were challenged by a suspicious voice.

"Hey, who are you guys?"

"First Machine-Gun Squad," Jacobs bristled. "Who the hell taught you to challenge, soldier?" The squad never slowed down, leaving the admonished rifleman rattled and with nothing to say. We soon found Caporali crouched behind a stone pillar at the intersection of a street that branched off to our right. Directly across the street, a large warehouse extended for a full block to our left. The only openings in the building were narrow, oblong windows beneath the roof overhang. A lane and a stream ran parallel to the building. An unkempt courtyard, surrounded by a picket fence, was immediately to our front and to the rear of the warehouse. A small church next to the courtyard faced the street to our right.

Caporali grabbed Jacobs by the arm. "We think that building is full of German vehicles, and we have them bottled up. They probably know we have armor, but they don't know it's not here, and that's why they're not willing to come out. I hope that means there's no German tanks among their vehicles. We have a bazooka team covering the front doors, but they're pinned down by the Krauts across the street."

"Germans! On the other side of the courtyard," Crooks suddenly yelled, bringing the .30-caliber to a firing position. He squeezed off short bursts at vague shadows in the darkness that darted along the far fence. I fed a new belt of ammunition into the gun as other members of the squad joined the fight.

The shadowy figures disappeared and I rose for a better view. A flash of light came from the bell tower of the church, and the whine of a bullet passed close to my head. Chips from the stone fence post next to me splattered on my helmet and shoulder. The post had saved my life. "Sniper in the bell tower," I shouted. But to my astonishment, no one fired. "Well, hell, if no one else is going to fire, I will," I snapped. I pulled my .45 pistol and fired two quick shots at the church bell.

"I can do better than that," Crooks calmly observed. His second shot struck the bell with a resounding bong. Everyone in the 1st Squad cheered.

Several riflemen to the rear started to laugh. "What's so damned funny?" Caporali growled.

"We just fired a rifle grenade at the sniper and forgot to pull the pin," came the sheepish answer.

"You boneheads," Caporali yelled. "If that grenade had exploded at that height, it could have killed all of us. Use your heads."

In the quiet that followed the lieutenant's tirade, the low rumble of engines could be heard inside the warehouse. Maybe the Germans were going to make a break for it. The bazooka squad was still pinned down by the front doors of the warehouse. Riflemen were spread out about every four feet along the side of the building. Jacobs' squad was ready to move forward to provide covering fire.

The unmistakable sound of a German burp gun broke the tension. The muzzle blast could be seen from the creek bed. It swept the entire side of the building and the courtyard, blowing chips of wood from the fence slats. I could almost feel the bullets as they passed on either side of me. I awaited the inevitable call for a medic. It never came. It seemed impossible that the bullets were spaced so they missed some thirty men who were lined up along the building and fence.

Almost every man fired at the muzzle blast and the burp gun fell silent. A runner came from the front of the building. "Lieutenant, Lieutenant, the Germans are surrendering. The sergeant wants you."

Caporali took off at a run. The war was over for the night. The sniper in the bell tower was forgotten. He undoubtedly had been killed, wounded, or escaped to join his surrendering comrades. No one went to find out. The engine noise stopped as the rifle platoons began rounding up prisoners. The machine-gun section was dispatched to the company command post for the rest of the night. A vacant school building served as the CP and aid station. The small number of minor injuries surprised me.

The division was engaged in a large-scale operation to mop up German troops bypassed during the rapid thrust of the VIII Corps through central Germany.

The 347th Infantry was last in the line of advance. C Company's 4th Platoon spread out and moved cautiously among the trees in a small patch of woods, surveying the treetops for snipers.

"Gene, you smell gas?" D'Arpino said, speaking very quietly, not wishing anyone else to hear.

"Yes," I replied. Like most of the original company members, I had long since pitched my gas mask so I could carry more K rations and personal items in the bag. There hadn't been any rumor of a gas attack since the 87th Division had been committed to action.

"Me, too," Crooks chimed in.

"Maybe it's swamp gas," D'Arpino quipped.

"That would be nice, but I don't see any swamp, do you?" I answered.

"Other things can cause that odor—dead animals, decaying leaves," Crooks observed.

"Come on, walk faster," D'Arpino urged.

A few minutes later, the odor disappeared. I felt the tension slowly drain from my muscles, and the knots in my stomach unwound. I hadn't thought it was a poisonous gas, but I still felt helpless. I remembered exactly when I had pitched the gas mask in the Saar four months ago. It seemed like an eternity. It was four months since my nineteenth birthday, yet I remembered everything that happened that day like it was yesterday.

My memories and the brief gas scare made me uneasy. The platoon was spread out single file, an easy target for a German ambush. The column slowed and Sergeant Black signaled for a break.

"Hey, Jake, we oughta have some flankers or scouts out," I said apprehensively. "We're sitting ducks if there're Germans out there."

"You worry too much, Garrison," Jacobs said.

"Better to worry than get killed. Give me your carbine and I'll go out."

"Here, but leave me your .45. I don't want to sit here with no weapon."

I took the carbine and gave my cartridge belt with the .45 to Jacobs. I checked the carbine's safety and sight adjustment, and moved toward a small cluster of trees about two hundred feet from the column. I had taken only about ten steps when I passed the trunk of a medium-sized pine tree. I noticed something in the underbrush that looked out of place.

I stopped in midstride behind the tree and leaned backward to get a better look. There was a German soldier aiming a rifle directly at me. Even at a distance of about a hundred feet, it seemed that I was looking down the barrel of the gun. I instinctively dropped to the ground as the German fired. The bullet missed; it plowed up dirt next to Hubbard, who scrambled for safety.

I was incensed. The war had always been impersonal—a blurred face or a shadowy form. Now, this enemy soldier had a face, and he was trying to kill me. I bounced to my feet, firing the carbine as I rose, clipping nearby trees with the bullets. "You son of a bitch," I shouted. I fired two more shots, but this time I took careful aim, and then I started running toward the German.

"Garrison, come back here! You want to get yourself killed?" Jacobs yelled.

My anger had subsided slightly, at least to the point that I recognized the wisdom of the order. I stopped and fired another shot. The German had disappeared in the underbrush, as, by this time, others in the column also had opened fire.

"Garrison, stop wasting my ammo," Jacobs scolded. "I only have two clips left."

I walked back along the column, pointing toward the area where the German had lain in ambush. The gunfire ceased, but now the troops were fully alert.

"Move out! Get some flankers out back there," Black shouted. The scuffle with the German had obviously convinced him that following proper procedures was prudent. "Watch out for those damn stragglers."

As the column moved out slowly, all eyes searched the surrounding undergrowth. We advanced about a half mile without any further encounters with the enemy. Periodic gunfire erupted from the front of the long, winding column.

Hand signals from the forward units brought the column to a halt. Soon, instructions came back down the line to set up defensive positions.

Crooks and I took the machine gun to a small knoll. Thick underbrush gave us frontal protection, and a row of pine trees provided cover to our right. D'Arpino, Hubbard, and a replacement ammo bearer, Tony Lupo, protected the machine gun's left flank. The mortar squads were to our immediate rear and the heavy weapons company was farther back.

Crooks flipped the gun's bipod down and positioned the .30-caliber on the crest of the knoll. I placed the ammo box to the left of the gun for use if the cutoff belt ran out. The ammo bearers began digging shallow foxholes. Jacobs was concealed to our right, at the base of a large pine tree, surrounded by bushes.

I noticed that the second machine gun was positioned about fifteen yards farther to our right and slightly behind us. Stec, Dudley, Jacobus, and Knight were sitting around the gun.

The minutes slipped by in complete silence. The sun cast warm beams of light through the pine branches. I slipped over the crest of the knoll to lay on my back. The muzzle of the .30-caliber was about a foot above my head. I unslung my gas-mask bag and broke off part of a pecan log candy bar from my mother's last gift box. I passed it up to Crooks and broke another piece for myself. The last letter from home dropped out of the bag. I leaned over to pick it up. I heard the gunshot at the same time the bullet scattered dirt over me. I instinctively dropped the letter, slid down the slope, and covered my head with my arms as Crooks fired the .30 directly over my head.

"Gene, get up here and feed the gun," Crooks cried.

I leaped back over the top of the knoll and had a new belt of ammunition ready to feed into the gun just as the cutoff belt emptied.

The Germans bobbed up and down about fifty feet away as they fired their burp guns. I focused my attention on feeding ammo into the gun properly, so it wouldn't jam. Jacobs crouched behind the shelter of the pine tree, methodically aiming and firing.

"Jake, stay down before you get killed," Crooks shouted.

"But I can see them," Jacobs said. "D'Arpino, can you see them?"

"Hell, no! I can't move! They're shooting right into my foxhole!"

"Hubbard, how about you?"

"No! I'm pinned down, too," Hubbard yelled.

"I can see them," Crooks shouted as he poured a steady stream of bullets toward the enemy troops.

"Garrison! Crooks! Get out of there," Dudley ordered. "Jake, come on. Move!" Dudley fired his .30-caliber from his waist with the gun, supported by the horse strap over his shoulder, and Jacobus fired a carbine as he walked directly toward the Germans. Taken off guard by this sudden, two-man counterattack, the Germans took cover.

"The Krauts are pinned down," Jacobs shouted. "D'Arpino! Hubbard! Lupo! All you ammo bearers, leave now."

The three barreled past Crooks and me. Hubbard was struggling to hold his ammo box, keep his helmet on his head, and prevent his carbine strap from slipping off his shoulder.

"Jake, you go. We'll cover you," Crooks said.

"No, you go," Jacobs replied.

"Dammit, Jake, shut up and go," Dudley shouted.

Jacobs left quickly, followed by Crooks and me. Dudley continued to fire in the direction of the fleeing Germans, even as he slowly retreated to a new defensive position.

The short firefight left some casualties. Gilbert was attending to two riflemen. He already had bandaged Waddelow, the machine-gun section runner, who had a shoulder wound and was sitting with his back braced against the trunk of a pine tree.

During the fighting, a German soldier had been taken prisoner.

"Let me take him back," Waddelow offered. "Give my carbine back to me. I'll take care of him."

Chaney interceded, "That's why you aren't getting your carbine. Battalion wants to talk to any prisoners we get."

"Screw Battalion. Somebody shoot him."

"Calm down, Waddelow," I said. "Your war's over. You get to go back."

"You go to hell, Garrison. You're always butting in."

I turned and walked away as Waddelow continued his tirade. I never saw him after that.

C Company had taken some casualties, but the Germans had fared much worse. A half-dozen field-gray mounds dotted the meadow beyond the knoll.

Forward elements of the 1st Battalion secured their objective, a very small village located at the intersection of two roads. A command post was established and the battalion set up defensive positions for the night.

The soldiers of C Company dug their foxholes, and, with an hour of daylight left, built small fires with K-ration boxes for some warmth against the chill of the early spring evening. Crooks and I had put the finishing touches on our machine-gun position when I made an unpleasant discovery.

"Damn it, I left my gas-mask bag back where the Germans attacked us," I snapped.

"What? You still had cookies and candy left," D'Arpino said. "Go back and get it."

An overwhelming desire to go back for my gear engulfed me. In it were the last vestiges of home—a box of chocolate chip cookies and candy, and the letters I took out to read over and over again.

"Don't you even think about it, Gene," Jacobs warned.

"My K rations were in it," I muttered. "Anyone have an extra one?" I looked at Jacobs, who always carried extra rations. Unlike the other squad members, Jacobs didn't eat much. Sure enough, Jacobs reached into his bag and pulled out a K-ration box.

"Here," he said, tossing the ration to me. "I get first pick on your next box from home." Everyone in the section laughed and went about preparing their fires and warming their cans of Spam.

By daylight the next morning Lieutenant Hammond had two small patrols sweeping the flanks of the column in hopes of preventing another Kraut surprise attack. The rest of the soldiers prepared their morning breakfast of K-ration eggs and extra strong, bitter coffee.

I preferred hot chocolate over coffee and gamely whittled away on my chocolate D bars with my trench knife. I not only had lost my K rations but also my pearl-handled knife. My trench knife just wasn't as sharp. Fortunately, Panther and Blanchard arrived with supplies, including C rations, or I would have had a very light breakfast of saltines and chocolate.

The order of the day was the same as the day before—sweep the area of bypassed Germans.

The morning started out badly for Chaney, who was in an unusually foul mood. Although generally cheerful, Chaney always was sure that something was going to happen to him. He and Jesse Knight were obsessed with thoughts of never seeing their loved ones again. Sometimes it was very depressing.

Chaney was barking at everyone in the section about everything. The squad mostly ignored him, except for D'Arpino and Dudley. D'Arpino's friendly banter seemed to help a little, but Dudley's "go-to-hell" attitude was like drawing a line in the sand. He and Chaney sniped at each other for the first hour of the sweep.

At the first break, while everyone flopped down to rest, Chaney stood erect, leaning on his rifle. I closed my eyes and tried to get a few minutes' sleep. I was jarred awake by Chaney's shrill, screaming voice. I saw Dudley rising from his resting place to meet a charging Chaney.

"I've taken enough from you, Dudley," Chaney shouted.

Dudley came up swinging. He missed by several inches but was close enough to stop Chaney's charge. They stood poised in front of one other, reminding me of pictures I had seen of the legendary prizefighters John L. Sullivan and James Corbett. It was obvious that they had never fought much, at least not in this manner. They both missed a couple of wild swings.

"That's enough," Jacobs barked.

The two combatants paid no attention and kept circling each other, looking for an opening. Most of the company watched the spectacle in complete silence.

I found myself walking toward them. "Damn it, Dudley, stop it! Chaney, back off! This is not the place for this crap. If you still want to fight, do it when the war is over, if it ever gets over. Stop. Now!"

My unexpected intervention surprised the two fighters. They both backed away. "Damn you, Chaney, get off my back," Dudley said through clenched teeth. "He started it," he added, looking around the section for confirmation.

Jacobs interceded and chewed them both out for a minute or so, even though Chaney outranked him. Properly chastised, the two men retreated to opposite sides of the road, Chaney by himself, Dudley with Jacobus and Stec.

"Gene, you should have let them go. If Dudley hurt him bad enough, there might be an opening for another sergeant," D'Arpino chuckled.

"Yeah, you weren't thinking ahead," added Crooks, who probably would be in line for promotion.

Only Jacobs' squad heard the remarks, and we all smiled. No one wished harm to either man. Strangely enough, Chaney and Dudley tolerated each other fairly well from then on.

CHAPTER 18

A Hospitable German Family

Daylight began to fade behind the pine forests as the trucks carrying C Company entered the small village of about twenty two-story houses, with stables either underneath or next to each house. The odor of manure permeated the air.

The 4th Platoon was directed to one of the houses. As Jacobs motioned for his squad to enter, the muffled cry of a child carried down the second-floor stairway. A tall man dressed in farm clothing descended the stairs. A small blond girl about five years old clung to his shoulder, her legs wrapped around his waist. A young woman pressed close behind him.

The entire squad stopped and watched the German family leave their home. I thought of my four-year-old sister. She would be terrified, just like this little girl.

"Jack, say something," I asked Crooks. "You took German."

"What should I say?"

"Tell her she will be okay, not to cry."

"I'll try."

"Madchen, nicht schreien bitte. Ist richtig. Ist okay. Nicht schreien, okay? Ist gut. Ist gut."

The girl twisted in her father's arms and looked at Crooks. She stopped crying. Crooks repeated, "Ist gut. Ist gut."

The German family continued down the steps. The girl kept her eyes on Crooks until they disappeared through the door.

"Hey, that was great," D'Arpino said. "What did you say?"

"I hope I told her not to cry," Crooks replied. "Whatever it was, it worked."

"Wonder where that guy stashed his uniform," Jacobs said.

"Yeah, he's probably SS," I added.

The stairway opened to a small hallway that led to three bedrooms and a sewing room that also had a built-in single bed. The men doubled up on the beds, leaving late arrivals to find soft spots on the floor.

We had just settled in when Sergeant Black entered. "I need two volunteers to unload the mess truck. Garrison, Hubbard, let's go."

"Did anyone hear me say anything?" I queried.

"Shut up and come on," Black snapped as he descended the stairs.

I groaned and followed Black. Hubbard's expression never changed. If they wanted him to unload a truck, he would unload a truck.

As we hurriedly moved equipment and boxes of food, we noticed a few townspeople watching. When we finished, a man and woman approached me. "Haben sie Hunger?" the man asked.

I stuffed four K-ration boxes in my pockets and responded, "Ja," expecting them to ask for food.

"Das ist gut. Kommen sie mit. Wir haben die Suppe, Kartoffel Suppe. Ser gut. Kommen."

I wasn't sure of the words I had heard, but I recognized "good," "come" and "potato soup." I looked for Hubbard, but he had disappeared. I shifted my .45 slightly and thought, Why not? I followed the couple across the town square and up a flight of stairs to a two-room apartment. I slowly looked around as the two people gestured and spoke in rapid German.

The woman busied herself at a wood-burning stove. Suddenly, the man said, "Please sit. You are tired." Before I could answer, the man continued, "I am Henry. Meinen Frau ist Emma. Her sister lives in Cleveland. Wir gehen zu Cleveland." They both smiled and nodded their heads.

I relaxed and smelled the aroma of the potato soup.

Henry pointed to a sink in the corner of the room. "You wash, you bathe, Jetzt! Essen spatter." He handed me a towel and washcloth with a small piece of soap. I saw no other soap and thought it might be their only piece. They both gestured, and finally I realized they wanted me to bathe. We all laughed about my reluctance to remove my clothes.

Henry placed an old blanket across two chairs, which partially shielded me from the family's view. I bathed, but I never removed all of my clothes. By this time, I had noticed that there was only one room, with a blanket separating the bed from the rest of the room.

When I finished washing, we all ate a bowl of potato soup. Henry and Emma continued to talk about her sister in Cleveland. Henry volunteered that he was no longer in the army. He had been wounded by the Russisch, had come home, and never went back. He didn't seem concerned about his desertion.

During my short visit, I periodically checked the square to make sure everything remained quiet. After about an hour, I decided it was time to leave and get some sleep. I thanked the couple, gave them two of my K-ration boxes, and started down the stairs. I turned and smiled. As I did, Emma said, "Wir sehen sie auf Cleveland." At least that's what it sounded like to me.

No one noticed me as I crossed the square and returned to the commandeered quarters. Hubbard had taken my place on the bed next to D'Arpino. I stretched out on the floor and promptly went to sleep.

The next day was overcast and dreary. The pace of march had slowed. Several vehicles were visible in the shelter of a small copse to the front of the column, suggesting that the troops were either preparing to board the 6×6s or bivouac. The column came to a halt. Noncoms walked back along the waiting men, apparently to brief them on a plan of action. Conversation buzzed up and down the line of men. Stec, who was forward with Black and Chaney, turned and shouted, "President Roosevelt died! President Roosevelt is dead!"

Several voices asked, "What happened? How did he die?"

"Don't know," answered another GI. "Said they just found him dead. Probably a heart attack."

The news stunned me. Roosevelt was the only president I could remember being in office. I briefly lost direction. What would happen to the country and to the war without Roosevelt? Who would become president? I answered my own question. Vice President Truman was probably already sworn into office. Wonder what he will do?

Then reality hit me. It wouldn't matter who was president; I would still be walking these damned muddy roads until the war was over, or until I got killed. Yet, somehow, it was different; it would never be the same. I couldn't understand my emotions. It was as if I had been cheated of some stability in my life.

The troops crawled aboard the trucks and settled on the hard wooden seats or in the middle of the truck bed, on the floor. We talked in hushed voices about what effect Roosevelt's death would have on the war. Our feeling of loss and uncertainty was obvious.

The trucks headed out again; another convoy, another day of pursuit. It was April 12, 1945. The President had died and the 87th Division was nineteen miles from the Czech border.

The 1st Battalion had been formed into a task force that moved rapidly, deeper and deeper into Germany. A jeep, or sometimes two jeeps, always headed the task force, each with a driver, an officer, and someone to man the .50-caliber machine gun. I had been selected to ride "shotgun" in one of the jeeps. Some days I would be with Carl Blanchard and some days I would be with Norm Panther. In a way, I enjoyed the thrill of being on the lead vehicle. I knew it wasn't the safest place to be, but as long as they asked for me, I would go.

One day, the task force raced through the central German countryside without encountering any German troops. I hoped the day would end that way. The sun already was beginning to set. The tops of the pine trees danced in the evening wind, casting shadows across the narrow road, which could have been either a logging road or a firebreak carved along the base of a twenty- to thirty-foot-high ridge. The young pine trees crowded both sides of the road, fighting for room to grow.

C Company led the regiment's advance. Enemy units ranged

throughout the area, some of them still full of fight as they withdrew deeper into their homeland, others just trying to get home. The fighting units consisted of either hard-core SS troops or midteen boys with hunting rifles and shotguns. Both were dangerous, but the SS troops set booby traps and ambushes.

Lieutenant Hammond, Blanchard, and I rode in the lead jeep, making slow progress. I continually swept the .50-caliber across the tree line, and the other two watched the road for snipers. I spotted a thin wisp of smoke drifting through the trees on the right of the road.

"Smoke on the right," I called as I swung the .50-caliber out to cover the tree line. I could hear Panther and Dudley in the jeep behind and knew that Dudley also had his machine gun aimed at the hillside.

Blanchard slowly drove the jeep forward. Hammond called back to Dudley, "Watch the left side of the road."

"There they are," I yelled.

Four roughly dressed men were squatting around a campfire just below the crest of the ridge. They completely ignored the column of military vehicles.

I shouted, "Hände hoch! Kommen Sie hier!"

Nothing happened. One of the men stirred the fire.

"I didn't know you spoke German," Blanchard commented. "What did you say?"

"'Hands up and come here,' I think." I fired a burst several feet above the men's campfire. Now I had their attention. Hammond motioned for the men to come toward him. They clamped their hands behind their heads and half slid and half walked down the slope. They obviously weren't German soldiers, but who were they? They spoke in guttural tones and kept saying, "Nicht Deutsch! Arbeiten! Arbeiten!"

Finally Hammond declared, "I think they must be either Russian or Bulgarian workers. The Germans must have put them in a forced-labor camp." He motioned for them to sit down by the roadside. "Let Battalion worry about them. Let's go."

He waved the column on to a rather uneventful day. We reached our designated map coordinates and camped for the night.

* * *

Although looting was morally wrong and strongly discouraged, it was a common practice at all levels of rank. Usually the higher the rank, the more expensive the booty. The greater the distance from the front lines, the worse the looting became. Rear-echelon troops had more time to explore and were not constrained by the rigors of combat.

Front-line soldiers had little time to seek souvenirs and no place to carry them when they did find something. When combat troops did manage to find some booty, officers, to their credit, recognized the situation and made space available for looted items on the company supply and mess trucks. These vehicles carried two or three chests of pistols, knives, swords, cameras, and other articles. From time to time, Rehkop, the mail clerk, mailed packages to the States. But sometimes the trucks could be overloaded with supplies and souvenirs.

The battalion task force rolled through yet another day in Germany, and I rode as the gunner in Panther's jeep. The next day, I was scheduled to ride with Blanchard, so I decided that it would be simpler to stay the night at the CP, where the jeep drivers slept, rather than rejoin my squad.

The two jeep drivers and I were drinking coffee that had been boiled by the cooks for the evening meal. Hot meals occurred more often now that the front was so fluid and the mess truck could join the company every evening.

Mess Sergeant Fry was rearranging the mess truck, grumbling and swearing when things didn't fit as he desired. Suddenly he exploded in a fit of anger as he tried to jam a mess box into a tight spot. He shifted the box and grasped something caught in the side rails. He yanked an exquisitely made .410-gauge German shotgun into view. The metal was engraved with a scene depicting a hunter aiming a gun at a pair of pheasants. The wood stock was carved with various designs. I had noticed it before and wondered about its owner. I wanted very much to obtain the gun and send it home to my father. To everyone's disbelief, Fry swore and swung the gun repeatedly against a tree trunk until it splintered and fell apart. Complete silence fell over the CP.

"Fry, you had no right to do that," I shouted, glaring at the mess sergeant.

"Fry, somebody will shoot you yet," Blanchard barked.

First Sergeant Pearson intervened. "That's enough. Fry, clean up that mess and get that truck parked for the night. You other men, settle down."

Blanchard started to say something but was cut off by Pearson. "That's enough. I don't want to hear any more about it."

Panther restrained both Blanchard and me. "Let it go. You'll just get into trouble."

The mess truck pulled away. I sat down and thought of Barr's comment in the apple orchard in France, when Corporal Herman had so needlessly lost his life. Immediately after hearing the rifle shot, Barr had said, "Ten to one someone killed either Fry or Breen." Too bad his first choice hadn't been correct.

The task force swept into Saalfield on April 14 with a decisive thrust. German forces either surrendered or fled to the surrounding hillsides. Lieutenant Caporali commanded the scout jeep with Panther driving and me manning the .50-caliber. Caporali had Panther race up and down the streets at top speeds, and Panther enjoyed every second of it. I was holding on to the gun to prevent my being thrown to the cobblestone streets. The riflemen quickly occupied the town with no casualties. I left the jeep to look for Jacobs and the rest of the squad.

The immediate area consisted of two- and three-story apartment buildings with various types of specialty shops occupying the ground floors. I recognized Brewer and Little standing on the corner of a side street. As I approached, three teenage German girls appeared from one of the shop doors. It looked to me as if they had been talking with Brewer.

"Hey, Garrison, you know some German. What do they want?" Brewer asked.

I couldn't understand anything they said, but it was obvious by their dress and actions what they wanted. One of the girls immediately moved toward me. Her blond hair was dyed and not well kept, her fingernails were broken, and her hands needed washing. I thought they might be camp followers of the German troops who had been stationed in the town. The town itself was too small to have girls of this type living there.

I also thought about the basic training films on diseases. The picture wasn't pretty. "I think they want the same thing as you do," I said to Brewer. Before I could say more, another voice interceded.

"If you don't want a dose of clap, you had all better get the hell out of here." It was Gilbert. "You guys know better."

"We were just walking by," Brewer retorted as he and Little moved away.

"Come on, Garrison, let's escort these ladies to the battalion aid station," Gilbert suggested. "They'll think we're going to shack up and it will be too late to get away when they find out where they are. They need to be tested."

The girls turned surprisingly docile and appeared relieved when they arrived at the hospital. I wasted no time leaving. I didn't like feeling guilty by association.

I found the 4th Platoon in a second-floor apartment about three blocks from the aid station. The large apartment was being shared with a squad from the 2d Platoon that had a squad leader who was an Air Corps replacement staff sergeant. Replacement noncoms were not always popular in the ranks, because they filled vacancies that should have gone to infantrymen. But the men seemed to overlook that in the case of Sergeant Jacobs and Sergeant Clark Holmes.

The squad leader was boasting that he had had sex with a German frau for two boxes of K rations. "I'm taking this floor lamp and going back for another one."

"You dumb ass, she's hungry," said Jacobs in his stilted Washington State accent. "If you take a lamp, she'll be able to see you, and she'll throw you out."

Jacobs' sarcasm evoked laughter from both squads. We laughed even harder when 1st Sergeant Pearson came in and asked, "Where are y'all taking that lamp?" And when he learned of the reason, Pearson thundered, "That's fraternization! Take that lamp back upstairs and stay away from her!"

The 1st Machine-Gun Squad had just finished breakfast the next morning when Chaney came in and pointed to Jacobs. "Jake, when you finish breakfast, take your squad to that field in the next block and dig in. Some Krauts are supposed to be surrendering from that direction, and we need some cover."

Jacobs didn't hurry, but eventually he called the squad together. We moved out to the field to dig shallow foxholes near the roadway, staggering the positions for maximum coverage. A few minutes after we settled in, D'Arpino called quietly, "Jack, someone is watching us from that second-story window in that yellow house on the corner."

"Yeah, I saw the curtain move," Crooks acknowledged.

"Probably a civilian, but point the machine gun in that direction and see what happens," Jacobs said.

Crooks very deliberately lifted the gun and placed it on my shoulder so it was pointed directly at the window. The curtain flew open and a dark head appeared in the window. It was Schneller, the company sniper, who doubled as company interpreter. He may not have always been grammatically correct, but he always got his point across. "Hey, Crooks," he yelled. "It's me! Don't fire!"

"You got a girl up there? You'd better get your ass back to the CP before the CO finds out where you've been," Jacobs roared.

Schneller didn't reply, but within minutes he emerged through the front door, waved, and headed for the CP.

D'Arpino laughed, "You put the fear of God into him, Jake."

The drone of an engine interrupted our conversation. Someone shouted, "Tank!" But the roads were empty.

"There, over the trees, it's a German plane. See the swastikas," I blurted. The .30-caliber still rested on my shoulder, so Crooks and I both pivoted to obtain a proper trajectory for a burst. "Should we shoot it down, Jake?" I asked.

"It's a passenger plane—no guns," Jacobs replied.

"That's even better. He can't shoot back," D'Arpino chuckled.

"You could fire a burst over the top of the plane," I suggested.

"No, I guess not. Never thought I'd pass up a chance to get a plane," Crooks sighed.

"You can see the pilot. He looks a little worried, doesn't he?" D'Arpino said.

"Fun's over. Let's get ready for any POWs if they come," Jacobs said.

The Nazi troops had either changed their minds about surrendering or the Germans had arrived by airplane, because no enemy troops came into town by road or field.

It was unfortunate that the Germans had not surrendered. Patrols sweeping the surrounding hills the next morning lost two replacements killed by snipers. A pitched battle ensued, and many of the German troops were killed, wounded, or taken captive. There probably would have been more prisoners if the snipers had not killed the two riflemen. Several GIs were wounded and one rifleman was captured during the brief skirmish.

Gilbert made a point to find me later that day. "You were lucky. Those three camp followers were all infected."

"I was just passing by, honest," I protested. "Ask Brewer."

"Sure, Gene. Who's going to believe that even a camp follower would be interested in Brewer?"

I continued to protest my innocence, but I knew that I would never convince Gilbert of the truth. Besides, D'Arpino thought the story was too good to let pass and ribbed me for not telling him. "Look at all the fun we could have had," he pleaded in mock disappointment. "Then we could spend the next month in the hospital."

"Yeah, and the next year in the stockade," I retorted.

"You always look at the dark side," D'Arpino laughed.

"Jake, isn't Tony supposed to be on guard duty or something?"

"Don't look to me for sympathy," Jacobs answered.

Jacobs' squad dug in along the C Company perimeter at the edge of a stand of birch trees and pines. The trees were not dense, so the field of fire was good. Sporadic firefights occurred throughout the day, luckily, with no casualties. It seemed the Germans didn't have sufficient troops to mount a full counterattack; there were just enough of them to be dangerous.

The *putt-putt* of a plane echoed among the treetops. The aircraft buzzing overhead was an L-4 observation plane. It had passed over us several times during the day and had drawn ground fire from the Germans on at least one occasion.

"I'll bet he has a nice, warm bed tonight," D'Arpino said.

No sooner had the words left D'Arpino's lips than small-arms fire erupted about a hundred yards to our front. The plane banked and attempted to gain altitude, but smoke poured from the engine. It suddenly dipped and disappeared. There was no sound of a crash, but the sound of the engine was gone. More gunfire ensued, and then there was a brief silence followed by another fusillade. It sounded like all of A Company was engaged. Once again, the gunfire quickly died down.

Sometime later, orders came to move forward. As the company made its way down the road, the plane became visible in a small clearing on our right flank. The left wing and nose were crumpled into the ground, and the right wing pointed skyward at a sixty-degree angle. The bodies of two GIs were sprawled on the field several feet from the plane. There was no sign of the pilot.

That evening, as we dug in to our defensive positions, we heard that the dead GIs had tried to save the pilot, but nearby German troops who had tried to capture the pilot had killed both Americans. A concerted attack by A Company drove off the Germans before they reached the crashed observation plane. The observation plane had performed its mission of locating enemy troops, but a heavy price had been exacted for its success.

A chilly late-afternoon wind whipped the canvas on the trucks carrying the 347th Regiment deeper into Germany. Remnants of German military vehicles lay scattered on the road and in the ditches alongside dead horses and shattered wagons. Shell holes from artillery and bombs covered the fields. The Americans had been extremely careful not to hit the road, which was needed for the Third Army advance.

The task force entered a town that was a jumbled mass of broken concrete and collapsed buildings. The convoy worked its way carefully through the streets, dropping off troops at designated spots. The truck carrying the 4th Platoon veered around several large concrete blocks and parked in front of a sign hanging by one end from a wrought-iron hook. The sign read GASTHAUS. Sergeant Black appeared at the tailgate. "Jake, your squad stays here. No warm meal. Get some sleep. I'll check with you as soon as I know anything."

Jacobs, Crooks, Hubbard, D'Arpino, and I slid off the tailgate and entered through what was left of the doorway. We descended narrow stone steps to the cellar, which was still partially covered by a timber-and-beam ceiling. Debris scattered around the basement indicated that this part of the building had been a restaurant. Nothing was left intact. Each man selected a niche in the rubble and settled down. I removed a D bar from a jacket pocket and gnawed on its broken corner.

A sudden explosion shattered our tranquillity. The vibration sent clouds of dust billowing into the cellar. Two more explosions sounded in rapid succession.

"Crap! What was that?" D'Arpino yelled.

"*Whose* was that?" Crooks replied. "We know *what* it was."

For the next two hours, the bombardment was sporadic; it never concentrated on one specific area of the town. But the shock waves had a powerful emotional effect. Everyone avoided conversation and direct eye contact.

I sat in a corner with my back braced against the concrete-and-stone wall. Two large chunks of concrete rested in front of me and to one side. My entire body trembled, and I had no way of controlling it. I was sure that everyone was watching me and sensed my fear. But every time I tilted my helmet so I could see, the other squad members were sitting in silence with their helmets resting on their knees. Only Jacobs seemed alert. He appeared to be reading a letter, probably from his wife.

The trembling gradually ceased, leaving a hollow feeling in my stomach. I raised my head. Jacobs was stretched out on the floor, snoring gently. No one else had moved. I lowered my head and slept.

Scattered German units bypassed by the spearheads of the 87th Division task forces lurked throughout the surrounding woods and occasionally sent harassing fire on the rest of the columns. The 1st Battalion had been dropped off to deal with the marauding enemy, but so far we had not made contact. The troops were foot-weary. The two or three hours we had walked seemed like two or three days. We continued our search, anxiously waiting for the trucks to pick us up again.

I was tired and had felt that way for several days. The box of ammunition I carried was heavy, and I frequently shifted it from one arm to the other. I noticed a tree stump, about three feet high, beside the narrow road. "Hey, Tony," I called to Hubbard. "I'm falling out for a few minutes. I'll catch up."

I carefully sat down on the uneven top of the stump, holding the ammo in my lap. As D Company slowly passed by me, hardly anyone glanced my way. Those who did said nothing and immediately looked back to the man to their front as if they might lose contact. I realized that these men also were exhausted. But they were still walking. They weren't sitting on a stump while their comrades were disappearing over the next hill. I leaned over and tugged on my combat boots, then set off at a rapid pace parallel to D Company. I tightened my buttocks and leg muscles and did my best to put a little parade march in my step, just like in basic training.

Jacobs stood by the roadside as I approached. "Where have you been?" he asked.

"Had to tie my shoestrings," I answered. Hubbard glanced at me, his ever-present trace of a smile on his face. The column continued toward the next hill.

CHAPTER 19

A Soldier's Number Is Called

P-51 Mustangs swooped parallel to the road that led to the village in the distance. Blanchard twisted in his jeep seat as he watched them pass. "I hope to hell they can tell the difference between the good guys and the bad guys," he said to Lieutenant Lyons and me, who were on the lead jeep of a mixed 1st Battalion task force. The jeep immediately behind us came from A Company.

I was uncomfortable having another .50-caliber behind us that was manned by a gunner I didn't know. It would be different if the GI was from my machine-gun section and was reliable and had my confidence. I couldn't help glancing back uneasily at the jeep.

Distant, heavy gunfire broke out ahead of us, leading Blanchard to comment, "I'm glad we aren't those poor bastards catching all that fire."

"Yeah, but there isn't supposed to be anybody in front of us," Lyons said.

The task force waited along the roadside. Lyons looked at his watch and said, "It's time. Let's move out."

We moved rapidly toward the village, where our job was to go through and secure the road that led away from the place. Any house-to-house fighting would be left to other infantry in the company, or as

Blanchard gleefully called them, "the ground troops." After one such reference, I tried to set the jeep driver straight. "Carl, I think we are 'the ground troops.'" To which Blanchard answered, "Not as long as we're in this jeep, we aren't!"

As the jeep entered the village, we saw white flags everywhere. From the looks of it, there wasn't going to be any need for ground troops. The task force sped over the cobblestone streets of the village, which displayed signs of a recent battle. Many of the buildings had shattered roofs and walls pockmarked from bullets and shrapnel. Several dead horses and broken carts littered the streets. Blanchard steered the jeep around the obstacles and out of town, stopping just short of the crest of a small hill. Lieutenant Lyons sighed as he left the jeep to confer with the officer in the second jeep, saying, "Well, we got through another one."

Blanchard and I looked at each other and laughed. Our laughter helped drain away the tension from our bodies. The lieutenant was right; each village we passed through on the way across Germany held the potential for a sudden and deadly ambush. I always kept Lieutenant Lyons in sight. Lyons was in his early twenties. Ever since that night patrol involving the mysterious Polish DPs and the missing soldier, both D'Arpino and I went to great lengths to make sure that everything went right for the young officer.

I watched Lyons taking part in a rather animated discussion with the other officers when I was startled by Blanchard's exclamation: "What the hell?"

The A Company gunner from the second jeep was holding the barrel of my .50-caliber. "How many clicks do you set the barrel on?" the gunner called out.

"No!" I warned, but it was too late. The gunner already had turned the barrel to a complete stop position. "I don't know," I angrily yelled back. "It worked. That's all that matters. Did you count the clicks when you turned the barrel?"

"No," the A Company gunner replied without concern. "My gun has been jamming, and I thought I would use your setting." With that comment, he rotated the barrel a couple of clicks forward and ran back to his jeep. He had no comprehension that he might have screwed up my gun.

"What did he do? I spent an hour last night making sure that gun was adjusted right," Blanchard snapped.

"I'll fix it, Carl," I said, still irritated. Thinking I had heard five clicks, I rotated the barrel all the way tight and then five clicks back. I hoped I was right. I wanted to test-fire the gun, but that would send the entire task force on alert.

A hand signal from another officer somewhere in the rear of the task force let Lyons know that he should get going. He stepped into the jeep, and Blanchard pulled back onto the road, still cursing the ancestry of the A Company gunner.

We topped the crest of the hill and were greeted by a scene of utter carnage. It became instantly clear that the gunfire we had heard earlier had come from the three P-51s. The fighters had practically destroyed an entire column of retreating Germans and probably also strafed the village. Bodies, vehicles, wagons, carts, and dead horses littered the road and ditches. The German Army had been reduced to using farm horses and wagons to haul supplies in order to save precious gasoline for tanks and command cars. A small number of German soldiers who had survived the air attack seemed surprised to see the task force. They made the mistake of not dropping their rifles and surrendering. Instead, they instinctively ran for cover.

I fired the .50-caliber, but it jammed after a short burst. In frustration, I picked up a carbine and fired at the base of a large tree, which provided cover for two or three soldiers. Gunfire came from behind us. I heard Blanchard swear. Lieutenant Lyons shouted, "Cease firing!" A white flag had appeared in the window of a small barn about two hundred feet from the road. The war was over for another group of Germans.

I turned to Blanchard. "What happened to you?"

"That dumb S.O.B. behind us almost killed us," Blanchard seethed. "Look at that road. Look at those marks. He fired that .50 right next to the jeep and up over our heads. He's an idiot! I ought to shoot the bastard!"

For once, Lieutenant Lyons asserted himself. "Calm down. I'll take care of it." Lyons, the A Company lieutenant, and a group of riflemen cleared the barn and surrounding area of Germans, of whom most had been wounded.

When Lyons returned, he said, "You guys killed a lot of Germans. The ditch was full of them."

I didn't like taking credit for killing anybody, even if I had done it, but especially if I wasn't responsible. "I don't think so, Lieutenant. Those P-51s did most of that."

Lyons just smiled and said, "Let's pull out. From what those prisoners said, that woods ahead should be clear." Blanchard nudged me and nodded toward the A Company jeep. The gunner was no longer there.

Blanchard maneuvered the jeep slowly through the carnage, which littered the road and continued down the rolling landscape and for about another thirty yards inside a dense thicket. Apparently, most of the German column had been caught on the open road, but the forward elements had escaped into the dense woods.

The task force encountered no other action that day. Blanchard and I calibrated the machine gun at the first opportunity.

The next day found Lieutenant Lyons, Blanchard, and me in the lead jeep again. It was midafternoon, and there had not been any serious problems all day. We had passed through two small villages without encountering resistance. Nevertheless, there had been sporadic gunfire for the past hour, and several search-and-destroy patrols had been dispatched on both sides of the task force. The Germans usually allowed the lead elements to pass, then sniped at the trucks loaded with troops. Any snipers discovered by the GIs weren't given a chance to surrender.

"I feel like a sitting duck," Blanchard groused as he drove the jeep over a small rise on a narrow road in a shallow valley nestled between forests of dark green pines. At the far end of the valley was a cluster of gray buildings surrounded by a stockade-type fence consisting of wooden boards and wire fencing. At first glance, it reminded me of a frontier town in the 1700s.

Blanchard pulled the jeep off the road as Lyons tried to get the attention of Captain Charles Green, the B Company CO, who was several vehicles behind us. Green was the officer in charge of our task force.

People poured through the open gates of the stockade into the open valley away from the road. I had the .50 trained on the gathering mass, but I sensed that they were no threat. I thought they must be prisoners of war, because they exhibited good discipline and avoided blocking the road and entrance to the camp.

Several officers congregated in front and to the right of the jeep to discuss a course of action.

"Fire at them! Fire at them! Dammit! I said fire!" A wild-eyed lieutenant came out of nowhere, waved his arms at Blanchard and me, and pointed toward the camp.

"Lieutenant, we don't know who they are," I protested. "They may be our troops."

"Damn you! I'll have you court-martialed," the lieutenant screamed.

The officer's threat stunned us. There was no way I was going to open fire. I looked to the other officers for help—and got it. Captain Green approached the jeep, calling to the irate officer, "What's the problem?"

"I want this man court-martialed," the officer demanded. "He refused a direct order."

Green glanced at me as he took the agitated lieutenant by the arm and walked toward the other officers. After some quiet discussion, the officers appeared to calm the lieutenant, who then accompanied Green as they returned to their vehicles. Green waved slightly as he and the lieutenant passed our jeep.

Lieutenant Lyons returned. "Let's go—right through the front gate. Green thinks all of the Germans have pulled out, but we should be careful of the POWs. They might be a little overjubilant."

Blanchard started the jeep. "What was wrong with that lieutenant?"

"A sniper killed his jeep driver a little while ago," Lyons explained, "and he took it really hard. He's only been on the line for a short time."

There was no hostile response as we neared the POW camp. The prisoners started to wave as the jeep drew closer. A clear British voice could be heard, "Hey, Yanks. Good to see you."

The POWs were very thin and haggard, and their clothes hung slackly on their gaunt frames. Despite their disciplined behavior, I still was a bit apprehensive. I had heard rumors of prisoners overwhelming their liberators in search of food. An onslaught of enemy soldiers you shoot, but there's no way to adequately protect yourself against a teeming mob of starving Allied soldiers. I prayed that everything would go well, because hundreds of POWs lined the roadside.

The entrance was clear, so Blanchard gunned the jeep and charged through. I gripped the handles of the .50-caliber, partly to keep my position in the jeep, partly in anticipation of what we might find inside the camp.

The camp consisted of a series of drab-looking one-story barracks with small porches. No German troops were in sight. Other POWs, more emaciated than those who had greeted us outside the camp, sat on the porch steps and leaned against the railings. Their eyes were dull and they appeared listless. Only one man greeted us by way of a weak gesture of his hand.

Blanchard called out, "Are you guys Brits?"

A man sitting on the steps smiled slightly. "Yes. All kinds are here, but no Americans."

Nothing else was said. The scene was the same at each building. The able-bodied POWs had left the compound to greet the liberating Americans. The sick and weakened ones didn't have the strength to move from the barracks. The camp compound was quiet but for the rumble of the jeep's engine. I kept expecting SS troopers to leap from behind the barracks and attack us, but it turned out the German guards had left before the Americans had entered the prison camp.

A sudden burst of cheering interrupted the silence, as if the home team had just scored the winning touchdown. An officer, we later learned, had greeted the POWs outside of the camp and had told them that food and medical help were on the way.

Lyons touched Blanchard's arm. "There's the rear gate. We need to scout the rear of the camp and be sure it's clear of Krauts."

"Good. This is depressing. These poor bastards have had a rough time," Blanchard said. "I don't want to be one who has to go into those barracks."

I was quiet. I rubbed the jacket on the machine gun's barrel for a while and hoped we would find some of the prison guards. But there was no enemy to shoot. We were soon joined by the rest of the task force and continued our pursuit.

"Hey, Garrison," Chaney called. "First Sergeant Pearson wants to see you right now."

"Why? I haven't done anything."

"Maybe that's why he wants to see you," Chaney retorted.

"I haven't finished breakfast yet."

"Well, finish and then go."

But I was already on my way. I never questioned Pearson. As I approached the CP, I saw Pearson and Lieutenant Baxter standing next to a jeep with two GIs, one in the driver's seat and the other sitting in the backseat. I hadn't seen Baxter since New Year's Day, when the lieutenant had been hit in the rear by shrapnel. I remembered that Baxter had been reassigned to B Company.

Sergeant Pearson saw me and said, "Garrison, you're on the .50-caliber with Lieutenant Baxter. You're on a reconnaissance patrol. Just one jeep, no support."

"You still goofing off, Garrison?" Baxter greeted me.

"Yes, sir. I never recovered from moving all of your luggage at Fort Jackson," I said with a grin.

Baxter smiled. "Come on. There are a couple small villages we have to check out."

The jeep driver took off at a high speed with Baxter and the other GI complaining to no avail. We soon saw a cluster of houses, but no people were visible.

"Circle the town, then stop in the square," Baxter ordered. "Garrison, if you see a problem, shoot first, and we'll sort it out later."

The sweep turned up nothing, and the jeep stopped in the village square. Baxter disembarked and shouted loudly, "Burgermeister! Kommen Sie hier!"

Immediately, an elderly man, dressed in a forest green suit and a cap with a feather, appeared.

"Gather up all the rifles, shotguns, and pistols and bring them here," Baxter told the aged civilian.

The old man must have understood English, for he left and began shouting orders. Soon, elderly men and women came with pistols and a couple of rifles of World War I vintage. By this time, white flags began fluttering from every house. Baxter laughed, "Let's get out of here before they invite us to dinner. I hope the next village is as easy."

The jeep driver bounced down the road even faster than before, and this time everyone complained. We rounded the next bend and entered another town. White flags hung everywhere as we arrived in the village square. We saw a table loaded with weapons and the burgermeister—a carbon copy of the old man in the previous town—standing next to it.

Baxter and the two B Company men leaped from the jeep and began loading the pistols. There were no rifles or shotguns. "Garrison, stay with the .50 and cover us," Baxter ordered. I continually swept the gun around to provide cover, although it was obvious that none was required. When I noticed several young men dressed in civilian clothes, I pointed them out to Baxter, who talked to a couple of them. After a brief conversation, Baxter returned to the jeep. "According to them, there hasn't even been a war," he said. "Forget about them; the war is over as far as they're concerned. Let's go back to the company. We have to go out again in the morning. You're supposed to be with us again, Garrison."

"Don't you have anyone in B Company who can use the .50?" I inquired.

The lieutenant grinned. "You volunteered. Be ready in the morning." I couldn't tell if that was good news or bad news, so I didn't press it.

Shortly after breakfast the next morning, Lieutenant Baxter parked his jeep in front of the two-story brick building where Jacobs' squad was billeted. The two machine-gun squads seldom stayed together, especially at night, so that a chance artillery shell wouldn't eliminate both squads. I left the building within minutes after seeing the jeep.

"Come on, Garrison," Baxter chided. "C Company sure has gotten lax since I left." I merely smiled, crawled into the backseat, and examined the .50-caliber.

The day was a repeat of the previous day, except we only liberated one village. Again, it seemed that the burgermeister knew we were coming and had several nonmilitary weapons ready to surrender. They probably had three times as many firearms that weren't turned in, but there was no will to fight. The villagers were tired of war.

The next morning brought the same routine, but this time I took advantage of an opportunity to get a souvenir. While covering the others with the machine gun, I noticed an elderly German dressed in a World War I uniform. The man stood erect with his shoulders squared, as he must have stood years before. His wife stood in a nearby doorway. Tears flowed down her cheeks as she told him good-bye, probably expecting never to see him again.

I also noticed a pistol holster attached to his belt. After a quick check to verify where Lieutenant Baxter was, I left the jeep and stopped the man. I unfastened the holster and took a watch and fob from his vest pocket. For years afterward, I felt bad about taking the old soldier's watch and fob. The pistol was an unused 9mm Walther and, as far as I was concerned, more desired than the larger and more cumbersome P-38. I turned to the man and said, "Gehen Sie," hoping it meant, "Go." The man appeared relieved, and his wife cried even harder as she said, "Danke, Danke!" An old soldier had done his duty. Baxter never noticed that I had left the jeep.

The next morning, when the battalion moved on through the German countryside, I was once more riding the jeep with Panther and Lieutenant Lyons. I never saw Lieutenant Baxter again.

The machine-gun section was wedged in the back of a 6×6 truck with other members of the 4th Platoon. The April weather was nice, but the wind had a chilling bite as it whipped through the sideboards. I had the collar of my field jacket turned up around my neck. I was glad for the protection that Crooks and Hubbard provided by being seated in front of me. I seldom rode the trucks since I had been riding shotgun on Panther's and Blanchard's jeeps.

The convoy stopped by a small group of buildings, hardly a village, with a large manor house and several smaller dwellings. The troops unloaded and were directed to the second floor of the large building. There was the usual hurried scramble for beds. Jacobs was efficient when it came to commandeering good sleeping quarters for our squad, and soon we were settled in two large rooms with beds and couches for everyone.

Jacobs, Crooks, and D'Arpino disappeared to look for food, souvenirs, or anything of interest. Hubbard and I selected beds and went to sleep. We were awakened sometime later when Chaney shouted, "Chow time. Fourth Platoon, get with it! We get a hot meal for a change!"

The warm food was welcome—and it even tasted good. After we washed out our mess kits, Hubbard and I were returning to our room when a gunshot ended our conversation. We had reached the hallway leading from the stairway to our room about thirty feet away. The gunshot had come from the end of the hall, possibly from our room. Guns ready, Hubbard and I slowly advanced from doorway to doorway, one on either side of the hall, peering into each room as we went. We neared the end of the hall, passed our room, and stopped by the last doorway.

"Who's in there?" I shouted.

"It's okay," came a reply. "I was just showing him my rifle." The speech was slow and slurred from drink. A rifleman sat on the edge of the bed with his rifle pointed toward the ceiling. A small German boy, with his hands over his ears, stood in front of him. The boy appeared frightened but was otherwise all right.

I had never seen the rifleman before and assumed he was a recent replacement. Luckily, we did not have to make a decision on what to do with the drunken soldier because Jacobs burst into the room.

"That boy shouldn't be here," Jacobs shouted. He took the boy by the arm and spoke directly to the intoxicated rifleman. "You get the hell out of here and report back to your squad. You're lucky I don't have you court-martialed."

The rifleman, who was sober enough to realize that he could be in big trouble, quickly staggered along the hall and disappeared down the stairway. Jacobs led the boy down the same steps.

"Can't let you boys alone for a minute, can we?" D'Arpino quipped as he and Crooks approached, followed by the entire 2d Squad. Hubbard and I took the next several minutes to explain what had happened. The incident was then quickly forgotten and the squad scattered.

I looked across the room at Crooks, who sat on the edge of his bed, holding a large book on his lap.

"What's that, Jack?" I asked.

"Stamps," Crooks replied.

"Hey, that's a big book. Is it worldwide, or just German?" I inquired.

"World, but there are a lot of German stamps."

"You gonna share those stamps, Jack?" I said.

"Yeah, just like the P-38," D'Arpino interjected.

"Right. Go find your own stamps," Crooks said.

"Did you guys see Nelson?" D'Arpino said. "He just came back from New Year's Day. He's in Stec's squad as an ammo bearer."

"He was an ammo bearer in the mortar section, wasn't he?" Crooks asked.

"Yeah. Guess we need more ammo bearers for the machine guns than they do for the mortars," D'Arpino reasoned.

"Get some sleep, guys," Chaney said as he poked his head into the room. "We may be pulling out this evening." He was greeted with the usual callous remarks, but everyone prepared to bed down.

A hand on my shoulder awakened me. It was Jacobs. "They want you at the CP. Guess you're on the .50 again."

"Better than walking," I said sleepily as I groped for my boots. I quickly assembled my equipment and trudged off to the CP.

"Gene, over here," Panther called. "You're with me. Hammond's on the jeep with us."

I crawled in the backseat of the jeep, placed my hands on the double handles of the .50-caliber, and rubbed my hand along the barrel, almost as a caress. I fervently hoped that if I needed to fire it, the .50 wouldn't jam, as it had once before. I settled down in the backseat, used my blanket as a pillow, and went to sleep. I was awakened sometime later by the jostling of the jeep over the rough road. "You decide to join us?" Lieutenant Hammond asked.

"Yes, sir," I replied, rather sheepishly. That provoked a laugh from everyone, but we quickly quieted down as we drove slowly along the dark country road. The 1st Battalion was strung out behind us. The road wound through a dense forest and consisted of many S curves. Distant artillery fire rumbled ahead of the column, but we didn't know if it was friendly or enemy fire.

Hammond kept looking at his watch. "Stop here," he commanded. "Turn off your engine and listen."

At first, all we heard was distant gunfire and the engine noise of the vehicles behind us. Then those engines shut down. Soon, between the sporadic shell bursts, came a muted undertone of not-too-distant vehicles. My stomach muscles tightened as I thought of German tanks.

"That should be the 346th Regiment," Hammond remarked. "We had to stop to allow them to cross in front of us. I'm glad we're not going into that artillery barrage. I really hope, for their sake, it's our artillery."

I dozed off, but the whine of an incoming German artillery shell brought me to instant alert.

"That one's well over our head," Panther said.

"I hope it misses the trucks behind us," I added.

"The way the road curves, it will probably land in the trees. The Krauts would almost have to have the exact coordinates to hit the road," Hammond said. "Here comes another one."

A third shell immediately followed the second, and then the shelling near us stopped. The detonations in front of us also gradually diminished. The engines of the 346th motor column were still audible. By now, it was about 2:00 in the morning. It took another few minutes for the 346th to pass, then the crossroads was clear.

Hammond was in touch with battalion headquarters and received clearance to proceed. "Let's go. We have to be in position by daylight," the lieutenant said. "One of those shells did a lot of damage in the company." We didn't say anything. We knew that if Lieutenant Hammond had any details, he would have shared them.

Dawn found the convoy in a densely wooded area where the troops unloaded to await further orders. Panther found the company headquarters and parked the jeep. Lieutenant Hammond left to report to battalion headquarters. I started to search for the machine-gun section.

I found Stec and Dudley's squad first, huddled over a small bonfire of K-ration boxes. They glanced at me as I approached, then quickly returned their gazes to the fire. I had an odd feeling in my stomach as I linked their behavior to Lieutenant Hammond's statement about damage to the company. Where was my squad?

"Hey, Gene. Over here," Jacobs said. Then I saw D'Arpino leaning on the .30-caliber. Hubbard was next to him, and Lupo behind him. Crooks was missing. I looked back at D'Arpino. "Where's Jack?"

"He's going to be all right," D'Arpino said soothingly. "We got hit by 88s, and Jack got it in the shoulder. This time it really is a million-dollar wound."

"Anyone else?" I asked as I glanced around. Stec and Dudley were watching me. They both looked back into the small fire.

"Chaney's dead," D'Arpino answered in a lower voice. "Jesse Knight got it, too."

I felt sick to my stomach. I leaned against a tree and slowly sank to the ground. Jesse. Why Jesse? Memories of all our conversations rushed into my mind.

"Come on, Gene. It could have been any of us," D'Arpino said. "They were just in the wrong place. There was nothing anyone could do."

"McDowell was killed," Stec said, adding to the casualty report. "Nelson was wounded, and he just came back on the line this morning."

"One of the truck drivers was killed, at least two riflemen were badly wounded, and a couple more were hit," D'Arpino continued. "You were lucky you were out joyriding with Panther in front of the column."

The squad spent the next half hour filling me in on the details of the shelling. When they heard the first shell coming, D'Arpino, Hubbard, Chaney, and some others had taken shelter under a truck. The explosion didn't cause any damage or casualties. For some reason, D'Arpino decided the truck was not safe, so he and Hubbard had sought safety in a roadside ditch. Crooks, Knight, and Nelson had joined Chaney and two truck drivers beneath or around the truck. The second and third shells were so close together that D'Arpino didn't know which shell hit the truck.

"What happened to Jack's stamp collection?" I asked.

"He had it under his other arm," D'Arpino said. "Wouldn't let go. Said he was getting something out of this damned war." We all gave a halfhearted chuckle and quickly lapsed into our own thoughts.

D'Arpino continued, "Archie Gilbert really had a rough time," he said of the company medic. "Chaney was still alive and hurting real bad. Gilbert was trying to patch him up, and Chaney kept begging him, 'Don't let me die.' Gilbert asked for help, so Blanchard, Williams, and Coble started working on Chaney. Chaney had so many wounds that he was covered with blood. Gilbert told them to keep patching Chaney, because he had to help the other wounded."

D'Arpino went on: "Jake, Dudley, and Jacobs tried to help Jesse, McDowell, and the truck driver, but they must have been killed instantly. Barr came from his truck when he heard Jack had been hit, and we put sulfa on all the open wounds. Gilbert examined Jack and thinks he has a broken shoulder. Funny, Jack never cried out once. When Gilbert told him about his shoulder, he just grinned and said, 'This time I'm going home.'"

D'Arpino paused. "Blanchard and Williams grabbed Chaney by the arms and shoulders. Coble got underneath Chaney so that Chaney's legs and butt were on his back. The three of them lifted Chaney onto the jeep. When Coble turned away his uniform was covered with blood. We got everyone loaded on the jeep to go back to the hospital, and Gilbert checked on Chaney. He had died. Chaney had a real deep chest wound, and Gilbert said he never had a chance." D'Arpino's voice trailed off, and there was total silence.

I lowered my head. I knew I was going to cry. Jesse Knight would never get to see his new baby. And there would be no one to tell his wife how much he loved and missed her. How many times had Jesse told me how he felt about his family? Jesse always came to me when he was really down about missing his wife and child. I was glad I wasn't an officer responsible for writing letters to the family. Damn Jack Crooks, anyway! Why did he have to get hit again? He should have known better. I closed my eyes and clenched my teeth in an attempt to stop the tears.

Chaney, the squirrel hunter, the expert marksman, was loud and sometimes overbearing, but I liked him. I thought about how he had been consumed with the possibility of dying. It was good that Crooks and Nelson would probably get to go home. That was more than I could expect. As long as I was on the line, my number could be called anytime. Being a .50-caliber machine gunner on the lead vehicle of a task force didn't help my odds any.

No one seemed to know the two riflemen. They were probably recent replacements. What about the truck driver? Did his unit even know that he had been killed?

It could have been a very long night, but fatigue and the emotional loss of my friends had drained my last reservoir of strength. I fell into a deep sleep.

CHAPTER 20

When the Last Man Is Gone, Will There Be Anyone to Miss Him?

I was glad when the order came down the next morning to move out, and I wasn't called to ride shotgun on one of the jeeps. The company was again sweeping the area for Wehrmacht stragglers and hard-core SS troops. C Company had been pulled in to patrol the outskirts of the lone village in the valley, and B Company was responsible for clearing the main square.

The company took positions along a fence line that separated a row of houses and a stock field. The type of fences changed from home to home—some were stone, while others were made of wooden slats or wire—but they all surrounded a garden.

I had positioned the machine gun next to a stone pillar from which I could see most of the houses. Dudley's gun covered what was left of the field of fire. Everyone was fairly relaxed but alert. It wasn't healthy not to be alert.

"Hey, Walt," D'Arpino yelled to Byrnes, who was leaving his position. "Where're you going?"

"I'll be right back," Byrnes replied as he disappeared through the back door of one of the houses. Minutes later, he reappeared with a jar in his hand. A German hausfrau was standing in the doorway, shaking her fist at Byrnes and shouting unintelligible German phrases.

Byrnes scurried behind the stone wall and opened the jar. "I think these are bing cherries," he chortled. He noticed the other squad members eyeing him. "You guys get your own."

We were all laughing as we alternately watched Byrnes and the German woman.

"Here, you guys want to share?" Byrnes said, suddenly changing his mind.

"What's wrong?" Barr asked. "Are they spoiled?"

"No, they're fine. I'm just generous," Byrnes laughed, while he handed the jar to D'Arpino.

D'Arpino probed into the jar, extracted a cherry, and popped it into his mouth.

"Damn, these aren't cherries. They're prunes," he half yelled, and then started to laugh. "Anyone want a prune?" A chorus of no's followed his offer.

Byrnes recapped the jar and, to our surprise, took it back to the hausfrau. Walt definitely did not need prunes.

The next morning the entire 1st Battalion attacked in force. The objective was Oelsnitz, a rather large town compared with the villages we had been encountering for days. There was not much resistance. The town was soon occupied and defensive positions were established.

It wasn't long before someone discovered a wine storage warehouse. Whole cases of wine and champagne disappeared before guards could be posted. Field jackets suddenly appeared unusually bulky, and we could hear laughter and singing from several houses.

D'Arpino, Hubbard, and I were wandering down a tree-lined, cobblestone street when Blanchard and Williams pulled their jeep to within a few feet of us. "You guys been to the distillery yet?" Blanchard inquired. "If you haven't, it's too late. Cobb's closed it down."

"We were looking for it. You don't have an extra bottle or three, do you?" D'Arpino asked.

"As a matter of fact, we do," Blanchard laughed as Williams pulled a half case of champagne from the back of the jeep. "We have to unload this stuff before we get back to the CP."

The jeep pulled back onto the street and disappeared quickly. We distributed the bottles of champagne to various pockets and headed back to our temporary quarters. It was obvious from the scene that greeted us that the rest of the platoon already had discovered the wine and champagne. There was no singing, but the alcohol noticeably loosened the men, who talked and laughed in loud tones. The only person who didn't participate was Jacobs. He sat apart, writing his daily letter home, but he was attentive to all of the actions around him. Dudley was absent from the 2d Machine-Gun Squad. He had liberated a German motorcycle and was giving people joyrides. When last seen, he announced that he wasn't coming back until he ran out of gas.

Jacobs had claimed a first-floor bedroom for our squad, and D'Arpino, Hubbard, and I sprawled on the two beds in the room. We each opened a bottle of champagne and took a swallow. The bubbles tickled my nose. I had never tasted champagne before. I tried another swallow and sneezed. D'Arpino and Hubbard began to laugh, and we all three placed our bottles on the floor. None of us were drinkers. D'Arpino said, "I'd rather have a soda."

"Or a chocolate malt," I added. Hubbard nodded in agreement. Soon we were asleep.

Upon awakening, we found that all of our bottles were gone. Lieutenant Colonel Cobb had issued an edict that all bottles of alcohol be surrendered immediately to the company commanders. Jacobs had collected every bottle he could find. Most of the enlisted men reluctantly gave up their liquor, but we suspected that a few of the officers managed to shanghai some of the better-tasting stuff and secrete it on the mess or supply trucks. Of course, that meant sharing with the mess and supply personnel.

The war seemed to have slowed down. The 87th Division remained stationary as we sent out large patrols, both day and night. I rode the jeep with Panther or Blanchard on an almost daily basis. Most of these patrols were either uneventful or encountered Germans troops looking to surrender. Large numbers of DPs and Balkans troops who had been forced into service by the Germans were in the area. All of them wanted to be friends of the "Americanish." They were routinely passed through the front lines for the rear-echelon units to process.

Rumors ran wild. Some said that the war was over and some that the battalion was supposed to go on the attack into Czechoslovakia. More than the usual number of passes to Paris were being handed out. I had given up on my chances of getting a pass. I concentrated more on staying out of sight while I carried out my duties.

The battalion moved from quarters in Oelsnitz to a small village on its outskirts. Shortly after throwing our gear in the machine-gun squad's new billet, D'Arpino, Hubbard, and I hurried to a small house that had been commandeered as a mess hall.

"These people don't seem to have been affected by the war," D'Arpino commented as we walked through the quaint little village, with its cobblestone streets and window boxes of flowers. The Germans were fond of flowers. I thought that it was too bad they didn't concentrate more on flowers instead of starting wars.

The presence of the Americans kept the civilians who were still in the village confined to their homes and cellars. The streets were hilly, following the contours of the land. To me, the village looked hundreds of years old.

We arrived at the converted mess hall and entered a small doorway. Forsythe, the assistant cook, greeted us from the serving line. We worked our way through the line as D'Arpino directed a barrage of jibes at the cooks and any administrative personnel he spied. His jocular delivery allowed him to say many things that others could not. He was often elected to be the squad spokesman in airing the men's complaints to officers and noncoms.

We located a table in the center of the small dining room and found ourselves seated next to Lieutenant Colonel Cobb and a captain. We all liked Cobb, but I thought the captain was a little too impressed by his position. Cobb acknowledged us, but the captain did not. I racked up another point against him.

About halfway through the meal, Lieutenant Lyons entered the room, balancing his mess gear in one hand and trying to keep his carbine from falling off his other shoulder. He saw Cobb, the captain, and the two empty chairs at the table. There were no other officers in the room. Lyons was intimidated by Cobb and had never recovered from the night patrol when a soldier had disappeared.

Very tentatively, Lyons approached the officers' table and asked if he might join them. Cobb nodded assent while the captain remained indifferent. I chalked another point against the captain. Lyons placed his carbine in a corner next to him and sat down. Almost on cue, the carbine slid down the wall and fell noisily to the floor.

There was instant silence in the room. I started to rise to retrieve the weapon, but D'Arpino touched my arm and shook his head. Lyons looked visibly crushed as he got up to set the weapon upright. The colonel obviously was embarrassed, but to my surprise, Cobb immediately engaged Lyons in friendly conversation. The atmosphere in the mess hall instantly changed and the hum of conversation resumed. D'Arpino looked at me and smiled. "I knew Cobb would come through."

Rumors that the war was over changed every day, but patrols and sentries were still essential. Either everyone took them seriously or they soon had dishpan hands and became experts in digging latrine trenches.

The battalion had moved once again to another village that looked like a copy of the previous one.

Small groups of Wehrmacht troops surrendered constantly, but care had to be taken in case a fanatic wanted to die for "Der Fuhrer."

Another rumor circulated through the ranks that a German field army was to surrender in the C Company area. No special arrangements for such a mass surrender had been made, so the 4th Platoon didn't take the rumor very seriously. Instead, the soldiers engaged in a cat-and-mouse game to stay out of sight of officers and noncoms.

D'Arpino and Byrnes were somewhere scrounging for eggs, Jacobs was at the company CP, and Hubbard and I were sitting at the base of a huge tree. I was writing a letter, while Hubbard dozed. Most of the platoon was billeted in a large two-story house. The road in front of our quarters was packed dirt and gravel, changing to cobblestones as it entered the village. Going in the opposite direction, it curved and twisted into a nearby forest.

I was intent on my letter, occasionally looking around as I searched for a new thought. Without warning, a German command car emerged from the forest. I saw two sentries cranking on their field telephone, apparently asking for instructions. One of the men stood, without his rifle, and very carefully waved the command car to a stop. It was Schneller. A brief conversation ensued, accompanied by several gestures toward the village.

I nudged Hubbard, and the two of us leaned against the tree in plain view of an enemy column advancing behind the command car. The column consisted of numerous vehicles packed with a rather motley-looking army of soldiers and female camp followers. The German troops sat on the hoods of the trucks, stood on running boards, or held on wherever they could. I noticed the large number of women present. I felt very naked with nothing but a .45 pistol on my hip.

"Damn. I hope they don't change their minds," Hubbard muttered.

There were hundreds of soldiers and dozens of women in all types of vehicles, including tanks. They were armed, but their demeanor was that of defeat. They had fought their war and now they wanted no more. Most of the officers in the command cars appeared haughty as they stared straight ahead. Others looked relaxed and glanced from side to side. None acknowledged the sentries or Hubbard and me.

Jacobs had returned from the CP and walked up next to me.

"Division just called and said to be on the alert for a large column of Germans. Whole damn army is coming to surrender," he muttered.

"A little late on their info, aren't they?" I replied. "These guys have been passing for fifteen minutes. I've already seen three cousins."

"I hope they looked better than you do," Jacobs answered. "You two just stay here and stay real relaxed. I'm going to the house and make sure none of those new guys lose it."

It was well over an hour before the last German stragglers passed the sentry post on horse-drawn carts.

I sighed, "Tony, maybe the war really *is* over."

Hubbard smiled. "Hope so," he responded. "Here come D'Arpino and Byrnes. Looks like they pilfered some food."

The next morning, members of the 1st Battalion awoke to find a sign posted on a tree at the edge of town that read:

ACHTUNG!
CLOSED SEASON ON ALL GERMANS
—By order of Lt. Col. R. B. Cobb.

The war was indeed over. It was May 9, 1945.

Stec, who took over as section leader after Chaney's death, strode toward the 1st Squad. Now that the hostilities had ended, his most important task was deciding which squad would go on guard duty first. "First Squad. Jake. Your squad's on guard duty. Your entire squad."

"The entire squad. How many men do you think it takes to stop the Russians?" Jacobs asked.

"That's what they want you to do. Set up your gun in the middle of the road in plain view of the Russians. I guess Patton wants a show of force. Lieutenant Hammond seems to think we have something more to fear than the Japs—the Russians. He thinks they may come charging down that road most any time."

D'Arpino laughed, "You sure know how to make a guy's day, don't you, Steve?"

The squad made its way to the dirt road that led to the border between Germany and Czechoslovakia. No one knew quite where the line was, except for a sign that lay beside the road approximately thirty yards from the American position. To our surprise, Lieutenants Hammond and Caporali were waiting for us.

"Listen up," Hammond said. "See that barricade the Russians built? They're telling us not to come any farther—the arrogant bastards. Place that machine gun right in the middle of the road so they can see it. They can also see D Company's heavy weapons and those artillery pieces on that hillside. We also have a squad of riflemen as your flankers. Those bastards had better not come any closer." With that, the two officers strode toward the command post.

"Well, I guess that takes care of me getting any autographs," D'Arpino chuckled.

"They probably can't write, and if they can, you couldn't read it," Jacobs said.

The squad dug foxholes on either side of the road and positioned the machine gun exactly in the middle. "I feel like I'm on display," I said.

"Me, too," D'Arpino responded. "I wonder where the border is. I always wanted to go to Czechoslovakia."

"I thought you wanted to go to Italy."

"There, too. Hey, what are those Russkies doing?"

Two Russian soldiers were casually strolling along the road toward the American positions. They looked to be unarmed except for possible sidearms. They obviously posed no threat, but every American weapon was trained on them. They stopped by the sign lying along the road, and after much posturing and gesticulating, located a specific spot and shoved the sign into the ground.

It was the Czech border sign. The Russkies pointed at the sign, waved at us, and returned to their own positions.

Sergeant Jacobs quietly said, "First Squad. Leave your weapons here. We have to respond. That sign is crooked."

Very calmly, Jacobs approached the sign. I wasn't calm; my stomach was tied in knots. I didn't want to be the first casualty in a Russian war. D'Arpino and Hubbard followed closely. Jacobs pulled the signpost until it was vertical, and the rest of us pressed the dirt down with our feet until the post felt firm.

"Well, guess we're in Czechoslovakia," D'Arpino said, as the squad stood on the Czech side of the line. The sign read ALLEMAGNE. "Alley-mag-nee," D'Arpino said slowly. "Thought we were in Germany."

As we milled around, none of us acknowledged the Russian troops. We moved to the German side of the sign. It read ČESKOSLOVENSKO.

"Wish we had a camera. I won't remember how to spell that word," I said.

"I don't imagine anyone would know the difference, anyway," D'Arpino replied.

"Wave some more at those bastards and let's go," Jacobs ordered.

During the entire time, Hubbard, typically, had never uttered a word.

The company was stationed at this checkpoint for several days, until the 117th Infantry Regiment of the 30th Infantry Division relieved the 347th Regiment.

After the 30th Division relieved us, the 347th moved to the small town of Oettersdorf near Schleiz.

For the first time since we left the apple orchard in France, we pitched pup tents using newly issued shelter halves. Surprisingly, we remembered how to put them together.

"Well, the good times are gone," D'Arpino remarked. "Let's see how fast these so-called noncoms turn chicken."

"No problem, Tony," I said. "We'll have to teach these Air Corps types how to march, and everything."

"It doesn't take much training to know how to send you to KP," Jacobs growled.

"Everybody out for calisthenics," Stec shouted.

"Hey, Gene. Stec finally did something right," D'Arpino laughed.

The troops assembled in an open area behind the bivouac area and did jumping jacks and push-ups for about twenty minutes before we were dismissed.

"All of you get back to your tents and check your equipment and clean those weapons," 1st Sergeant Pearson instructed. "You're going to start acting like soldiers."

"He's starting to act like a first sergeant," D'Arpino said.

"I heard that, D'Arpino," Pearson shot back. "Get with it."

The men broke into laughter, but everyone carried out the order. Pearson was respected as well as liked by the troops. I followed the squad back to our area. I noticed that my legs felt weak. It must have been those exercises, I thought. Later, at chow time, the food didn't smell good to me and I had no appetite. I sacked out early that night, missing the campfire and bull session.

The next morning at breakfast I barely ate, prompting D'Arpino, who knew that breakfast was my favorite meal, to ask if I felt okay. I barely managed to survive the calisthenics and drew a sharp rebuke from Black about loafing.

Later in the day, some of the platoon members engaged in wrestling matches. In spite of our small size, D'Arpino, Hubbard, and I usually gave a good account of ourselves. But this time I not only did not win a match, I was a quick loser.

"Gene, you're stronger than that. You have something?" D'Arpino asked.

I was slow to answer. "I think I'll rest for a while."

Sometime later, I awakened to find Gilbert touching my forehead.

"The whites of your eyes are yellow," the medic said. "D'Arpino says you have no appetite. Is your urine a reddish color?"

"Yeah, I guess it is," I answered.

"You have yellow jaundice," Gilbert concluded. "You get to go to the hospital, because it's contagious."

"Better than doing this basic training stuff," I laughed weakly.

"Check your equipment in at Supply," Gilbert said. "No point in carrying it with you."

"We better not catch anything from you," Jacobs said.

"Hurry back; you don't want to miss going to the Pacific," D'Arpino called out as Gilbert led me away.

"Garrison," Dudley yelled. "If you go to the hospital, I'll get to go to Paris again."

"That figures," I said. "See you guys later. Hey, Tony, with me going to the hospital, you're the only one left from Fort Jackson."

D'Arpino started to answer but couldn't get the words out. His gaze turned into a blank stare.

When I went to the supply tent, I hadn't yet realized that I would never see most of my comrades again. "Hey, Watson," I said to the supply clerk, "I'm going to the hospital and I'm turning in everything except my .45!"

"That, too," Watson replied.

"Hell, no," I retorted. "I'll never see it again. In fact, give me my two pistols."

"Come on, Gene. You'll be back. I don't want to dig through that crate."

"Okay. Stay out of trouble."

"You're the one going to a hospital with nurses."

We both laughed as I left the tent and crawled into Panther's jeep.

I waved to Jacobs, D'Arpino, and Hubbard as the jeep pulled away.

The war was over. I was going to a hospital where I could relax, shower, maybe see movies, and eat. My buddies would go back to doing calisthenics, train, and maybe even go on marches. I thought about D'Arpino, who now was the only surviving, original member of both machine-gun squads. Oh, well, I thought, I would soon rejoin the company.

I couldn't help but remember my feelings of long ago: "When the last man was gone, would there be anyone to miss him?"

CHAPTER 21

Closure

After I said good-bye to the 4th Platoon, I was evacuated by train to an army general hospital in Liège, Belgium. I was released from the hospital the day after the 87th Infantry Division boarded the American luxury liner *West Point* to embark for the United States. I remained in Belgium and France until assigned to the Army of Occupation in Munich, Germany, where I served for another eight months before returning home for discharge. I consider my biggest accomplishment during that time period was never again putting myself in a position where I had to salute an officer.

I never achieved closure with the deaths of those who shared my countless foxholes, my fear, my laughter, my misery, and my sense of duty. Paul Gullet and I, knowing that we would probably die, had the courage to charge a forest defended by enemy soldiers who were trying to kill us. But I never could gather sufficient courage to meet the families of my fallen comrades. I always wanted to, but I never did. If I had, perhaps I would not have a periodic sense of guilt. Who else could have told some of them how a son or husband met his fate?

After I was discharged I went home to Middletown, Ohio, re-enrolled in Miami University, and completed bachelor of arts and master of science degrees. I took a job as a procurement officer for the Department of the Air Force at Wright-Patterson Air Force Base in Dayton, Ohio, and at Tempelhof Air Force Base, Berlin. I retired in 1981.

In 1948 I married Juanita Hodge, whom I met on a blind date, and together we've had a marvelous life. We were blessed with four children and eight grandchildren.

In 1953, I received a note from someone whose name I can't remember now, telling me that a reunion of the 87th Division was to take place in Philadelphia. It had been more than eight years since I left the remaining members of C Company on the field near the Czech border, and I was curious to see if any of them would show up at the reunion. The only person I recognized was Chuck Yanachek, who was with Lieutenant Henry Wise when Wise was killed after crossing the Rhine River.

I continued to attend the 87th Division Association reunions sporadically after that. Except for Chuck Yanachek, Norm Panther, Armand Verdone, and a few others who sometimes came, not many of my former comrades attended. They, like me and millions of other World War II veterans, were busy putting the war behind us and getting on with life. It wasn't until 1987 that I started to attend the reunions regularly and finally was reunited with Tony D'Arpino and other members of C Company.

These days, we're a company again, albeit aging and losing members almost yearly. We swap stories and share laughter and tears. This has helped to bring some closure to the incredible experience that took a year out of my life and exposed me to things as a nineteen-year-old youth that most people don't endure in a lifetime. Some other surviving members of C Company and the 4th Platoon, for reasons known only to them, decided they wanted no further contact with their former foxhole buddies. I find this sad, but I have to respect their choice.

Each time one of us passes on, those remaining miss him dearly. It inevitably will continue that way until the morning comes when one among us will wake up and realize he is the last man left. I wrote this book in the hope that, through it, the men depicted here will always be remembered by the generations that follow us. That way, when the last man goes, he too will be missed.

Carl Blanchard returned to the United States with the 87th Division. After separation from military service, he returned to Colorado and worked in fire suppression until his retirement. He married Connie, and they raised their family in Colorado. They now reside in Pueblo.

Walter Byrnes was transferred at the end of hostilities in Europe. He completed his Army career attached to the War Department, working on the rocket development program. Upon separation, he attended the University of Michigan and Syracuse University. He married Dorothy, and they have four children. He retired after a thirty-year career as a senior engineer–manager in systems development with IBM. He and his wife live in Cary, North Carolina.

Robert B. Cobb had seen combat as a battalion commander with the 9th Infantry Division in North Africa and Sicily before he joined the 87th Division. After World War II he spent more than three years in the Army of Occupation in Austria before being rotated back to the United States, where he attended the U.S. Army Command and General Staff College. After duty in Washington, D.C., he was assigned to Korea, where he completed his tour as chief of staff of the 24th Infantry Division. During his tour in Vietnam, which started in 1964, he was a senior training advisor working with the Vietnamese. At the time of his retirement as a full colonel, he had been awarded more than twenty medals, including the Distinguished Service Cross with Bronze Oak Leaf Cluster. In 2001, he was inducted into the University of Idaho Hall of Fame and awarded an honorary doctoral degree. He and his wife had three children. He is now retired in Phenix City, Alabama.

Pat Coluccio's shoulder wound of New Year's Day never healed properly. Shortly after VE Day, he was evacuated to a field hospital and returned to the United States for further treatment at Halloran General Hospital in Staten Island, New York. He was discharged in November 1945 and entered a successful family construction, land development, and gravel-mining business. He and his wife, Jean, have three boys and live in Poughkeepsie, New York.

After being wounded, **Jack Crooks** was evacuated from the 87th Division in April 1945. Some twenty years later, Crooks and I met several times at Wright-Patterson Air Force Base. He told me he had married his high school sweetheart and earned an engineering degree. He became a program engineer for a California aerospace company. We reminisced about our wartime experiences. Crooks confided that he thought that the bravest thing he had done during the war was that night on the Siegfried Line when he took the first guard duty and let me get some rest and warmth in the pillbox. He said he had never been so cold, and thought that he might freeze before he was relieved.

After several years, Jack wrote me that he had taken early retirement. That was the last contact I had with him. At an 87th reunion, Harold Barr related that he was best man in Crooks' wedding in Bethlehem, Pennsylvania, but had never heard from him since.

Richard Cunningham returned Stateside with the 87th Division. He used his GI bill to earn a civil engineering degree from Clarkson College. In 1950 he got a job with the Atlantic Refining Co. and became regional engineer for the New England area. He married Nancy in 1953, and they have two daughters. He lives his retirement with his wife in Prescott, Arizona.

Anthony D'Arpino returned to the United States with the 87th Division on the troop ship *West Point*. He lacked sufficient points for discharge, so when the 87th was deactivated he was transferred to Fort Dix, New Jersey. D'Arpino returned to Utica and attended Utica School of Commerce and Utica College. He worked for eighteen years for a division of Remington Rand, and then worked another eighteen years at the Mohawk Data Co. He married Dorothy, a schoolteacher, and they have two sons, two daughters, and six grandchildren. They live in Herkimer, New York. Tony remains one of my closest friends.

After his return from Europe with the 87th in July 1945, **Robert Fulton** was discharged in October 1945, and became head artist for the RKO Orpheum Theater in Denver. He and his wife entertained for clubs and conventions throughout Denver and Colorado. He later opened

Display Art and continued doing contract work for the theaters. Bob retired in 1985. He and his wife have three children.

Archie Gilbert was evacuated from the 87th shortly after the end of the war and sent to a general hospital in France to recover from a severe kidney infection. He was finally discharged from the army in October 1945 and reunited in Parkersburg, West Virginia, with his wife, Lois, and their first son, born on the day C Company crossed the Rhine. Sadly, his son died six weeks after Gilbert returned home.

Gilbert started in 1949 with the Baltimore & Ohio Railroad as a switchman. He and Lois raised another son and a daughter. In the early 1960s, he joined a National Guard Special Forces unit. He stayed with the B & O until his death from leukemia in 1973.

Frank Grieco was severely wounded by a 20mm shell crossing the Rhine River. He was evacuated to a hospital but lost an arm at the shoulder. I happened to meet him at Griffiss Air Force Base in the mid-1950s, while both of us worked for the Department of the Air Force. Pat Coluccio made contact with him in the mid-1990s near Utica, New York, and they played a round of golf. (Grieco won despite playing with only one arm.) He lives in California. I tried to contact Frank in recent years, but he never responded.

Paul Gullet nearly lost his feet from frostbite and trench foot. He was finally given a medical discharge and returned to Middletown, Ohio. He married his high school sweetheart, Rose Marie. He was active in the family's floral business until the late 1980s, when he retired to the west coast of Florida. He passed away in 1996. Although I saw him briefly after the war, he and I went our separate ways.

Tony Hubbard was transferred to another military unit prior to the 87th Division's return to the United States. I met him one time after that, in 1959, at an 87th Division Association reunion. At the time he lived somewhere in the southeast Ohio–northern Kentucky area. Tony was still quiet and good-natured and had his ever-present smile. He unexpectedly left the reunion that night without saying good-bye, and I never saw or heard from him again until earlier this year, when I got a surprise call from Tony. We plan to get together at the next reunion.

Tom Katana was wounded three times on New Year's Day, 1945.

He was evacuated to the general hospital in Reims, France. Elmer Zeichner, also wounded that day, lay on the bed next to his. After an operation at Reims, Tom was moved to the 94th General Hospital in England and lost touch with Elmer. He returned home on the *Queen Mary* in March 1945. He was processed to the general hospital at Camp Pickett, Virginia. Tom had married Marie at Fort Jackson in July 1944 before going overseas. Shortly after VJ Day he was given a medical discharge and returned home on crutches. He was rehired by Westinghouse, worked in various capacities, and retired after forty years. Tom still has steel in his chest and undergoes periodic medical examinations. He and Marie have three children.

Daniel Mendelsohn returned Stateside with the 87th Division. He was involved with the musical industry before and after his military service. He was an accomplished musician and did many big-band arrangements, and reportedly became music director for the Martha Graham dance group. He attended at least one mini-reunion with Richard Coble. At that time, he lived in New York City.

Norman Panther returned with the 87th Division to Fort Benning, Georgia. After VJ Day, he was transferred to Fort Devens, Massachusetts, and discharged in January 1946. He married Barbara in January 1948. He joined the Army Reserve and was recalled to active duty shortly after the start of the Korean War. He was inducted at Fort Lewis, Washington, then shipped to Japan and Korea. Panther was awarded his second Combat Infantryman's Badge in March 1951 and discharged that November. Later, he was employed by the L.P. Gas Co. in El Paso; then transferred to Ohio and Peru, Indiana; then he retired in 1992. He and Barbara now live in Garden City, South Carolina. They have four children, seven grandchildren, and four great-grandchildren.

John Thomas was nominated for officers' candidate school at the end of the war. He stayed in military service and retired as a major. While serving in Europe, his wife, Becky, and their daughters visited Lahneck Castle, at the junction of the Lahn and Rhine rivers—the same castle we captured. It had been converted to a restaurant. John, now a widower, lives in St. Petersburg, Florida.

Armand Verdone was captured the night of December 16, 1944, and shipped to the POW camp Luckenwald. Being Italian, he managed to mingle with the Italian prisoners. One of them was from the same town in Italy as Verdone and his family, so when the Italian soldier returned home, he notified Verdone's parents in Albany, New York, that Armand was a POW (and not missing in action). Armand made two escape attempts. The first failed, but the second time he reached American troops and was placed aboard a C-47 aircraft that was shot down by a German fighter. A second C-47 took him safely to France. Verdone returned to Albany and joined his father in running a car dealership. He married Josephine and moved to Phoenix, Arizona, where he and his sons ran several car dealerships. He passed away in 2000.

Guy Wick was also captured the night of December 16, 1944. His first reunion was in 1987 in Albany, New York. His experiences as a prisoner of war were not pleasant and he declined to discuss them at the 87th reunions. At one of the reunions, Gus stated that one of the reasons he had never attended earlier was that he was unsure how he would be received. He felt there was a stigma to being captured. He was assured that there was not. Guy and his wife, Nancy, attended every reunion from 1987 until his death in 2001. Nancy still resides in Charleston, West Virginia.

On New Year's Day, 1945, **Elmer Zeichner** was wounded by rifle fire and also lost his right leg below the knee from a shrapnel wound. After being released from a military hospital, he enrolled at Johns Hopkins University in the fall of 1945. He earned an engineering degree and took a job with a glass company in Baltimore, Maryland, until 1960. He then was hired by the Department of Defense until his retirement in 1986. During that time, he was assigned to a position with the U.S. Army in Germany for three years. He met his wife, Helen, on a blind date and they married in 1954. They had three children. Elmer died in 1993.

GLOSSARY

Ammo: Ammunition

ASTP: Army Specialized Training Program

BAR: Browning automatic rifle

Bazooka: A tube-shaped, portable rocket launcher that fires a missile capable of penetrating the armor plate of a tank.

BBC: British Broadcasting Company

Bed Check Charlie: Any German aircraft that flew surveillance flights at dusk.

Booby traps: A hidden bomb or mine that can be set off by an unsuspecting person who steps on it, touches a trip wire, or the like.

Bouncing Betties: Antipersonnel land mines that spring upward one to three feet when activated by a trip wire or similar device, scattering shrapnel over a large area.

Burp gun: A German Schmeisser 9mm machine pistol similar to the American grease gun.

CO: Commanding Officer

CP: Command Post

C rations: Five-inch-high, OD-color tin cans of spaghetti, hash, or beans with hot dogs

D bar: Solid chocolate bar; extremely hard.

DP: Displaced person.

Dragon's Teeth: Inverted, triangular-shaped concrete blocks approximately three feet high. Blocks are spaced every few feet apart to deter armored vehicles.

Fifth Column: A group of people who act traitorously and subversively out of secret sympathy with an enemy of their country.

40 × 8: Railway cars capable of holding forty men or eight horses.

GI: Government issue. A nickname for American soldiers.

Grease gun: A .45-caliber, automatic submachine gun with a collapsible stock. American made.

Halazone tablets: A water purification tablet. One tablet in a full canteen of water. One capful of treated water will purify another canteen of water.

Half-track: A caterpillar tread that runs over and under the rear or driving wheels of a vehicle but is not connected with the forward wheels. The vehicle can be armed with 20mm or .50-caliber guns and is capable of transporting a small contingent of troops.

KP: Kitchen police; work in the mess hall.

K rations: Meals packaged in waxed cardboard boxes about eight inches long by three inches wide by one and one-half inches thick.

Kraut: World War I nickname given to Germans because of the perception that they ate large quantities of sauerkraut. The name carried over to World War II.

Nazi: The name given to the ruling political party under Adolf Hitler's regime.

NCO: Noncommissioned officer

Ninety-day wonder: Enlisted men's nickname for an officer who graduated from a ninety-day officers' candidate school.

OCS: Officers Candidate School.

OD: Olive drab color.

OR: Orderly room; location of the commanding officer and administrative functions.

"Over the hill": Take unauthorized leave.

Panzerfaust: The German version of an American bazooka. Designed as a throwaway, firing only one shell.

Pillbox: A relatively small fortification of boxlike or rounded, usually concrete construction built for machine guns or antitank weapons.

Potato masher: German grenade with a handle about eight inches long for ease in throwing.

POW: Prisoner of war.

PX: Post exchange; a government-operated store for military personnel.

RAF: Royal Air Force

Rifle grenade: A small striated pineapple-shaped shell containing an explosive, adapted to be fitted and fired from the end of a rifle bore.

Section 8: A military discharge based on unacceptable actions.

Siegfried Line: A zone of fortifications in western Germany that faced France. Erected prior to World War II.

6×6 trucks: $2^1/_2$-ton trucks, nicknamed deuce-and-a-half.

TD: Tank destroyer; a vehicle, tanklike in appearance, armed with a 90mm gun and built with a lightweight armor shell.

USO: United Services Organizations

West Wall: Name given to the western perimeter of the Siegfried Line.

A NOTE ON SOURCES

This book is my memoir. It is not intended to be a definitive history of the fighting in Europe, of the 87th Division, or even of my company. It is simply the way I remembered my experiences as an American soldier fighting his way with others across Europe. It is based upon my recollections, letters home, correspondence and interviews with former comrades, and similar sources. I used general histories of World War II and other published sources to help me flesh out certain details such as dates, movements, and other aspects of the war that have faded from my memory.

Three sources in particular that I relied upon are:

Golden Acorn News, published by the 87th Division Association (various issues).

History of the 87th Infantry Division, Army & Navy Publishing Company, Baton Rouge, La., 1946; reprinted, 87th Infantry Association, 1988.

The 347th Infantry Regiment, 87th Infantry Division, An Historical and Pictorial Record. Army & Navy Publishing Company, Baton Rouge, La., 1946.

ABOUT THE AUTHORS

Gene Garrison attended Miami University after his discharge from the Army. He retired after a thirty-year career with the Department of the Air Force. Gene and his wife, Juanita, have four children and eight grandchildren.

Patrick Gilbert has worked as a journalist and editor for thirty-five years. Twice nominated for a Pulitzer Prize, Patrick is the recipient of many local and national journalism awards. He is the associate director of publications for the Johns Hopkins Medical Institutions, Johns Hopkins University. He lives in Baltimore with his wife, Catherine, and their two children.